The
EVERYTHING
Jewish History & Heritage Book

Dear Reader:

The great Yiddish writer Yitzhak Leib Peretz once wrote, "A people without a memory is like an individual with amnesia." Each generation is a link in a chain stretching back to Abraham and forward to the end of time. And according to the Nobel laureate Elie Wiesel, it is precisely this memory that has connected Jews throughout the ages.

Memory has kept the Jews together as a people through four millennia—memory of a shared history and a rich heritage that we are proud and honored to write about. Every Jew has a responsibility to keep that memory alive, and one way to do this is to know about the lives of those who preceded us.

Although this is a book concerning Jewish history, it is intended for everyone. Dispersed among the nations of the world, the saga of the Jews also informs us about Western civilization—its people, nations, and religions.

Enjoy the adventure that follows, for it is truly an amazing story!

Julie Gutin

The EVERYTHING® Series

Editorial

Publishing Director	Gary M. Krebs
Managing Editor	Kate McBride
Copy Chief	Laura MacLaughlin
Acquisitions Editor	Eric M. Hall
Production Editor	Khrysti Nazzaro

Production

Production Director	Susan Beale
Production Manager	Michelle Roy Kelly
Series Designers	Daria Perreault
	Colleen Cunningham
Cover Design	Paul Beatrice
	Frank Rivera
Layout and Graphics	Colleen Cunningham
	Rachael Eiben
	Michelle Roy Kelly
	Daria Perreault
	Erin Ring
Series Cover Artist	Barry Littmann
Interior photographs	Israel Ministry of Tourism and Brand X Pictures

---

Visit the entire Everything® Series at everything.com

THE
EVERYTHING®
JEWISH
HISTORY & HERITAGE
BOOK

From Abraham to Zionism, all you need to
understand the key events, people, and places

Richard D. Bank & Julie Gutin

Adams Media Corporation
Avon, Massachusetts

History is about generations and family. To my "history":
Ruth and Louis Bank, Rose and Herbert (alav ha-sholom) Jacobs,
Frani, Ari, Cory, and Joy.

In memory of Asya Poleyes and Zinaida Samsonovich.

An Everything® Series Book.
Everything® and everything.com® are registered trademarks of Adams Media Corporation.

Published by Adams Media Corporation
57 Littlefield Street, Avon, MA 02322 U.S.A.
www.adamsmedia.com

ISBN: 1-58062-966-0
Printed in the United States of America.

J   I   H   G   F   E   D   C   B   A

Library of Congress Cataloging-in-Publication Data
Bank, Richard D.
The everything Jewish history & heritage book /
Richard D. Bank & Julie Gutin.
p.   cm.
(Everything series)
ISBN 1-58062-966-0
1. Judaism–History. 2. Jews–History. 3. Bible. O.T.–History of
Biblical events. I. Gutin, Julie. II. Title. III. Series.
BM155.2.B26   2003
296'.09–dc21   2003008264

This book is available at quantity discounts for bulk purchases.
For information, call 1-800-872-5627.

Contents

Acknowledgments

I don't think I could have faced 4,000 years of Jewish history without knowing Julic Gutin was by my side. Her keen eye for detail insured the accuracy of this book. I would like to thank my editors, Gary Krebs and Eric Hall, for making this project a reality; Jack Herzig, Esq., for providing research material; and my agent, Carol Susan Roth.

—Richard Bank

I would like to thank my family—Nonna, Faina, and Leonid Gutin—for all their love and support. I would also like to thank Richard Bank for his expertise and all the hard work he put into this project. And of course, many thanks go out to Eric Hall, Kate McBride, and Gary Krebs at Adams—I couldn't have done this without your help. Finally, I would like to acknowledge the Jewish Federation of the North Shore for helping Russian families like mine find new homes in the Boston area.

—Julie Gutin

Top Ten Events
That Changed the Course of Jewish History

1. Abraham and his family leave Mesopotamia and travel to Canaan, led by God's promise that Abraham will become the father of a great nation.

2. Moses leads the Israelites out of Egypt and receives the commandments at Sinai. After forty years of wandering in the desert, the Israelites enter the Promised Land.

3. King David establishes the capital in Jerusalem and his son Solomon constructs the Temple.

4. The kingdom of Israel is destroyed by the Assyrians; the Ten Israelite Tribes are exiled and disappear.

5. The kingdom of Judah is conquered by the Babylonians and many Jews are taken into exile, but the Jewish community in Babylon remains strong and does not succumb to assimilation.

6. When Greek culture threatens to destroy Judaism, the Maccabeans stage a revolt and reclaim the Temple.

7. The Romans vanquish Jerusalem and destroy the Second Temple as the Jews are exiled, marking the beginning of the Diaspora.

8. After centuries of persecution, the Jews of Western Europe are emancipated and become full citizens of their countries.

9. The Holocaust claims the lives of six million Jewish people and threatens to destroy Jewish European culture.

10. The creation of the State of Israel marks the end of the Diaspora as all Jews from around the world are invited to return to their ancestral home in Israel.

Introduction

▶PREPARE YOURSELF FOR AN EXTRAORDINARY ADVENTURE! In the following pages, you'll traverse a time continuum spanning more than 4,000 years as you learn about the history of the Jewish people.

We'll begin in the area known as the Fertile Crescent, the cradle of civilization and the home of the early Hebrews. Then, we'll move forward in time and place to follow the footsteps of Abraham and descend with Jacob's clan into Egypt, emerging years later as a nation searching for freedom and the Promised Land. We will witness the founding of the kingdoms of Judah and Israel, their destruction, the re-establishment of the Second Temple, and how it, too, was destroyed.

The loss of the Temple led to a 2,000-year exile, the Diaspora. During this time, the Jews dwelled in all parts of the world, often strangers among their countrymen. The pressure to give up their religion and their culture was great, but despite all the hardships—including social and cultural isolation, as well as religious persecution—the Jewish people persevered. Then, out of the ashes of the *Shoah* (Holocaust), one of the most horrific acts ever visited upon a people in human history, arose the modern State of Israel.

What kept the Jewish people together over the two millennia of exile and separation is a mystery unique in civilization. One answer is their adherence to Judaism—a shared set of beliefs, practices, and laws. (If you'd like to learn more about Judaism, you can turn to Richard Bank's *The Everything® Judaism Book*.) However, there is another explanation—their cultural heritage, which we will examine as we explore Jewish history.

Because the narrative of the Jews begins so long ago, the only sources for their earliest history are the Bible and the oral tradition—the stories that have grown around the biblical narrative. What is more, the first part of the Bible, or Pentateuch, is essentially uncorroborated by independent data. Whether the incidents related in it are truth or fiction is, at least to some extent, a matter of belief, but the fact remains that this is indeed how the Jewish people view their history. We see heroic figures, prophets, kings, and scholars in all their glory and with all their blemishes and foibles. We see a people with a repetitive history of turning away from God, repenting, and turning away yet again. We see the Jews as slaves and as conquerors, showing mercy as well as cruelty. It's because this saga is so human that it speaks to everyone—Jew and gentile alike.

For the non-Jews, *The Everything® Jewish History & Heritage Book* should make for interesting and rewarding reading on a number of levels, not the least of which is the fact that Christianity and Islam trace their roots to Judaism and the Jews. Christians believe that Jesus of Nazareth was a divine figure, but they also recognize that he was a Jew who lived in Palestine before the destruction of the Second Temple. Muslims accept as history the story of Abraham and his two sons, Isaac and Ishmael, and they honor Moses as a major prophet. And because of the Jewish Diaspora, much of Jewish history is deeply interconnected with the history of the rest of the world.

For Jewish readers, however, this book serves an additional purpose— to help them remember those who have come before us. Why do the Jews cling so tenaciously to memory, especially when that memory is replete with so much suffering? According to Nobel laureate Elie Wiesel, it's because they must: "It is human nature to forget what hurts you. . . . But the Jews live by other rules. For a Jew, nothing is more important than memory. He is bound to his origins by memory. It is memory that connects him to Abraham, Moses and Rabbi Akiba. If he denies memory he will have denied his honor."

Memory is what all Jews have in common, whether they are Orthodox Jews from London, Reform Jews from New York, or nonpracticing Jews from Tel Aviv. As the story of the Jewish people unfolds in the following pages, bear in mind that it is the collective memory of the Jews from one generation to the next that is the cornerstone of the Jewish people. And it is this memory, perhaps more than anything else, that has held them together for over four millennia and continues to be a unifying force today. Ⓔ

Chapter 1

The Age of the Patriarchs

According to the Jewish tradition, Jewish history begins with Abraham and the other patriarchs, leaders of the nomadic Hebrew tribes that came from Mesopotamia and wandered throughout Canaan, eventually ending up in Egypt. Not much is known about this early period. The two sources are the Bible and archaeological findings. Unfortunately, they don't always present the same version of the story.

Where Jewish History Begins

While no one can say for certain where the first human beings appeared on the planet, it is believed that civilization germinated in the Middle East, in an area known as the Fertile Crescent. Geographically, the Crescent was a fertile agricultural area surrounded by arid deserts. The fecundity of the terrain was ensured by four mighty rivers that surrounded or flowed through the region. To the west, it was supported by the Nile in Egypt; to the east it was nourished by the Tigris and Euphrates.

Archaeologists believe that humans first settled down to farm the land around 5000 B.C.E., in the region between the Tigris and Euphrates Rivers, known as Mesopotamia (parts of modern-day Iraq and Turkey). Eventually, prosperity in agriculture paved the way for the emergence of powerful city states. It is to this region that we trace the origins of the early Hebrews.

Abraham's Covenant with God

Abraham was born in the city of Ur, also known as Ur Kasdim (Ur of the Chaldees), in the southern part of Mesopotamia, sometime between 1950 and 1800 B.C.E. The baby boy's father, Terah, gave him the name of Abram. When Abram was still a youth, Terah moved with his family to the city of Haran in northern Mesopotamia, and that is where Abram grew into adulthood.

FACT

For centuries, the existence of Ur Kasdim was shrouded in mystery, and it was not until the nineteenth century that archaeologists began excavating this ancient city. Established over two and a half centuries B.C.E., Ur was one of the major cities of Ancient Sumer, an empire that thrived in southern Mesopotamia until its fall to the Babylonians.

Terah was a Semitic merchant of idols but, legend has it, his young son was not convinced by the logic of idol worship. One day, young Abram went into his father's shop and smashed all the idols, save the largest one. When Terah returned, he was dumbfounded—all the idols were destroyed, except the largest one, which was holding a hammer. Aghast, Terah demanded an explanation, so Abram calmly told his father that the biggest idol destroyed all the smaller ones.

"Ridiculous!" his father exclaimed. "Idols can't move!" Abram rejoined that if that were the case, there's no point to worship them. How could his father worship these statues if he believed them so powerless as to be unable to destroy one another?

This legend foreshadows a change in Abram's beliefs—that there is one God. Today, all three monotheistic religions—Judaism, Christianity, and Islam—credit Abram for this belief, which is central to their faith.

God Calls on Abram

From the Bible, we have the story of how God called on Abram and bid him to leave his home and family and go to Canaan, where he would make Abram the father of a great nation and bless him and his descendants. According to the Book of Genesis, God said, "Go forth from your native land and from your father's house and I will make of you a great nation and curse him that curses you and all the families of the earth shall bless themselves by you." Abram obeyed, and that is how the covenant *(b'rit)* between God and the Jewish people was established.

Part of God's promise to Abraham's descendants was territory (hence the concept of the Promised Land). In the Bible, God is very specific in delineating the boundaries of the region that stretches from the river of Egypt to the Euphrates River and includes the land of the Kenites, the Kenizzites, the Kadmonites, the Hittites, the Perizzites, the Rephaim, the Amorites, the Canaanites, the Girgashites, and the Jebusites. However, in another biblical passage, the Promised Land only includes Canaan.

A Nomadic Lifestyle

Abram left the city of Haran and headed west, accompanied by his wife, Sarai, and his nephew Lot, as well as a full entourage of servants. Thus Abram assumed the lifestyle of a nomad, and his wanderings led him all the way to Egypt and then back to Canaan.

Abraham was a formidable warrior as well as a savvy diplomat, employing his might or his wits—whichever proved most appropriate—when dealing with petty kings and local chieftains. Eventually, he amassed a great fortune, and was lucky in all but one respect: He and Sarai remained childless.

Sodom and Gomorrah

One day, three strangers came to visit Abraham. In keeping with the well-established custom of hospitality, he invited them into his tent and he set out a feast before them.

The three strangers were messengers from God, and they informed Abram that God intended to destroy Sodom and Gomorrah, two cities whose inhabitants were wicked and cruel. Despite all the crimes and transgressions of Sodom and Gomorrah, Abram pleaded with God on their behalf, pointing out that even ten just men didn't deserve to die for the crimes of the rest of the town. Apparently, though, the citizens of Sodom and Gomorrah were so depraved, that not even ten just men lived among them. The only righteous family was that of Abram's nephew Lot, who resided in Sodom. Because he was a good man, God's messengers traveled there to bring him out of the city before God annihilated Sodom and Gomorrah.

Lot's family had to flee quickly, and they were told not to look back. However, Lot's wife couldn't bear to leave her home behind without one last look, and so she turned around—and instantly turned into a pillar of salt. Today, visitors to the Judean Desert in Israel stop at a rock that, tradition holds, is Lot's wife, staring back at what used to be the city of Sodom.

The tale isn't necessarily meant to be taken literally, but it reveals something about the man whom the Jewish people see as their patriarch. Even in the face of evil and depravity, Abram was prepared to argue with God in favor of justice. Despite Abram's absolute loyalty to God, he was willing to question God's judgment.

Father of Two Nations

Eventually, Abram grew old. He began to doubt that God's promises would come true and that he would have as many children as there are stars in the sky—already, his wife had grown too old to bear children. Knowing that she could not provide a son, Sarai offered her maidservant Hagar as a wife to Abram. Polygamy was common to the peoples of the region, and making the union even more desirable was the fact that Hagar was Pharaoh's daughter, who had been given to Abram when he had traveled through Egypt. Soon, Hagar had a son, and he was named Ishmael.

However, God told Abram that Ishmael would not be a part of His promise. Instead, he would become the father of another nation. Eventually, Hagar and Ishmael were sent away; according to the Bible, the angel of God continued to watch over them and in time Ishmael became the father of the Arab people.

Arabs trace their lineage from Ishmael and believe themselves to be descendants of Abram. In fact, the story of Hagar and Ishmael figures prominently in the Qur'an. According to a Muslim legend, Hagar and Ishmael found refuge in the desert, at a site that is now the Muslim holy city of Mecca.

From Abram to Abraham

God promised Abram that he would have a son from his wife Sarai and that this son, Isaac, would inherit God's Covenant, which would be established between God and all of Abraham's and Isaac's descendants. From then on, Abram would be known as Abraham, "father of many"; Sarai, which means "my princess" in Hebrew, would be known as Sarah, "*the* princess."

As a sign of the Covenant between him and Abraham, God decreed that throughout the ages, every male child is to be circumcised at the age of eight days. The rite of circumcision was also binding upon Abraham who, it is said, circumcised himself at the age of ninety-nine. Circumcision, as a mark of the covenant between God and Abraham and all his descendants, has been a practice carried out throughout all generations of the Jewish people to the current times, even when they lived among people who did not practice it.

Circumcision, or *brit milah,* is one of the oldest Jewish traditions. The ceremony, which takes place eight days after a baby boy's birth, is a very special occasion for Jewish families because with this act the baby is included in the covenant made between God and Abraham, as well as all of his descendants.

As God promised, Sarah did indeed conceive and gave birth to a son at a place now known as Beersheba. The boy was named Isaac or Yitzchak (from the Hebrew word for "laughter"), because Sarah laughed when she heard that she would have a child in her old age and because the name reflected Abraham's joy in becoming a father.

©Itamar Grinberg. Courtesy of the Israel Ministry of Tourism.

▲ Tel Sheva, the excavated walls of the biblical city of Beersheba (Be'er Sheva).

The Story of Isaac

From what we know from the biblical narrative, Isaac appears as a somewhat weak, enigmatic figure. One of the most dramatic stories in the Torah is the story of Isaac's sacrifice.

As a trial of Abraham's faith and obedience, God commanded him to sacrifice Isaac, and Abraham dutifully set out with his son to carry out God's commandment at Mount Moriah. When they reached the summit, he bound his son and placed him upon the sacrificial rock. As he raised up the knife to kill his son, God spoke to him and told him to spare Isaac and sacrifice a ram instead.

Marriage and Family

When Isaac grew up, a family servant went to Haran to find him a wife. The servant returned with Rebecca, and she and Isaac got married; soon, Rebecca became pregnant with fraternal twins. It is said that the rivalry between the two boys was so strong that they were even fighting in the womb, causing a difficult pregnancy for their mother. After they were born, their battle of wills only intensified.

FACT

Abraham died when he was 175 years old and was buried in a tomb next to Sarah, in a village that is now the city of Hebron. His son, Isaac, would, as promised, become the next patriarch of the Jewish people.

Jacob and Esau: A Story of Sibling Rivalry

Though twins, two people could not have been more different than Isaac's sons. Esau, the older of the two by a few minutes, was swarthy and hairy while Jacob was lanky and smooth-skinned. Their personalities differed as well. Esau was a man of action. He loved to hunt and was quite adept at it. Jacob, on the other hand, was more spiritual in nature, prone to contemplation before deciding upon his course of conduct.

The sense of competition between Jacob and Esau was fueled by the fact Isaac favored Esau while Rebecca preferred Jacob. Because Esau was the elder, he was entitled to the blessing of the firstborn, which meant that wealth and power would pass on to him. But with the riches and authority also came the responsibility to continue with the mission of his grandfather and father, and this was something Esau did not desire.

Birthright for a Bowl of Stew

Esau gave little thought to his birthright; he sold it to Jacob for a bowl of lentil stew because he was hungry and, he reasoned, what can a man who dies of hunger do with a birthright?

When the time came for Isaac, who had grown old and blind, to give his blessings to each of his sons, Rebecca schemed to trick her husband into giving the blessing of the firstborn, with its entitlements, to Jacob instead of Esau. While Esau was hunting, Rebecca covered Jacob's arms with a goat skin. Though Isaac recognized the voice of Jacob, he felt the hands and arms of Esau and bestowed the blessing upon Jacob that had been meant for Esau.

Returning from the hunt, Esau learned that Jacob had received the blessing that was meant for him. Esau begged his father for the second blessing, but Isaac realized that Jacob was meant to continue the mission of his forefathers—that he would have the ability to instill in his people the values of learning and spirituality. Esau, a man of the sword, would be the father to a mighty nation of Edom—the Roman Empire.

Understandably, Esau was very angry, and Rebecca was afraid that his anger would lead him to murder his brother. And so, wishing to get her favored son as far away from danger as possible, she dispatched Jacob to her brother's house in Haran, where he was to take a wife.

Jacob Becomes Israel

Jacob arrived in Haran without means or prospects and had to rely on the benevolence of his uncle Laban. Setting his eyes on his cousin Rachel, Jacob was immediately smitten and he asked for her hand in marriage. Seizing the opportunity, Uncle Laban demanded that Jacob work for him for seven years before the marriage could take place.

At the end of the required time, the marriage ceremony was held, but Laban had tricked Jacob and substituted his older daughter Leah in Rachel's stead. Undeterred and still determined to take Rachel for his wife, Jacob worked an additional seven years for his uncle and then married Rachel. Subsequently, Jacob married the respective handmaidens of Rachel and Leah, Zilpah and Bilhah, and with these four wives, he sired twelve sons and one daughter.

Time to Go Home

Although Jacob worked for his miserly uncle/father-in-law, he was able to amass substantial wealth, and he eventually decided to return to his homeland—despite having to face Esau's wrath. Upon hearing of his brother's return, Esau set out to meet him with an army of 400 men. Rather than risk a violent confrontation, Jacob dispatched gifts to his brother and sent his caravan ahead, spending the night alone.

During the night, a stranger appeared. Jacob wrestled with the man until dawn, at which time Jacob, who overpowered the stranger, demanded that he receive a blessing. The stranger, who then revealed himself to be an angel, blessed Jacob and bestowed upon him the new name of Israel (*Yisrael*), which means "the one who wrestled with God."

ALERT!

The offspring of Jacob/Israel in Canaan became known as the Israelites, and even today, the Jewish people are called "the children of Israel." The founders of the Jewish state in Palestine were mindful of this connection when they named their new country *Eretz Yisrael*—the Land of Israel.

Jacob's Sons—the Twelve Tribes of Israel

Emerging from the night-long struggle with the angel, Jacob went on to meet his brother Esau. Jacob's good-faith offerings succeeded and peace prevailed when the siblings met. Although still not enamored with the brother who had deceived him, Esau saw the wisdom in combining his strength with the ingenuity of his brother, and he invited Jacob to accompany him and take up residence in Har Sa'ir. Jacob agreed to join his brother but he never did.

Jacob spent very little time in Canaan; with the exception of Benjamin, all his children were born in Mesopotamia or Syria. Toward the end of his life, Jacob's travels took him to Hebron where his grandfather Abraham had lived and his father Isaac dwelled. At the age of 180 years, Isaac died, and Esau and Jacob buried him.

During Jacob's lifetime, his followers came to regard themselves as linked to the land of Canaan. Indeed, even after Jacob and his tribe went down to Egypt, a good many Hebrews remained in Canaan.

QUESTION?

Who were the forefathers of the twelve tribes of Israel?
Jacob's twelve sons, who were born to his four wives. Leah gave birth to Reuben, Simeon, Levi, Judah, Issachar, and Zebulun; Joseph and Benjamin were born to Rachel, who died while giving birth to Benjamin; Bilhah had Dan and Naphtali; and Zilpah bore Gad and Asher.

Who Were the Early Hebrews?

So far, we have covered the biblical narrative of the Age of the Patriarchs, but the Bible is a religious text written much later than the events it described. Because we are reaching back more than 4,000 years, there is little we know for certain about the early Hebrews. In fact, we cannot even be sure of the origin of the word "Hebrew," though there are plenty of theories on the subject.

According to one, the term did not appear until much later, when the Hebrews dwelt in Egypt, since it derives from the Egyptian word *apiru,* or "foreigner." Another possibility has to do with the fact that Abraham came from the "other side" *(eber)* of the Euphrates River and was thus called a "Hebrew." A third argument is that the Hebrews believed themselves to be descendants of Eber, one of the ancestors mentioned in the complex biblical genealogy.

However they came about their nomenclature, the early Hebrews were a nomadic people who wandered in tribal groups organized around the rigid hierarchy of kinships. It is certain that they lived side by side with other groups, but there was one thing that separated the Hebrews from their neighbors—their beliefs.

Today, we know that the Hebrews were a Semitic people who lived in Ancient Palestine and claimed to be descendants of Abraham, Isaac, and Jacob. In the Pentateuch, the word "Hebrew" refers to "the children of Israel," and is meant to emphasize their status as a distinct people.

A New Concept

While other tribes worshipped multiple deities, it appears that the early Hebrews had developed a cult of one god whom they thought superior and more powerful to all others. Although this was not yet the monotheistic faith it would gradually evolve into, it probably set the Hebrew tribes apart and united them together, providing them with a common identity. Perhaps it was in one of these groups that a leader such as Abraham emerged and established that there was only one true God responsible for creating the entire world. (E)

Chapter 2

From Slavery to Freedom

From the story of Abraham, Isaac, and Jacob, the epic continues to the next period of Jewish history—the Hebrews' migration to Egypt, their enslavement, and then their liberation and departure, celebrated by Jews during the holiday of Passover as one of the central milestones of Jewish history.

Jacob's Favorite Son

As you already know, Jacob had twelve sons—and Joseph, the eleventh son, was the special one, ever since the beginning. For a long time, Jacob's favorite wife, Rachel, could not conceive, and so her son Joseph's birth was a long-awaited and much anticipated event. Unfortunately, being the center of his father's attention did not bode well for Joseph.

When Joseph was seventeen, it was time for him to join his brothers, who herded their father's livestock. For this important occasion, Jacob gave his favorite son a lavish gift, a "coat of many colors." Naturally, this made his brothers even more envious. What is more, Joseph's personality only exacerbated the relationship with his siblings. He never hesitated to report to Jacob any of his brothers' misdeeds. Even Joseph's special talent for dream interpretation, which would prove so useful during his sojourn in Egypt, would have been better set aside when he explicated his dreams to his brothers. His explanation of a dream he had where sheaves of wheat belonging to his brothers bowed to the sheaf owned by him and later, another dream where eleven stars bowed to him, transformed his brothers' envy into homicidal hatred, and they devised a plot to murder Joseph.

FACT

The story of Joseph is told in Genesis, which is the first book of the Pentateuch (literally, "five books" in Greek). Then, the story of the Hebrews in Egypt as well as their liberation is continued in the Book of Exodus.

Sold into Slavery

Fortunately, the oldest brother, Reuben, prevailed with a less lethal plan—to sell Joseph to Ishmaelite traders as a slave. After traders took Joseph away in chains, the brothers dipped his coat of many colors in goat's blood and took it to Jacob as evidence that Joseph was killed by a wild animal. Jacob's grief was great and he mourned his beloved son.

In Egypt, Joseph was sold to a nobleman named Potiphar and was set to work as Potiphar's personal attendant. Unfortunately for Joseph, who was a handsome man, Potiphar's wife was attracted to him. When he refused her advances, the spurned woman told her husband that Joseph seduced her, and Joseph found himself imprisoned, with barely any hope of getting out.

Interpreter of Dreams

In jail, Joseph soon gained a reputation as an interpreter of dreams by successfully interpreting the dreams of Pharaoh's butler and baker, who were fellow inmates. Later, when Pharaoh was troubled with cryptic dreams, he was told about a Hebrew prisoner named Joseph. Curious, the Pharaoh summoned Joseph and told him his dream. Pharaoh saw seven fat, healthy cows come out from the Nile and stand grazing on the river bank; then, seven more cows emerged from the Nile, but these were gaunt, skinny cows, and they came up to the seven plump cows and swallowed them up.

Joseph listened to the dream and responded with an explanation: There will be seven years of plentiful crops followed by seven years of famine. To survive those seven lean years, the country would have to be prepared. Joseph advised the Pharaoh to store food supplies during the good times in preparation for the years of scarcity.

In a Position of Power

Pharaoh believed Joseph, and he put Joseph in charge of all the logistics of preparing for the famine. When the famine really came to pass after seven years, Egyptians were prepared—and Pharaoh was grateful. As a reward, he made Joseph his viceroy, or next in command. Joseph assumed an Egyptian name, Zaphenath-paneah, and married Asenath, a daughter of the priest of On, who bore him two sons, Menashe and Ephraim.

The famine spread throughout Egypt and to surrounding lands, including Canaan where Jacob and his family lived. Learning that food supplies were available in Egypt, Jacob dispatched all his sons except for Benjamin, the youngest, to purchase what they could and avoid starvation. It was time for a family reunion.

Israel Enters Egypt

And so, Joseph's dream came true. His brothers came to him and bowed down, humbly begging the Egyptian official—they had no idea it was their brother Joseph!—for food supplies to take back to Canaan. Joseph recognized his siblings and decided to play a trick on them—he accused them of being spies. Of course, the brothers denied the accusation, asserting that they were shepherds from Canaan and that they had a father and brother back home. To prove their claim, Joseph demanded that they leave and return with their younger brother, Benjamin; to ensure their compliance, he kept his brother Simeon as a hostage.

Despite his reluctance to part with his youngest son, Benjamin, Jacob had no choice but to send him with his other brothers to Egypt. Much intrigue followed as Benjamin was falsely accused of robbery and thrown in prison, but when the brothers told Joseph how their father would be overwhelmed with grief and become inconsolable after having already lost one son, Joseph relented and revealed his true identity.

Expecting revenge, the sons of Jacob feared for their lives, but Joseph forgave them, saying that it must have been God's plan that he be sold into slavery so that ultimately he would be in the position to save his family. Joseph instructed his brothers to depart for home and return with their father and his household, and they could live in the town of Goshen.

A Family Reunion

Jacob rejoiced when he heard the news that his long-lost son, Joseph, was still alive, and was a successful man. At the age of 130, the patriarch took his family and household, consisting of seventy people, and set off for Egypt. When the time came that Jacob knew he was about to die, he blessed all his sons, as well as his grandsons born to Joseph, Menashe and Ephraim, promising them that they would become the forefathers of two additional tribes of Israel. Joseph and his brothers returned to Canaan to bury their father at the cave of Machpelah.

FACT

Joseph was 110 years old when he died. Before his death, he made one more prediction—he told his brothers that God would bring them out of the land of Egypt and into the Promised Land and asked that at that time his bones be carried in a coffin from Egypt and buried in Canaan.

A Clan Grows into an Enslaved Nation

Up to this point, the story has largely relied upon the biblical narrative, but here it seems that the presence of the Hebrews in Egypt is authenticated by other sources. There is no question that West Semitic people and other immigrants came to reside in the northern portion of Egypt as early as the end of the third millennium B.C.E. Occasionally, this heterogeneous population would become unruly, and the Egyptians expelled individual groups. The Egyptian rulers oppressed these foreigners, taxing them heavily and using them as labor for building projects.

Apparently, the descendants of Jacob intermingled within this population, but they held on to their identity as the sons of Israel. Unlike the other foreigners living within Egypt, the Hebrews did not assimilate. They continued to speak their own language, dressed in a distinctive style, and gave Hebrew names to their children. But perhaps even more important, they rejected the pantheon of Egyptian gods and held steadfast to their belief in the one and only God of Abraham, Isaac, and Jacob.

The Israelite communities grew so rapidly that they became a cause of concern to the Egyptians. To deal with the problem, Egyptians enslaved the Hebrews, in part to take advantage of cheap labor and in part to decrease the size of the Israelite population, whom Egyptians saw as a threat to their security. However, the cruel conditions under which the Israelites labored were not enough to destroy them. When astrologers informed the Pharaoh that a male child born to the Israelites would grow up to overthrow him, a decree was passed that every Israelite male newborn be drowned in the Nile River.

A Jewish Hero Is Born

One Israelite family was not willing to accept the murder of their baby boy. Shortly after he was born, his parents Amram and Yochbed placed him in a basket and floated him down the Nile. The boy's sister Miriam followed the basket at a safe distance. She watched and waited until she saw Pharaoh's daughter, Bityah, find the basket and lift it from the river. Bityah called the baby boy Moses because he was drawn from the Nile.

FACT

In the Jewish tradition, Miriam is seen as a prophet who predicted her younger brother's birth and eventual role as the liberator of Israelites. She was a strong woman who never lost her hope in a better future for her people. When it was time to leave Egypt, she was the first one to start making hurried preparations to set off into the unknown.

The Prince of Egypt

Adopted by the Pharaoh's daughter, Moses was raised as a prince in the Pharaoh's palace. One day, he saw an Egyptian overseer striking a Hebrew slave. When the overseer would not stop the beating, Moses killed him. Then, realizing what he had done and fearing for his life, Moses fled to Midian, where he became a shepherd. Soon, he married Tziporah, the daughter of Jethro, a Midianite priest.

The Bible narrates how one day, while he was tending his flock, Moses came upon a burning bush that was not consumed by the flames. It was then that God spoke to Moses, instructing him to return to Egypt and demand the Pharaoh to let the Israelites leave Egypt.

ESSENTIAL

At first, Moses was reluctant accept God's assignment. All he wanted was to lead a quiet life as a shepherd, among his new family and friends. Ultimately, however, he took on the responsibility placed on him by God and returned to Egypt.

Who Was Moses?

The story of Moses' life is described in the Book of Exodus. But did a historical Moses really exist? Many believe that he did, though his figure remains mysterious, shrouded by time and numerous legends.

Because "Moses" is an Egyptian name, some now believe that Moses was an Egyptian prince who adopted the Hebrews as his people and led them out of Egypt. Another theory has it that there were two men, an Egyptian and a Hebrew, or even a Hebrew and a Midianite, both called Moses. The matter is complicated by the fact that Moses spent so much time among the Midianites and married the daughter of a Midianite priest.

Regardless of the historical accuracy of the portrait of Moses, it seems fairly clear that the story of this man altered the course of history, uniting a people by providing them with a common law and distinct way of life.

Deliverance from Bondage

The Bible tells us how God advises Moses to seek the help of his brother Aron, and how they together come to the Pharaoh to convey to him God's demand to free the Hebrews. As expected, the Pharaoh did not give in easily; worse, life for the Hebrews became even more difficult. To prove that he was God's messenger, Moses called down the ten plagues to be visited upon Egypt:

1. Blood
2. Frogs
3. Lice
4. Wild beasts
5. Pestilence
6. Boils
7. Hail
8. Locusts
9. Darkness
10. Slaying of the firstborn males

After each plague, Moses asked Pharaoh to change his mind, but the Pharaoh was stubborn. Finally, Moses threatened him with the tenth plague, the slaughter of firstborns, which would include the Pharaoh's own son. On the eve of the tenth plague, before the fifteenth day of Nisan, God instructed Moses to tell Israelite families to slaughter an unblemished lamb and smear its blood over the doorposts and thresholds of the Jewish homes.

According to Jewish oral tradition, the lamb was one of the Egyptian deities. By selecting a lamb for slaughter, the Israelites rejected pagan beliefs and demonstrated their devotion to God.

The Passover Meal

During the night, the Hebrews ate the roasted lamb, unleavened bread (because there was not sufficient time for the dough to rise), and *maror* (bitter herbs), a meal that was the original *seder* (Passover dinner). While they recounted the many miracles God had performed for them, at exactly midnight the Angel of Death swept through Egypt, killing all the male firstborns. Because he *passed over* the homes of the Israelites, which were marked with the smeared blood of the sacrificial lamb, the holiday that celebrates the Jews' eventual liberation from Egypt is known as *Pesach* (Hebrew for "Passover").

The Israelites Leave Egypt

The next day was the day of mourning for all Egyptians. The Pharaoh, in turmoil over the loss of his son, ordered the Israelites to immediately leave Egypt. Moses instructed the Israelites to visit all the Egyptians they knew and ask for their gold and jewelry, some of which would later be used to construct the Golden Calf. Rushed as they were, the Hebrews did not have time to bake their bread and the dough they kneaded did not have the opportunity to rise, which is one reason Jews eat *matzah* during Passover.

Under the leadership of Moses, it is believed that as many as two million descendants of Jacob/Israel emerged from Egypt on the fifteenth day of Nisan. However, Pharaoh soon regretted his decision. The Egyptian army set off to pursue the Israelites, catching up with them on the twenty-first day of Nisan at the Sea of Reeds (also known as the Red Sea).

©Itamar Grinberg. Courtesy of the Israel Ministry of Tourism.

▲ Bedouin traveling on camels along the Red Sea.

With the sea directly ahead of them and Pharaoh's mighty army at their backs, the Israelites were trapped. It was then, according to the Book of Exodus, that a miracle happened. God parted the water and allowed the Israelites to cross over to the other side. When every single one of them finally reached the other shore, the water rushed back to reclaim its territory. The Egyptian soldiers were caught in the middle of the rushing waves and drowned. The Israelites were safe. Gathered together, they sang songs of praise to God.

FACT

Many scholars believe that Ramses II (1300–1234 B.C.E.), who was especially notorious for his deployment of slave labor to construct his building projects, was the Pharaoh who enslaved the Israelites. However, it is likely that it was Ramses' son Merneptah who was the Pharaoh at the time of the plagues and the exodus of the Israelites from Egypt.

Celebrating Passover

Passover is a holiday that celebrates an event central to Jewish faith, history, and culture. It commemorates God's redemption of his people, liberation of a nation, and the connection between the ancient Hebrews and the Jews of today. In fact, one important aspect of the celebration is imagining yourself in the place of the Israelites and experiencing anew slavery, freedom, and eventual arrival in the Promised Land.

During the centuries following the exodus from Egypt, the Jewish people celebrated Passover in many different ways. When the Temple was constructed in Jerusalem and sacrifices were made according to the proscriptions of the Torah, the Jews would make the annual pilgrimage to Jerusalem to offer the sacrificial lamb as the paschal offering. After the destruction of the First Temple, the Jews continued to observe Passover while in exile in Babylon, but they did so without being able to offer the necessary sacrifice. In 516 B.C.E., when some Jews returned to Israel and rebuilt the Temple, the traditional observances resumed.

During the era of the Second Temple, the Pharisees added to the religious observances by establishing the *seder* and instituting the drinking of wine, reclining, and leisurely discussing the Passover narrative. Outside Jerusalem, where (by then) the majority of Jews lived, Passover was observed in the home and at synagogue, and new customs were added to the *seder*.

Say "NO" to Chametz

Over the years, Passover has evolved into a holiday that is celebrated primarily in the home. There is much to do in order to prepare the home and make it ready for the holiday. For starters, observant Jews must remove all traces of *chametz* from the home. Exactly what is *chametz?* Anything that is made from the five basic grains—barley, wheat, oats, rye, and spelt—and has not been completely baked within eighteen minutes after coming into contact with water. What this complicated definition means is that all bread and products made of grain not made especially for Passover must be taken out of the home. (Observant Ashkenazic Jews also avoid rice, corn, peanuts, and beans, since they may be used to make bread.) For the duration of Passover, Jews eat *matzah* and *matzah*-based products.

Obviously, making one's home "*chametz* free" is a very demanding task. Not only must all *chametz* be removed from the house, but no utensils, dishes, pots, and pans that had come into contact with *chametz* may be used throughout the eight-day holiday. Therefore, it is not uncommon to see some Jewish families who have a separate set of Passover kitchenware or who use paper products during the holiday.

QUESTION?

Why do the Jewish people eat *matzah* during Passover?
In memory of the Hebrew slaves, who left Egypt without time for preparing leavened bread. According to one popular explanation, they carried the flour on their heads, and it was so hot that the flour mixed with their sweat and was baked by the desert sun to form *matzot.*

The entire home, and particularly the kitchen, must be cleaned and scrubbed and made *chametz*-free. Once this is done, a formal search, called *bedikat chametz*, is conducted on the day before Passover. Any *chametz* that is found is carefully set aside, wrapped, and burned the following morning. It is customary that a renunciation of ownership is declared regarding any *chametz* that has not been detected.

Another ritual observed at this time is *mechirat chametz*, the sale of *chametz* to a gentile or a rabbi with power-of-attorney. In fact, those who sell their *chametz* intend to repurchase it after Passover.

The Seder

Although there are special Passover services held in synagogue, the central part of the Passover celebration is the *seder*—the Passover meal and related ceremonies conducted in the home on the first night of the holiday (though many Jews living outside Israel conduct an additional *seder* on the second night). The word *seder* is Hebrew for "order" or "order of the service," because the order and specifics of the *seder* ceremonies hold great importance.

The Haggadah

Conducting a *seder* is made fairly simple and straightforward because all one must really do is to follow the *Haggadah*. The title comes from the Hebrew *lehagid* (to tell), because the *Haggadah* is a book that tells the story of Passover; also, it includes *midrashim* (passages of interpretations that expand on incidents in the Bible in order to derive explanations and moral lessons), poems, and various ceremonies in the order in which they are performed during the Passover *seder*.

The *Haggadah* was developed by Diaspora Jews—it is likely that the first of these appeared as early as the eleventh century. And we know that the first illustrated *Haggadah* was printed in Spain in the year 1482. Today, *Haggadot* come in a wide variety of versions such as traditional, secular, feminist, mystical, and vegetarian.

Setting the Table

Setting the *seder* table has its own very specific requirements. Most of the objects present on the table are highly symbolic and play a ceremonial role in the dinner. The *seder* table should include the following:

- Napkin or doily to cover the middle piece of *matzah* (the *afikoman*).
- A *kiddush* cup for everyone and one special goblet to serve as the cup of Elijah.
- A pitcher and bowl for washing hands.
- At least one bowl filled with salt water to be used for dipping.
- Cushioned chairs or pillows on each chair so that everyone can recline and be comfortable during the *seder*.
- A copy of the *Haggadah* for each person.
- A *seder* plate.

The *seder* plate, or *ke'arah*, includes a section for each of the five symbolic foods eaten at the *seder*:

1. *Karpos:* A green vegetable (usually parsley, watercress, or celery) that symbolizes the green of spring; during the *seder*, the *karpos* is dipped into the salt water.

2 *Charoset:* A mixture of chopped nuts, apples, wine, and cinnamon, eaten in memory of the mortar used by the Hebrew slaves when they toiled in Egypt.

3. *Maror:* Bitter herbs or horseradish, a dish that represents the bitterness of slavery.

4. *Beitzah:* A roasted (hard-boiled) egg that symbolizes the continuity of life and the commencement of spring.

5. *Zeroa:* A roasted shankbone that represents the sacrifice of the paschal lamb.

Of course, in addition to these symbolic foods, the *seder* includes plenty of other dishes. It's amazing how many delectable foods can be prepared with *matzot* and *matzah* meal. In addition, some Ashkenazic Jewish families serve foods like gefilte fish and *matzah* ball soup, while specialties of Sephardic Jews include such delicacies as roasted eggplant and saffron rice.

Because Passover is a holiday centered upon the home and the family, the children are very much included. During the ceremony, the youngest child recites the Four Questions about the celebration of Passover. Another custom is the search for the *afikoman,* a piece of *matzah* hidden by the adults. The child who finds the *afikoman* receives a ransom for returning it and allowing the *seder* to continue.

According to the Order

With the table set, everyone is ready to commence with the *seder.* All over the world, families and friends gather to partake of the Passover meal and to recount the Passover narrative. No Jewish tradition or holiday is more widely observed by the Jewish people.

Once the holiday candles are lit, the *seder* begins with the blessing over the first cup of wine—there will be at least three more cups of wine (or grape juice, for children and those who cannot drink alcoholic beverages) before the end of the night. The four cups of wine represent the four promises made by God to the Israelites: that God will free them from the burdens of bondage, deliver them from slavery, redeem them with an outstretched arm, and take them to the Promised Land.

The final part of the *Haggadah* contains songs and praises to God, and the remainder of *Hallel* (Psalms 113–118) is recited. The *seder* is concluded with a poem and song, ending with the words *Le shana ha-ba'ah b'Yerushalayim* (Next year in Jerusalem).

Passover's Universal Message

No Jewish holiday has a more universal appeal than the celebration of Passover. Not only does it tell the story of the Exodus and commemorate the time when the Hebrews embarked from slavery into freedom, but it heralds the day when freedom will come to people everywhere and no one will ever need to endure the yoke of oppression. The story about a group of slaves who won their freedom from a powerful nation is a beacon of hope to all people the world over. For instance, the story of slavery in Egypt and subsequent liberation was one of the central themes of spirituals sung by African slaves in the American South.

But Passover has another message as well. The Torah says that God instructed the Jews to "Remember that you were a slave in the land of Egypt." And on four separate occasions in the Torah, the Hebrews are commanded, "You shall tell your child" of the exodus from Egypt.

In these two words, "remember" and "tell," the message is clear: All people are reminded of their responsibility both to the past and to the future.

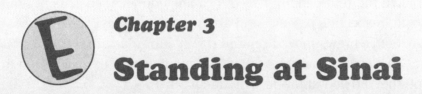

Chapter 3

Standing at Sinai

It was around the year 1250 B.C.E., that the Children of Israel gathered at Sinai to receive God's commandments, an occasion celebrated during the holiday of Shavuot. Following this monumental occurrence, the Israelites spent forty years wandering in the desert, until they finally entered Canaan, where they would become a unified nation and would assume their identity as the Jewish people, an identity they have held onto until this very day.

Into the Desert

After deliverance at the Sea of Reeds, the Israelites did not follow a direct path to Mount Sinai, but instead traveled about the region beginning with the Shur Desert, where they took a respite in an area called Marah. The Jewish oral tradition teaches that while the Israelites were in Marah, God instructed them in certain *mitzvot* (commandments) such as honoring the Sabbath, respecting parents, and an assortment of civil laws. After a while, the Hebrews moved on and traveled to Ailam, and then through the Seen Desert. Finally, less than two months after they departed from Egypt, they arrived at the foot of Mount Sinai.

The biblical narrative informs us that when the Israelites ran out of food, God provided manna for them to eat. Like dew, manna fell from the sky during the night and had to be gathered before sunrise, or else it melted in the sun. It remains uncertain exactly what manna was. According to Rashi's biblical commentary, the word *manna* comes from the Hebrew for "what is it?"

It should be noted that the territory surrounding Mount Sinai was occupied by the Midianites, with whom Moses had lived before returning to Egypt as God's messenger and where he had married Tziporah, daughter of the Midianite priest Jethro. At Sinai, Moses was reunited with Jethro, and many Midianites joined the Children of Israel, for a total population of two to three million people.

Moses Receives the Commandments

For the most part, what we know about the events at Mount Sinai is limited to the biblical narrative and the oral traditions. According to one scenario accepted among religious Jews, each and every one of the Israelites had an encounter with God, and out of this experience, shared by the entire people, was born a nation with a Jewish national identity. Shortly after, this nation received, with the intercession of Moses, the commandments that would govern all aspects of their life.

The Ten Statements

One of the great misconceptions about receiving the commandments is that Moses only received ten. In fact, when Moses spent forty days on Mount Sinai, God taught him the 613 commandments that would be recorded in the Torah. What many people think of as commandments is a mistranslation of "Ten Words," "Ten Statements," or "Ten Utterances." The Decalogue, as it has also come to be known, is only the heart of what is an elaborate system of laws that can be divided into three groups:

1. Laws that deal with relations between God and humans.
2. Laws that deal with relations among people.
3. Laws that deal with relations between parents and children, considered to be a bridge between the first two types of commandments.

FACT

It is believed that the Ten Statements were inscribed directly by God onto stone tablets which Moses brought with him when he descended the mountain on the seventeenth day of Tammuz.

The Ten Statements appear twice in the Torah, in Exodus 20:2–14 and Deuteronomy 5:2–18. (There are a few minor discrepancies between the two.) The following list is taken from Exodus:

1. I am the Lord your God who brought you out of the land of Egypt, the house of bondage: You shall have no other gods beside Me.
2. You shall not make for yourself a sculptured image, or any likeness of what is in the heavens above, or on the earth below, or in the waters under the earth. You shall not bow down to them or serve them. For I the Lord your God am an impassioned God, visiting the guilt of the fathers upon the children, upon the third and upon the fourth generations of those who reject Me, but showing kindness to the thousandth generation of those who love Me and keep My commandments.
3. You shall not swear falsely by the name of the Lord your God; for the Lord will not clear one who swears falsely by His name.
4. Remember the Sabbath day and keep it holy. Six days you shall labor

and do all your work, but the seventh day is a Sabbath of the Lord your God: you shall not do any work—you, your son or daughter, your male or female slave, or your cattle, or the stranger who is within your settlements. For in six days the Lord made heaven and earth and sea, and all that is in them, and He rested on the seventh day; therefore, the Lord blessed the Sabbath day and hallowed it.

5. Honor your father and mother, that you may long endure on the land which the Lord your God is giving you.
6. You shall not murder.
7. You shall not commit adultery.
8. You shall not steal.
9. You shall not bear false witness against your neighbor.
10. You shall not covet your neighbor's house: you shall not covet your neighbor's wife, or his male or female slave, or his ox or his ass, or anything that is your neighbor's.

©2001 Brand X Pictures

▲ The Ten Statements.

A Day of Shame

Forty days after scaling Mount Sinai, Moses returned, bearing the tablets on which God had inscribed the Ten Statements. This was supposed to be a joyous occasion, with the Israelites welcoming God's gift and thanking him for delivering them from Egypt and slavery. Instead, the seventeenth day of Tammuz became a cursed day that would coincide with other calamitous events that would befall the Jewish people.

FACT

On the seventeenth of Tammuz many years after the incident at Sinai, the walls of Jerusalem were breached by the Babylonians, and the First Temple was destroyed. And on another anniversary of that fateful day, the Romans sacked Jerusalem and destroyed the Second Temple, beginning the 2,000-year Diaspora.

To his dismay and outrage, instead of a solemn throng preparing to embrace the Law, Moses witnessed the Israelites engaged in an orgy and worshipping a Golden Calf they had fashioned out of the jewels and gold they had brought from Egypt. In his shock, Moses dropped the stone tablets and proceeded to smash the Golden Calf. Then, he ordered the Levites to execute those responsible for the transgression. Yet, despite his disappointment, Moses didn't turn against the Israelites. The Bible tells us that when God threatened to blot them out and make a new nation, Moses reminded him of his covenant with Abraham, Isaac, and Jacob, and God relented.

The 613 Mitzvot

Tradition holds it that on Mount Sinai Moses received the Torah, which includes the 613 *mitzvot* (or commandments). According to the Book of Exodus, God had dictated the commandments to Moses in order to provide the framework for a way of life for the people with whom God had established a covenant.

The term "Torah" has several meanings. In Hebrew, it means "law" or "doctrine," so it can be used to refer to Jewish Law as a whole. Often,

Jewish people use it to refer to the Hebrew Bible. However, another—narrower—definition is the Pentateuch, or the first five books of the Bible given to Moses at Sinai.

ALERT!

The Talmud recognizes that Moses could not have received the Torah in its present form at Mount Sinai since it describes events that hadn't yet happened at that time. The sages explain that Moses received the *mitzvot* orally and the Torah was compiled later. Nevertheless, we can still say that the Jews *received* the Torah at Sinai.

A Code of Law

In Judaism, the rules that the Jews must obey are known collectively as the *halakha,* and it is astonishing how comprehensive they are. *Halakha* is an interesting mixture of the secular and the religious. Some rules concern themselves with worshipping God and civic matters, while others cover such topics as dietary habits, hygiene, and sexuality. Some of the commandments apply exclusively to certain individuals or groups of people, such as the *kohanim* (temple priests) while others are pertinent only to the land of Israel.

A significant portion of these commandments are not germane to contemporary times. And yet, many of them still apply to Jews today. Being familiar with these laws is helpful in grasping what it was that united the Jewish people all over the world during the 2,000-year Diaspora. The following categories will provide you with an overview of the extent to which these commandments pervade Jewish life:

- God
- Torah
- Signs and symbols
- Prayer and blessings
- Love and brotherhood
- The poor and unfortunate
- Marriage, divorce, and family

- Criminal laws
- Punishment and restitution
- Prophecy
- Idolatry and idolatrous practices
- Agriculture and animal husbandry
- Clothing
- The firstborn

- Sexual relations
- Times and seasons
- Dietary laws
- Business practices
- Employees, servants, and slaves
- Vows, oaths, and swearing
- Sabbatical and Jubilee years
- Court and judicial procedures
- Injuries and damages
- Property and property rights

- *Kohanim* and Levites
- Tithes and taxes
- The Temple and sacred objects
- Sacrifices and offerings
- Ritual purity and impurity
- Lepers and leprosy
- The king
- Nazarites
- Wars

Interestingly enough, not all of these commandments are prohibitions. What makes *halakha* unique as a social and moral code of law is that in addition to prohibitions, it also contains obligations—of the 613 *mitzvot*, 248 are obligations.

Celebrating Shavuot

The revelation of the Torah to Moses is commemorated by the Jewish holiday of Shavuot. Shavuot is Hebrew for "weeks"; it occurs exactly seven weeks after the second day of Passover, a time period that represents the interval when the Israelites left Egypt but had not yet received the Torah. The interval between Passover and Shavuot is a time of solemnity, study, and meditation.

Starting with the second day of Passover, religious Jews practice the custom of counting the *Omer* (Hebrew for "sheaves of a harvested crop"). When they reach the fiftieth day, it's time to celebrate Shavuot. Traditionally, the counting was done in order to know when to begin harvesting, because Shavuot also celebrates the harvest.

Despite the deeply religious significance of Shavuot, the Torah itself first mentions Shavuot as an agricultural festival that marked the transition between the barley harvest and the start of the wheat-ripening season.

Before the destruction of the Temple, Jews used this brief respite from work to travel to Jerusalem, where they celebrated the Torah and offered sacrifices at the Temple. After the destruction of the First Temple, many pilgrims continued to come to Jerusalem. Communities that could not send all their members dispatched a representative delegation.

After the razing of the Second Temple in 70 C.E., pilgrimages to fulfill the earlier purpose of Shavuot became impossible. Hence, the focus of the holiday shifted from its dual agricultural and spiritual importance to emphasize the spiritual aspect.

FACT

Shavuot is known by many names: *Hag Habikkurim* (the Festival of the First Fruits), *Hag Matan Torateinu* (the Festival of the Giving of Our Torah), and *Hag Hakatzir* (the Feast of the Harvest).

A Dairy Feast

There are many customs and traditions associated with Shavuot that have been practiced for centuries and are embedded in Jewish heritage. During this festival, which lasts for seven days, certain blessings are recited and ceremonies are held in the home. Traditionally, the first Shavuot dinner is a dairy meal, and no meat is served.

One explanation for this custom is that it serves as a reminder of God's promise to deliver the Israelites into a land flowing with milk and honey (Exodus 3:8). Another reason offered is that when they received the Torah (which includes dietary laws), the Israelites did not yet have separate meat and dairy dishes and restricted themselves to dairy until they could have proper utensils. A more symbolic explanation is that the Jews eat dairy because at Sinai, the Israelites were as innocent as newborns whose only food is milk.

Holiday Greens

It is common practice on Shavuot to decorate both the home and synagogue with flowers, plants, and tree branches, because Shavuot is the holiday of the harvest. Other explanations exist as well. The plants are reminiscent of the foliage at Mount Sinai, which was forested and lush with greens, and may also serve as a reminder that Pharaoh's daughter found Moses among reeds in the Nile.

Reading the Book of Ruth

In the synagogue, the weekly Torah reading includes the revelation at Mount Sinai and the giving of the Ten Statements, and a portion of the Ten Statements is recited in a special chant.

It is also customary to read from the Book of Ruth, which relates the inspiring story of a Moabite woman who, after the death of her Jewish husband and her father-in-law, voluntarily chooses Judaism in order to stay with her mother-in-law. Likely as not, you will have heard some version of Ruth's famous unselfish pledge to her mother-in-law: "For wherever you go, I will go; wherever you lodge, I will lodge; your people will be my people and your God my God" (Ruth 1:16).

Observant Jews follow another Shavuot tradition—staying awake all night to study the Torah. This practice is called *Tikkun Leil Shavuot,* and it began sometime in the sixteenth century in Safed, Israel, where Jewish mysticism (*Kabbalah*), flourished (more on that in Chapter 16).

The saga of Ruth is particularly relevant to Shavuot because Ruth voluntarily accepts the Torah and Judaism as the Israelites did at the foot of Mount Sinai. Because it is central to Jewish belief that all Jews—past, present, and future—were present at Sinai, each and every Jew, like Ruth, freely takes upon himself or herself the privileges and responsibilities connected with accepting the Torah. And there is another reason for our remembering of Ruth. According to the Bible, Ruth was the great-grandmother of King David, who in turn would be the forefather of the messiah.

The Ark of the Covenant

The Torah relates that one of God's commandments to the Israelites was to construct the Ark of the Covenant, a sanctuary for God's spirit that would provide a dwelling place where God could make His presence known to the Israelites while they traveled. To this extent, the Ark of the Covenant was the only physical manifestation of God's presence.

The Ark was a wooden acacia box two and a half cubits in length (one cubit is approximately eighteen inches), one and a half cubits in height, and one and a half cubits wide. The box was plated in pure gold both inside and out, and four gold rings were affixed to the bottom through which two acacia poles coated in gold could be attached. Appended to the box's gold covering *(kapporet)* were two sculptured golden cherubs that faced each other with their wings touching.

When at rest, the Ark was situated within a large tent known as the Tent of the Meeting or Tabernacle. In the tent, there was an outer room that held a seven-branched candelabra, or menorah, a table with twelve loaves of bread on it, and an incense altar. The Ark was situated in an inner room called the Holy of Holies. When the Israelites kept on moving, they carried the Ark with them, hoisted upon the shoulders of the family of Kehath, of the tribe of Levi.

ALERT!

The construction of the Ark did not go against the prohibition to worship "a sculptured image" or any "likeness" of God. The Ark of the Covenant was not in itself the object of veneration, though it was believed that the Spirit of God dwelt within it.

The contents of the Ark remain a mystery that has piqued the interest of many throughout the centuries. Traditionally, it is believed that the Ark contained two sets of the Ten Statements—both the first set that was broken and the second, intact, set inscribed by Moses. Another version of the story relates that there might have been two Arks, each containing one set of the Ten Statements.

The Family of Priests

Many Jews carry the name of Cohen, Kohen, Kagan, Kahana, Kaplan, Rappaport, Aaronson, or Katz, as well as many other variations. Any one of these names signals that the person who carries it may be a *kohein*, or priest.

At Sinai, God designated Moses' brother Aaron as the priest and proclaimed that Aaron's descendants would be responsible for priestly duties. The *kohanim* were in charge of performing sacrifices specified by God in his commandments and carrying the Ark of the Covenant. Later, the *kohanim* would take on the responsibility in conducting services at the Temple in Jerusalem. Because of their special role, the *kohanim* were subject to the special *mitzvot* that had to do with ritual cleanliness and purity.

Today, most Jews don't know for certain whether they are direct descendants of Aaron, but those who carry the *kohein* names still adhere to the prohibitions specified in the Torah. One such restriction forbids *kohanim* from touching the dead or even passing through a cemetery. *Kohanim* are also afforded special honor. For instance, during religious services they are the first ones to be called up to read the Torah.

At the Doorstep of the Promised Land

Under the leadership of Moses, the Hebrews wandered in the wilderness for forty years, gradually moving through the Sinai Desert and toward Canaan. Why did it take them forty years to reach the Promised Land? One explanation is that it was their punishment for refusing to enter Canaan after the spies they sent ahead returned with a deceitful report, claiming the inhabitants were too fierce to be overcome. According to another explanation, God waited until the generation of those who were slaves in Egypt passed away so that the Israelites who would enter the Promised Land would be those who were born free.

Moses was denied entry as well, as a punishment for a transgression that remains unclear to this day. The reason most frequently offered has to do with a biblical episode when the Hebrews demanded water and God instructed Moses to order a nearby rock to provide water to the

Israelites. Instead of speaking, however, Moses struck the rock with his rod, thereby deviating from God's specific directions. Embellishing upon this incident, others have postulated Moses' infraction had more to do with giving the impression that he and Aaron supplied the water. In any event, Moses did not enter the Promised Land.

Sukkot—The Feast of Tabernacles

Given their migratory habits during this period, the Israelites lived in temporary dwellings, or *sukkot* (plural of *sukkah*, a booth or tent). In Leviticus 23:42–43, God commanded: "You shall live in booths seven days in order that future generations may know that I made the Israelite people live in booths when I brought them out of the land of Egypt." And up to this day, the Jews celebrate the seven-day holiday of Sukkot, which usually is in the fall.

Celebration of the Harvest

Historically, Sukkot was also a festival of the fall harvest, sometimes referred to as *Chag Ha-Asif* (the Festival of the Ingathering). When farmers completed their harvest, they would make a pilgrimage to the Temple in Jerusalem to celebrate and offer God their gratitude for a good harvest. Traditionally, they spent seven days in Jerusalem, during which time they lived in *sukkot*.

Dwelling in a *sukkah* has a symbolic element. Just as God protected the Israelites during the forty years wandering in the desert with the "clouds of glory" that enveloped them from above, below, and all around, the *sukkah* surrounds and protects whoever enters it.

Dwelling in the Sukkah

Even though residing in a *sukkah* at least for a period of time during the seven-day holiday is a *mitzvah,* there are exemptions to this duty. For example, if sitting inside the *sukkah* causes physical discomfort—if, for instance, it's raining heavily or killer bees are swarming about—it's okay to abandon it for the comfort and safety of your home. Nevertheless, building a *sukkah* and spending some time in it is usually an enjoyable experience and is something many Jews look forward to. It is time to get away from our busy lives and also a time of contemplation.

The primary function of the *sukkah* today is to eat there. In fact, there is a special obligation to eat in the *sukkah* on the first night of the holiday even if it is raining (although the elderly and sick, as well as mothers with small children, are not bound to keep this commandment). A bride and groom are also exempt from dwelling in the *sukkah*.

Many Jews invite guests to their *sukkah*, to fulfill the *mitzvah* of hospitality (*ha-chnasat orechim*). In accordance with another custom, called *ushpizin*, seven symbolic biblical guests are invited to the *sukkah* each day: Abraham, Isaac, Jacob, Joseph, Moses, Aaron, and David. Recently, some Jews have begun extending this invitation to female biblical figures—Sarah, Rachel, Rebecca, Leah, Miriam, Abigail, and Esther.

Building Regulations

The construction of a *sukkah* is subject to very specific requirements. The *sukkah* must be at least three feet high and at least twenty-six inches in length and in width. The walls cannot exceed thirty feet in height (although some sources specify that they may be as tall as forty feet). A *sukkah* can be constructed from cinder blocks, lumber, canvas, or nylon sheeting attached to a frame of wood, metal piping, or any other suitable material.

The rules governing the *sekhakh* (covering) are very explicit. Because the *sukkah* is meant to be a booth, the *sekhakh* must be temporary, and the material allowed for its construction is limited. Only organic material such as wood, leafy branches, and evergreens can be used for the *sekhakh*.

The *sekhakh* must be spaced evenly, with gaps no wider than eleven and a half inches, so that the covering is ample enough to provide shade. Furthermore, the boards or beams used should be no wider than sixteen inches, so that people inside can still see the stars at night. Should it rain, more material may not be added to fill the gaps on the *sekhakh*. Otherwise, the *sukkah* will no longer be kosher.

When the *sukkah* is complete, it's time for decoration. The Talmud (a collection of biblical commentaries and oral traditions) includes a number of suggestions for decorating a *sukkah*: hanging carpets and tapestries, nuts, peaches, grape branches, and wreaths made from ears of corn. More contemporary decorations are fruits, Indian corn, pictures of Jerusalem and other Jewish symbols, and New Year greeting cards.

The Four Species

God commanded that on the first day of Sukkot, "you shall take the product of goodly trees, branches of palm trees, boughs of leafy trees, and willows of the brook, and you will rejoice before the Lord your God seven days" (Leviticus 23:40). These are known as the Four Species:

1. *Etrog,* a citrus fruit, resembling a lemon, native to Israel.
2. *Lulav,* a dried palm branch.
3. *Aravot,* two willow branches.
4. *Hadasim,* three myrtle branches.

The *lulav, aravot,* and *hadasim* are bound together in a precise manner and may be referred to collectively as the *lulav*. During specific times of the synagogue service, the congregants shake and wave the *lulav* and *etrog*. According to tradition, the Four Species may symbolize four types of Jews. The *etrog* has taste and smell, and stands for those who possess knowledge and good deeds; the *lulav* has taste but no smell, representing knowledge but not good deeds; the myrtle, having smell but no taste, portrays those who have good deeds but no knowledge; the willow has neither taste nor smell and represents those without either good deeds or knowledge. Ⓔ

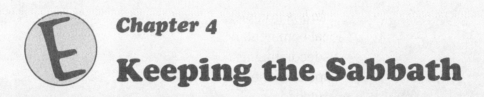

Chapter 4

Keeping the Sabbath

Shabbat, Sabbath, or the Sabbath Queen, as it is respectfully called, has been with the Jewish people since they encamped at the foot of Mount Sinai almost 3,400 years ago, where they received God's *mitzvot* and became a nation. Therefore, it is fitting that we examine the nature of this most exceptional day at this period in history—when the Jews are about to enter the Promised Land.

The Commandment to Keep and Remember

For the Jews, Shabbat is the most important day of the week. What is more, the Jewish tradition considers Shabbat more sacred than any other holiday—even Yom Kippur (the Day of Atonement). It is the only holiday specifically addressed in the Ten Statements, where God commands the Jews to "Remember the Sabbath day and keep it holy." This charge, a sign of the covenant between God and the Jewish people, carries with it both a blessing and a responsibility.

QUESTION?

What is a *midrash*?
A *midrash* is a commentary or a story that deals with a biblical passage and attempts in some way to explain it or elaborate on it. A *midrash* may be understood in opposition to a *peshat,* or the literal interpretation of a particular biblical passage.

Shabbat is such a unique time that it has been compared to the Messianic Age. A *midrash* explains that when God was preparing to give the Torah to the Israelites, He said that He had something extraordinary to give them if they would accept His commandments and the Torah. The Jews asked what that could be and God replied that it was the "world-to-come." The Israelites wanted to know what it was like, and God answered that it was just like Shabbat because the world to come is simply one long Shabbat.

The word *Shabbat* comes from the Hebrew root *shin-bet-tav*, which means "to rest" or "cessation of labor." It is also referred to as the Sabbath Queen, the Queen of the week, or the Bride because Jewish mystics believed that on Sabbath eve, God's Presence or *Shekinah* (often considered to be God's feminine component) descends to earth.

Observing Shabbat

On the Sabbath, the seventh day of the week, Jews rest and turn their minds toward prayer and toward home. Observant Jewish families gather at home to welcome the Shabbat as well as to end it the following evening. Because Shabbat is so important to the heritage and history of the Jewish people, we will examine exactly how this day is traditionally observed.

FACT

In the Jewish tradition, the day does not begin in the middle of the night or with the sunrise, but in the evening, at sunset. Hence, Shabbat begins exactly eighteen minutes before sunset and ends on Saturday night, after three stars appear in the sky (approximately forty minutes after sunset).

God commanded the Jews to "remember" and "to observe" Shabbat (Exodus 20:8 and Deuteronomy 5:12), a twofold injunction. *Halakhah* (Jewish Law) and all of the *mitzvot* having to do with Shabbat are designed to fulfill this purpose. However, Jewish people in different times and different places have observed Shabbat in many different ways. Today, those who practice one of the four branches of Judaism (Orthodox, Conservative, Reform, and Reconstructionist) follow their respective protocols when celebrating Shabbat. Jews from different parts of the world also share specific customs and traditions that may seem foreign to other Jews.

The following description of observances is from the Orthodox tradition, which is more rigorous in its adherence to all the rules and commandments concerning Shabbat. But it's important to note that despite the differences in observance, Shabbat is held in the highest esteem by all branches of Judaism.

Prohibitions on Keeping Shabbat

Mitzvot associated with observing Shabbat include affirmative obligations as well as prohibitions. These prohibitions are known collectively as *melachah,* a term that can be loosely translated to mean "work," but that should really be defined as any work that is creative or that exercises dominion over the environment. *Melachah* does not necessarily include any expenditure of energy or physical activity.

For example, flipping a light switch does not require much energy or effort, but because it is a creative act it is prohibited during Shabbat.

Walking up a flight of stairs, on the other hand, is permitted. Although it does require an expenditure of energy, climbing a stairway is not a creative act and does not exercise control over the environment.

There are two underlying explanations regarding the prohibition on turning on a light. The first has to do with the interdiction against cooking, because it involves heating metal. Secondly, because turning on the light completes (or builds) a circuit, it is prohibited by the injunction that the act of building cannot be performed on Shabbat.

Working within the definition of what is prohibited on Shabbat, the rabbis have established thirty-nine categories of forbidden acts, which they set forth in the *Mishna* (Code of Jewish Law). For instance, it is prohibited to take an object from the private domain into the public or transport an object in the public domain for over seven feet. Other categories include the following:

- Plowing
- Baking
- Slaughtering
- Writing ("creating" words)
- Building

- Kindling a fire
- Hitting with a hammer
- Weaving
- Tying

The Purpose of Melachah

On Shabbat, more observant Jews do not drive, turn on the lights or the television set, go out to dinner, see a movie, or even make a freshly brewed cup of coffee. With all these restrictions, you might seriously question whether "the world to come" is an event one should look forward to. But such an attitude misses the point. These restrictions are designed not to punish but rather to remove the devout from the mundane life and help them experience fully the wonders of Shabbat.

©Israel Ministry of Tourism. Courtesy of the Israel Ministry of Tourism.

▲ The ancient Hurva Synagogue in Jerusalem, destroyed in the 1967 war and later rebuilt by architect Louis Kahn.

Greeting the Shabbat Queen

Because work on Shabbat is prohibited, preparing for it usually involves such practical steps as cleaning the house, setting the Shabbat dinner table and preparing the Shabbat meal, bathing, and dressing up for the occasion. On Friday afternoons, for thousands of years, all over the globe, Jews have bustled about in preparation to greet Shabbat.

As Shabbat begins, the mother will traditionally light two candles, which represent the *mitzvot* to remember and observe. (Some families follow a slightly different tradition and light a candle for every person present at the table.) The candles may be of any color, but they are usually white. Usually, a blessing is said before lighting the candle, but in the case of Shabbat candles, you light them before saying a blessing because the blessing is what begins the Sabbath and you can't light candles on Shabbat. Then, the man of the house recites the special blessing, the *Kiddush,* over the wine.

FACT

The woman's role in welcoming the Shabbat by lighting the candles and saying the blessing is representative of women's responsibility of conducting the way Jewish traditions and practices are held in the home. However, if no women are present, a man can carry out the blessings. Inversely, if no men are present, it is appropriate for a woman to say the *Kiddush.*

The family can then greet each other with the words *shabbat shalom!* (in Hebrew) or *gut shabbes!* (in Yiddish), for the Sabbath has begun. At this time, some families attend a brief Shabbat service (*kabbalat shabbat*) at the synagogue and then return home for dinner.

Shabbat Dinner

For Shabbat dinner, the table is usually set with the family's best china and silverware. People often add a vase filled with fresh flowers and a white tablecloth. In addition to the festive decorations, the Shabbat dinner table requires a *Kiddush* cup, wine or grape juice, two *challahs* (special Shabbat bread loaves) with white covers, and candles.

Just before dinner, people wash their hands, and make a blessing over the *challah.* (This blessing is known as the *motzi,* or blessing of the bread.) Another beautiful custom that may take place at the Shabbat dinner is the blessing of the children.

It is also customary to sprinkle salt over the *challah* or dip the *challah* in salt. One explanation for this custom is that salt was a valuable commodity in the Roman Empire and was available only to free people. Another reason has to do with the fact that ever since the destruction of the Temple, the home has become a small sanctuary. Given that sacrifices were offered with salt, sprinkling salt on the *challah* is a link to the era of Temple Judaism.

On the Menu

Except for the bread and wine needed for the blessings, there are no special requirements for what is served at a Shabbat dinner, as long as the food is kosher, or subject to the Jewish dietary laws of *kashrut,* and was prepared before Shabbat began. Of course, Jews from different parts of the world do have their preferences.

At an Ashkenazic table, you may see dishes like gefilte fish, chopped liver, chicken soup with *matzah* balls, roast chicken, brisket of beef, and noodle or potato *kugel.* Among Sephardic Jews, traditional meals may consist of fish, eggplant salad, lamb roast, stuffed grape leaves, and white rice.

QUESTION?

Who are Ashkenazim and Sephardim?
Ashkenaz is the Hebrew term for "Germany," and Ashkenazic Jews are the Jews from Germany or Eastern Europe who speak Yiddish. Sephardic Jews take their name from *Sepharad,* or Spain—they are the Jews who were exiled to Spain and settled in Southern Europe, Northern Africa, or the Middle East.

During dinner, conversation is open to any subject, but it is a time for the family to move beyond the perfunctory small talk that exemplifies a typical evening meal. During or after the meal, some families will sing Sabbath songs. At the meal's conclusion, they recite the *birkat ha-mazon* (grace after meals).

Public Worship

Judaism is a religion shared by a community, and public worship has always been an integral part of Jewish life. Today, the synagogue is the place Jews go to worship together as a community, and at no time is this more appropriate than on the holy days of Shabbat.

The *kabbalat shabbat* service welcomes the Sabbath; it is followed by the evening or *ma'ariv* service, which includes additional prayers. In some synagogues, particularly those that practice Reform Judaism, this may be the main Sabbath service. Following services, most Reform, Reconstructionist, and Conservative congregations have an *oneg shabbat* (joy of the Sabbath), where refreshments are available and the congregation has the opportunity to socialize.

On Saturday, Sabbath observances continue with the morning service, which has three parts: *shacharit* (morning service), the Torah reading, and *musaf* (additional Shabbat prayer service). Again, following this service there is a *Kiddush* where wine and perhaps cakes and cookies are served. At this time, the family can return home to enjoy the rest of Shabbat.

FACT

It takes a full year for the congregation to read through the five books of the Torah. Upon the completion of the last weekly reading, which falls on the second day after Sukkot, Jews celebrate Simchat Torah, literally "rejoicing in the Torah."

During the afternoon, people may engage in a wide variety of activities so long as they are not prohibited by *Halakhah*. Generally, people occupy themselves with praying, reading, and studying, but you may also see some people playing games, such as chess or checkers, taking family walks, or engaging in other leisure activities. The point is for people to try and remove themselves from the ordinary and enter the holiness of Shabbat.

Separating from Shabbat

Because Shabbat is so extraordinary, simply ignoring its end when the sun sets on Saturday evening would be rude, much like not saying good-bye to an honored guest in your home. Hence, separating from Shabbat has its own ceremony and customs. When the day ends and three stars appear in the night sky, usually about forty minutes after sunset, devout Jewish families perform the *Havdalah* (separation) ceremony.

During *Havdalah*, blessings are made over the wine, a specially woven or braided multiwick *havdalah* candle, and a box called a *bsamim*, which contains sweet-smelling spices. Each of these objects represents something.

- **The wine cup:** Filled to the brim, the cup expresses hope that the upcoming week will be filled with divine blessings.
- **The *havdalah* candle:** Blazing like a torch, the *havdalah* candle's flame signifies light and guidance through life.

- **The spice box:** The spices contained in the spice box are meant to remind the devout to make an effort to bring some of the sweetness of Shabbat into the coming week.

It is customary to invite a stranger, traveler, or poor person to be a guest at a Shabbat dinner. Another common practice is to set aside a sum of money for charity before the lighting of the Sabbath candles and the welcoming of Shabbat.

Children are often included in the *Havdalah* ceremony—their parents entrust them with holding the candle and the spice box. At this time, the family recites the final blessing regarding the division between the consecrated and the worldly, which reflects how the Sabbath is distinct from the other days of the week.

A Pillar of the Jewish Community

The idea of the weekend, a time away from work at the end of each week, is a modern concept. And yet, thousands of years ago the Jewish people established one day of the week as a complete day of rest. Of course, the Sabbath is much more than a day free from toil, because it marks the covenant between God and the Jewish people.

During Sabbath prayer services, emphasizing this unique relationship between God and the Jews, the following words from Exodus 31:16–17 are recited: "The Israelite people shall keep the Sabbath, observing the Sabbath throughout the ages as a covenant for all time: it shall be a sign for all time between Me and the people of Israel. For in six days the Lord made heaven and earth, and on the seventh day He ceased from work and was refreshed."

The concept of the Jews as the "chosen people" has often been misinterpreted by gentiles. The special covenant between God and the Jews has nothing to do with the notion the Jews are superior to other people. Nor does it mean they are elected to salvation. All that it signifies is that God entered into a covenant with Abraham and his descendants that they would be loyal to one another. The Jews understand that this relationship comes with the responsibilities of following all of God's commandments, which do not burden the gentiles.

ALERT!

The way the Jewish people understand their covenant with God might explain why Judaism does not encourage conversion. Those who accept the Jewish faith and join the Tribe of Israel must also take on all the responsibilities of serving God and fulfilling all the *mitzvot.*

However, this notion of the Israelites being God's "chosen people" has not boded well for the Jews throughout the ages—particularly among the nations in which the Jews found themselves during the Diaspora. With the same jealousy leading to the murderous rage Jacob's sons displayed to their brother Joseph for being favored by their father, the nations and peoples of the world have vented their anger upon the Jews.

A Day of Hope

For millennia, Shabbat has served a special function of providing a beacon of light in the wilderness of the Diaspora by helping the Jews stay true to their path and their heritage. Each and every week of the year, this one day helped preserve the spirit of Jewish life even under the most adverse conditions.

Even if there was no synagogue to attend, there was the home and family where the Jews could welcome and celebrate Shabbat. If there was no home or shelter, there was always this special time of the week when each and every Jew could take a respite from worldly concerns and be reminded of the covenant with God. No matter how omnipotent their oppressors might have appeared and no matter how awesome their power seemed, nothing could ever stand in the way of the arrival of the Sabbath Queen every week.

Shabbat is a day that is central to both Judaism and the Jewish people. Perhaps this has been best expressed by Achad Ha-Am, a Jewish writer, who wrote: "More than Israel has kept the Sabbath, the Sabbath has kept Israel." E

Chapter 5

In the Promised Land

The Israelites reached the threshold of the Promised Land in the thirteenth century B.C.E. Through battle and negotiation, they soon installed themselves in the land that had been promised to them by God. For the next 200 years, they would live as separate tribes, led by their tribal elders and the Judges, fighting to hold onto their homes in the struggle with the Canaanites and later the Philistines.

The Conquest of Canaan

The Promised Land was Canaan, a place named after the son of Ham and the grandson of Noah. Located between the Jordan River, the Dead Sea, and the Mediterranean, it was bounded to the south by Egypt and to the north by Assyria. (At some points, it also included Transjordan, the area to the east of the Jordan River.)

Canaan was inhabited by Canaanites, a Semitic people speaking a language very similar to Hebrew. The Canaanites were mostly farmers and a few were nomads, but they had a civilized and advanced culture. The seven Canaanite tribes dwelled in thirty-one fortified city-states that were constructed using the great Mesopotamian cities as their model. Each city-state was ruled by its own sovereign.

©Itamar Grinberg. Courtesy of the Israel Ministry of Tourism.

▲ A modern Israeli hotel perched between the Negev desert and the Dead Sea.

Joshua Leads the Hebrews

The Book of Joshua goes into a great deal of detail over how God had commanded the Israelites to conquer Canaan and drive out the

Canaanites. After the death of Moses, sometime around the year 1250 B.C.E., God called upon Joshua, the son of Nun of the tribe of Ephraim, to cross the River Jordan and take with him the nation of Israel to the place that God had promised to the descendants of Abraham, Isaac, and Jacob.

FACT

There is also archaeological evidence to support the fact that at about this time in history, the Canaanites were indeed engaged in battles and their cities were threatened (and, in some cases, obliterated) by an invading force determined to make the land its home. There is also independent data suggesting that these people were led by a great military commander.

Joshua did not come to the job without considerable experience. He had been Moses' security chief and the commander of the guard of the Tabernacle. He engaged in combat during the years of wandering in the wilderness, particularly in the battle with Amalek and his army (one of the first conflicts Israelites had to deal with after leaving Egypt). Hence, Joshua was well prepared to assume the role of general and he would become the Israelites' first great military commander.

However, the Canaanites were formidable adversaries. They had better weapons and benefited from more experience in military tactics. Moreover, their individual city-states were well fortified. Clearly, a full-scale invasion would be out of the question, so Joshua sought to strike at the entrance to the heartland of Canaan—the city of Jericho. The conquest to claim the land promised by God was underway.

ESSENTIAL

Joshua preferred to negotiate peaceful settlements wherever possible, a practice he subsequently would follow before attacking besieged cities. Therefore, Joshua sent an envoy to the Canaanites asking them to leave peacefully. One tribe did in fact leave, but the others remained.

The Crumbling Walls of Jericho

The heavily fortified city of Jericho dates back to the seventh millennium B.C.E. and had withstood many attacks, so no direct assault on the city could ever have had any hope of succeeding. The Bible tells us that at God's instructions, the priests carried the Ark of the Covenant around the city walls while trumpeting on rams' horns. They continued these actions for six days. On the seventh, the walls of Jericho came tumbling down.

Whether the story told in the Bible describes actual events or whether it is a metaphor of the Israelites' quiet persistence and their trust in God, the walls of Jericho did fall. Excavation results suggest that the destruction of the city's ramparts was probably due to an earthquake. If you believe that God may have acted by way of nature, the occurrence of an earthquake at the time the city lay under siege by the Israelites supports the biblical explanation.

Victory over Hazor

Another large city-state to fall to the Israelites was the city of Hazor, a vast town with perhaps as many as 50,000 inhabitants. Archaeological evidence indicates that the city was conquered during the thirteenth century B.C.E., the time of Joshua's invasion of Canaan.

The Bible tells us that Joshua's men were instructed to destroy the religious altars in Hazor, where the populace had constructed a temple for Baal worship. Excavation reports have shown that the temple and its contents were indeed mutilated during the city's invasion.

FACT

Despite a few early impressive victories, the Israelites suffered defeats as well. The Torah specifies that they lost the battle for the city of Ai as punishment for the act of one man, Achan, who stole valuables from the people of Jericho after its demise, disobeying God's mandate not to loot or plunder the fallen city.

Emerging Victorious

The conquest of Canaan was a slow and painful process. The struggle continued even after Joshua's death, and more than two centuries would elapse before the Israelites were finally entrenched in the Promised Land, toward the end of the second millennium B.C.E. Even then, the region experienced times of peace followed by times of unrest, and sometimes Israelites would be driven out from areas they had previously occupied. Frequently, they were consigned to reside in some of the worst terrain in Canaan.

Ultimately, the Israelites settled in the central hill country and a few places in the Jordan River valley. Their wandering days behind them, they stowed their tents and constructed crude stone huts and founded tiny villages and towns on the slopes and along the mountain crest. Forests were cleared and cisterns were dug as the Israelites learned to plant wheat, flax, and barley, and press olives for oil and grapes for their wine.

The Ark of the Covenant

Throughout their conquest of Canaan, the Ark accompanied the Jews, making its most spectacular appearance at Jericho. Once Canaan was conquered, the Ark was permanently established in Shiloh and later in Even-Ezer; in a subsequent battle with the Philistines, the Israelites were defeated and the Ark was captured. The Philistines moved the Ark to Ashdod and then to other cities.

The Bible relates how wherever the Ark lodged, a plague would strike the inhabitants of that city. Finally figuring out the connection, the Philistines returned the Ark to the Israelites.

It would be up to King David to take the Ark of the Covenant to Jerusalem. When David's son, King Solomon, built the First Temple in 825 B.C.E., the Ark found a permanent home in the Temple, where it remained until the Temple's destruction at the hands of the Babylonian Empire in the fifth century B.C.E. What happened to the Ark after that time is not known, but the Ark of the Covenant unquestionably holds a singular place in the history of the Jewish people.

The Judges of Israel

The Era of the Judges spanned a period of more than 200 years and began with the death of Joshua. What we know about the Judges is derived from the Book of Judges, comprised of stories that provide a historical narrative of Jewish life during that period of time.

Because the Israelites were spread thinly across the region during this epoch, they did not comprise a unified nation. Rather, they remained divided into separate tribes, which governed themselves according to tribal logic. There was no central authority or main Temple to worship God. In fact, we are told that "In those days there was no king in Israel, everyone did what was right in his eyes" (Book of Judges 21:25).

Tribalism seemed well suited to the needs of the Israelites at that time. Self-rule by tribal council conformed to that streak of individualism that has always been prominent in the Jewish character throughout history. The aversion to the concept of a sovereign may explain why kings appeared for only the briefest period in Jewish history.

A Religious, Political, and Military Role

However, this did not mean anarchy prevailed among the tribes of Israel. The tribes had judges, *shofetim* (*shofet* in the singular), who served a twofold task. On the one hand, they were expected to resolve disputes among the tribes, adjudicate Jewish law, and provide spiritual leadership. On the other hand, they were frequently called upon to fulfill the role of military commander.

The judges attained their position by popular appeal and their charismatic personalities. Although no formal process of election existed, neither was the post inherited. When Gideon was offered the kingship of Israel after his victory over Midian, he refused, saying, "I will not rule over you, and my son will not rule over you. The Lord will rule over you."

They were a diverse group of a colorful cast of characters. Many were born to poor families, or worse—Jephthah, the son of a prostitute, defeated the Ammonites with his gang of bandits. On the other hand, Eli and Samuel were priests, and Deborah was a prophetess. Gideon was a simple farmer while Ehud was an emissary. And then we have Samson, a Nazarite known for his love of violence, vandalism, debauchery, and a penchant for wicked women.

Along with Samson and Jephthah, there were a total of sixteen judges of Israel:

- Othniel
- Ehud
- Shagmar
- Deborah
- Gideon
- Abimelech
- Tola

- Yair
- Ibzan
- Elon
- Abdon
- Eli
- Samuel

ALERT!

The Book of Judges often explained the military losses and attacks on the Israelites as results of the Israelites' turning away from God. One of the responsibilities of the judges was to deal with the Israelites' proclivity for neglecting the Law.

Judged by a Woman

One of the first judges was a woman named Deborah, the wife of Lapidoth. Deborah was a prophetess and an advisor to her people—she used to sit under a palm tree where anyone could approach her for advice. She was a military leader as well: She issued battle orders and Barak, the leading military figure at that time, would not go into combat without her.

Leading the troops at a key engagement in Sisera, Barak and Deborah faced the Canaanite army supported by 900 iron chariots. On the eve of the confrontation, Barak questioned how they could prevail without any chariots of their own, but Deborah insisted they proceed. The next day, it rained and the Canaanite chariots got stuck in the mud. The Canaanites panicked as the agile Israelites attacked and quickly won, thereby fulfilling Deborah's prophecy that the Lord would deliver Sisera.

Samson and Delilah

Most of you have probably heard of the story about Samson and Delilah. Samson was a Jewish hero whose legendary strength kept at bay the Philistines, who posed a very serious threat to the Israelites. Inhabitants of the coast of Israel and Lebanon in the area of what is now Gaza, Ashdod, and Jaffa, the Philistines had perfected iron weapons and employed them to their advantage over their neighbors. Without Samson, the Israelites were no match for them.

The story goes that the Philistines convinced Delilah to find out the secret of Samson's strength. Beautiful Delilah seduced Samson and tricked him into confessing—Samson's power lay in his hair, which had never been cut. At night, Delilah cut off Sampson's long hair and then called in the Philistines. Without his superhuman strength, Samson was captured. The Philistines blinded him and brought him into a temple, where he was chained to two large columns and was left to await his execution.

When the time of execution finally came, Samson's hair had already begun to grow back and he had regained some of his strength. After the Philistines had gathered at the temple, Samson grabbed at the columns with all his strength and toppled them, letting the entire structure crumble to the ground, killing all those who were inside (including himself). Thus, Samson redeemed himself and slew many of Israel's enemies.

Turning from the Law

When the slow and painful process of occupying Canaan was as complete as it would ever be, the Israelites found themselves living nearby or even amidst the Canaanites, and it was unavoidable that they would come into contact with the Canaanite religion.

FACT

The Canaanite religion was polytheistic but there was one chief god known as Baal, the ruler of the universe and the source of life and fertility. Many temples were erected throughout Canaan in honor of Baal. During certain periods, the Baal cult had an effect upon the religious rituals practiced by the Israelites.

Israelites who faced bad weather and famine sometimes copied the Canaanite practices designed to appease various gods and goddesses that supposedly controlled nature, despite their own religion's strict injunction against pagan practices.

The biblical narrative is filled with examples of the repercussions experienced whenever even a small segment of the Jews abandoned their obligations under the covenant with God. Indeed, a pattern is established throughout Jewish history that when the Jews betray the Law, adverse consequences occur, usually in the form of defeat at the hands of an enemy.

Samuel Prophesies a State

The last judge of Israel, Samuel was more of a priest and prophet than a military leader. He spent many years traveling throughout the land adjudicating the law and providing guidance to the people, and he earned great respect from them, but he lived in a time when the people needed a military commander to lead them in the fight against the Philistines, who had once again gained the upper hand in Canaan. The Bible narrates how old Samuel looked toward his two sons, but neither was popular with the people and could not fill their father's shoes as a judge. In any event, emboldened by the return of the Ark, the tribal heads had something other than a judge in mind.

For four centuries, the Hebrews had never experienced central leadership. Now, faced with the awesome might of the Philistines, the elders believed the time had come to adopt the ways of their neighbors and swear allegiance to a king who would unite the disjointed tribes and lead them in war. Of course, God would remain their sovereign, but through Samuel, they believed, God would choose a temporal monarch whom all the tribes would accept.

Samuel also recognized the need for unity if the Philistines were to be defeated, and with God's help he anointed the first king of Israel to lead the Israelites. Though Samuel would continue to act as a spiritual leader in his own right, the time had arrived for the kingdom of Israel to come into being. Ⓔ

Chapter 6

The Kings of Biblical Times

The kingdom of Israel, which included the twelve tribes of Reuben, Simeon, Levi, Judah, Issachar, Zebulun, Joseph, Benjamin, Dan, Naphtali, Gad, and Asher, did not last for very long. However, its achievements remain legendary, from the construction of the First Temple in Jerusalem to the writing of the Psalms of David and the Song of Songs of Solomon, as well as the military conquests that were nothing short of miraculous.

Saul Is Anointed the First King

Though Moses had prophesied the time would one day come for a king to be appointed from among the Hebrews and the elders had convinced Samuel of the need for a secular monarch to unite the Israelite tribes, the last judge of Israel still had his misgivings. In part, his reluctance was based upon a sincere belief that the people's desire for a king was an act of disobedience towards God and that, in the end, they would suffer for this. However, it is also likely that Samuel was uncomfortable about sharing the power he had exercised over the Israelites in all their affairs.

The Jewish tradition does not state definitively how it came about that Saul, from the tribe of Benjamin, was anointed as king of Israel. Though it's hinted that Samuel received the direction from God, he may have also been guided by popular opinion, tribal leaders, or some other force. In any case, sometime before the end of the eleventh century B.C.E., in a place called Mizpeh near Ramah, Samuel anointed Saul the first king of Israel in a ceremony held before representatives of all twelve tribes.

ALERT!

As Samuel anointed Saul's head with oil, sanctifying his new role, he did not give Saul the title *melekh* (hereditary king), which would have automatically passed the kingship to Saul's sons. It seems that Samuel had his reservations about Saul's future conduct as king.

Why Saul?

Saul was a well-received choice for many reasons. His physical traits lent the new king an aura of royalty. He was tall, standing a head above his peers, handsome, and was full of confidence, if not outright bravado. Most importantly, he had earned a reputation as a military leader, which was the main reason for establishing the throne in the first place. His knowledge of guerrilla warfare had proven successful against the better armed and trained Philistines and other enemies of Israel. Saul organized the first standing army and would achieve many military victories, although he could not completely rid the land of the Philistines.

Saul's Failures

Saul was no diplomat, and only rarely did he exercise his monarchical authority for anything other than military purposes. He never attained great wealth during his relatively brief reign and did not enjoy the powers normally wielded by monarchs. Though he was comfortable among the two southern tribes of Benjamin and Judah, he lacked the political savvy to garner the support of the other ten tribes in the north. But the real problem Saul faced was not with the tribal leaders nor with the general population but with one man—Samuel, the judge who had anointed him.

Samuel resented Saul's inability or refusal to execute God's instructions as they were imparted to him by Samuel. The final break between Saul and Samuel occurred when Saul waged war against the Amalekites and the Israelites emerged victorious. All the Amalekites were to be executed, but Saul did not obey and spared the life of the Amalekite king, Agag. When Samuel heard the news, he became enraged and took it upon himself to slay Agag. Unfortunately, he was too late. By that time, Agag had already sired a male child.

According to Jewish tradition, the evil antagonist of the story of Purim, Haman, was a direct descendant of Agag's surviving son. That is how all the Israelites were punished for Saul's failure to obey God.

This was the final straw for Samuel, who set out to find another person worthy of being king. The judge did not desire civil war and determined that the new king would only assume the monarchy after Saul's death. But because of Saul's mistakes, the crown would not pass down Saul's line.

A New King in Waiting

During the course of his travels, Samuel found himself in the town of Bet Lechem (Bethlehem), where he visited Jesse, of the tribe of Judah and met Jesse's seven sons. Despite their physical and intellectual attributes, Samuel did not find a future king among them and asked if Jesse had any more sons. It was then that Jesse summoned his youngest son, David, a shepherd. The Bible tells us that Samuel knew at once that David would be the future king of Israel. Then and there, he poured oil over David's head and anointed him *melekh* and a successor to Saul.

With Samuel's blessing, David left his father's house and joined Saul's entourage. Quickly, he earned a reputation as a formidable fighter, thanks to his skillful use of a sling and his agility in battle, as he did not wear armor. You have probably heard of the legendary fight between David and Goliath, in which the young David slew the giant Goliath, a miraculous victory that inspired the Israelite forces to defeat the Philistines.

FACT

There is also another aspect of David's personality that endeared him to Saul. Saul was plagued with a dark, saturnine disposition—it is possible he suffered from bipolar disorder. During the periods of depression, Saul could only find comfort in David, who would play the harp and sing as a way of soothing the melancholy monarch.

David and Jonathon

Soon, Saul began to treat David as a son, and his son Jonathon, who was supposed to inherit his father's kingship, did not grow jealous of his father's attention to this young man and also bonded with David. In fact, David and Jonathon were as close as brothers. At Jonathon's suggestion, Saul arranged a marriage between David and Saul's daughter Michal.

Since David could not pay a worthy dowry, Saul asked for the lives of 100 Philistines, a bloodthirsty request affording insight into Saul's morose nature. Rising up to the challenge, David slew 200 Philistines. The marriage solidified David's position in the court, but his growing popularity among the Israelites was becoming a threat to the king.

When Saul heard the people sing that "Saul has slain his thousands, and David his tens of thousands," he fell into a fit of rage and threw a spear at David. Although he missed, it became clear to Jonathon and

David that David must flee for his life. David retreated back to Judah, where he carved out a fiefdom for himself, supported by Samuel and the priestly establishment.

Israel Is in Danger

Saul became so preoccupied with catching David that he ignored the enemies of Israel. When the Philistines attacked the Israelites at Mount Gilboa, in the Galilee region (around 1005–1004 B.C.E.), Saul was unprepared, but he did not want to give in without a fight, so he engaged the superior Philistine forces. This time, the Israelites were no match for the Philistines, and Saul saw his army defeated, and all of his sons killed. Rather than be taken alive and murdered, Saul committed suicide by falling on his sword. Thus, the fledgling kingdom of Israel was without a king. David's time had come.

The Reign of King David

David was an extraordinary man. The stories related about David describe him as a handsome man with dark features and a ruddy complexion, a man of great spirit and faith, well versed in poetry and music—the Jewish tradition ascribes to him the authorship of the Psalms. He was also a formidable warrior and shrewd statesman who brought many victories to his people and consolidated the kingdom of Israel.

At the time of Saul's death, David already had control over the tribes of Judah and Benjamin, in the south. However, control of the lands of the other ten tribes, also known as the Northern Kingdom, went to Ishmael. It was only after Ishmael was murdered that the northern tribes offered the throne of the Northern Kingdom to David, and that is how he united the lands of the twelve tribes into the kingdom of Israel.

A Strong Leader

History afforded David a unique opportunity. At this time, Egypt and Assyria were in a state of decline and did not pose a threat to Canaan. Thus, David was able to concentrate all his efforts on internal struggles with the Philistines. His military victories were numerous, and David succeeded in transforming Israel into a small kingdom with a political system that can best be described as an absolute monarchy.

Unlike Saul, David exercised leadership in nonmilitary matters such as legislation, religious matters, and even public development. David was ambitious, clever, and popular among the people, a card that he played to his advantage.

In the New Capital of Israel

Perhaps one of David's greatest military achievements was the conquest of Jerusalem, which he declared the capital of the Israelite Empire. With the Ark of the Covenant safely lodged in Jerusalem, the city became both a political and a spiritual center of Israel, and it would retain this important role for millennia, even during the times of Diaspora, when the Jews could not claim the city as their own.

David was a devout man, and he wanted to construct the Temple for the Ark of the Covenant, but there were political problems that forced him to delay the construction. David did not wish to provoke the northern tribes, who would be angered that the Temple was being constructed in the southern city of Jerusalem. Furthermore, the resplendent edifice he envisioned sounded more like a pagan temple than the Tabernacle, where the Ark of the Covenant had been housed. It would be up to David's son Solomon to erect the magnificent structure of the First Temple.

The Story of Bathsheba

Despite his glorious military triumphs, his popularity among the people, and his unrivaled ability to govern, David was not a man without faults. The story of David and Bathsheba certainly shows David in a less than favorable light.

One night, David was resting on his rooftop, when he spied a beautiful woman bathing.

This woman, Bathsheba, was the granddaughter of Ahithophel, David's counselor, and the wife of one of David's military commanders, Uriah, a Hittite who had adopted the ways of the Hebrews. David had to have Bathsheba, regardless of the fact that she was married. When Bathsheba later informed him that she was pregnant, David decided that he would summon her husband back from the battlefield. If Uriah would sleep with his wife, he would later assume that the child was his own.

However, it was customary to abstain from sexual conduct when on leave from battle. In keeping with this tradition, Uriah refrained from going home to his wife. Seeing that his devious scheme failed, David went even further. He dispatched Uriah back to the battlefield with sealed instructions to his commander that he be assigned to the front lines and ordered to remain there even after all others retreated. Uriah perished in battle, and after a period of mourning Bathsheba was married to King David.

Technically, David did not violate the *mitzvah* regarding adultery because it was the practice of David's troops to give their wives conditional divorces in the event they would go missing in action, thus making it impossible for their wives to ever remarry. Therefore, at least according to the letter of the law, Bathsheba was not married. But clearly, David acted immorally regarding his conduct with Bathsheba and he was the one responsible for the death of Uriah.

FACT

In accordance with Jewish law, a woman who cannot prove that she is a widow (that is, if there is no proof of her husband's death) is known as *agunah*, and cannot remarry.

Overcome with guilt, David confessed to his confidant, the prophet Nathan. Because David, a monarch, showed humility and remorse, he was forgiven, but Nathan declared that the child born to Bathsheba would not live long. And indeed, the boy was frail and soon died. And yet, Bathsheba would have another child, a boy named Solomon, who would one day assume his father's role as king of Israel.

Solomon the Wise

As fortunate as David was when it came to ruling the land and winning military battles, he was not so lucky when it came to his sons. His first-born son Amnon, born to Ahinoam of Jezreel, lost his birthright after raping his half-sister Tamar, who was David's favorite daughter. The next in line was Chileab, David's son with Abigail; unfortunately, he died as a youth. Another one of David's sons, Absalom, made an attempt to depose David and was clearly not going to be rewarded with the monarchy. Adonijah was next in line, and then there was Solomon, born to Bathsheba, David's favorite wife.

©Israel Ministry of Tourism. Courtesy of the Israel Ministry of Tourism.

◀ It is a great honor to become bar mitzvah at the Western Wall.

David did not formally name his successor until he was on his deathbed, and the choice fell on Solomon. Summoning the priest Zadok to his chambers, David arranged for his son to be anointed and blessed the twelve-year-old with words that have become the traditional Bar Mitzvah blessing: "You shall be strong, therefore, and show yourself a man, and keep the charge of the Lord your God to walk in His ways, to keep His statutes and His commandments and His testimonies." David died around the year 965 B.C.E., after a forty-year reign as the greatest king of the Israelites.

A Secular King

Unlike his father, Solomon was neither spiritual nor deeply religious. Instead, he ruled by his wits and focused his energies on more secular concerns, such as increasing trade and commerce, and constructing grand buildings like the majestic palace within the city walls of Jerusalem. Indeed, Solomon modeled himself more on the Mesopotamian kings than he did upon either David or Saul.

One practice common to the area that he followed was to forge political alliances and establish trade routes by marrying the daughters of foreign sovereigns and affluent merchants. It is said that Solomon may have carried this custom to an excess—he had 700 wives and 300 concubines, most of whom were not daughters of Israelites. It is not coincidental that the Jewish tradition credits Solomon with composing the Song of Songs, a lyrical love poem that may be read metaphorically as describing man's love for God.

QUESTION?

Did Solomon break Jewish law when he married non-Jewish women?
Halakhah prohibits Jewish men from marrying non-Jewish women, although a gentile woman can convert to Judaism prior to the marriage. Because Solomon allowed his wives to continue practicing their pagan religions, he incurred the wrath of God, who threatened to break apart the kingdom of Israel after Solomon's death (1 Kings 11:9–13).

Solomon was an astute king. His rule extended for almost four decades, until the time of his death. Solomon displayed a keen ability as a statesman and also as an organizer in fortifying his power. But along with this wisdom, there was a streak of ruthlessness in his personality that became most apparent as he pursued his dream to erect an imposing edifice to be remembered for the millennium to follow.

Construction of the First Temple

Perhaps Solomon's greatest achievement was the construction of the Temple, as it was envisioned by David. No doubt, this was a magnificent structure, but it came at a tremendous price.

First, there was the matter of labor to undertake the massive project. It is believed that as many as 180,000 men were needed to complete the Temple's construction. To provide the manpower, Solomon used foreign-born slaves and laborers from the Jewish lower class, who were drafted for shifts that would last from one to three months. In order to finance the project that involved importing expensive products such as gold, copper, and cedar, the people of Israel paid heavy taxes. Although this did not endear Solomon to a large segment of the populace, he was undeterred.

There were other political problems as well. Although the idea of a Temple to house the Ark of the Covenant was popular among many Israelites, some felt that Solomon's Temple was more a model of an advanced pagan society than a reflection of the spiritual religion of the Hebrews that arose in the vastness of the desert. Indeed, some people at the time completely rejected the notion of a central place to worship or having a royal temple. One such sect was the Rechabites, who refused to recognize the Temple.

Moreover, many Israelites from the ten northern tribes resented that the center of their religion was to be in the southern part of the kingdom, in the land of Judah. They saw a problem with Jerusalem's claim that only ceremonies held at the Temple would be valid in the eyes of God.

A Glorious Undertaking

All the problems aside, the Temple really did turn out to be a magnificent structure. Because of the rocky terrain, a flat platform had to be built and set in place before the construction of the Temple could begin. The actual Temple, built in the shape of a rectangle, may have been as large as 180 feet long, ninety feet wide, and fifty feet high (this is according to the Bible; other sources indicate it was somewhat smaller). Side chambers about twenty feet high surrounded the Temple. Since Solomon hired Phoenician architects to work on this project, the design reflected a Phoenician motif with gold and ivory overlays and figures of sphinxes.

By contrast, the most important room in the Temple was practically barren. The Holy of Holies, located at the far western wall, was a thirty-foot windowless cube illuminated by oil lamps. Under the sculptures of two cherubim, fifteen feet in height with human heads and the bodies of lions, lay the Ark and the Ten Statements. The only time anyone was permitted inside this sanctum was once a year on Yom Kippur, when the high priest would enter and pray to God on behalf of the Israelites.

Outside the Temple there was a large altar. This is where the priests performed daily ceremonies and sacrifices, and where special offerings were made to God during holidays and festivals.

A Nation Divides

Solomon died sometime between 926 and 922 B.C.E., and his son, Rehoboam, was anointed the next king of Israel. But despite the centralization of the government established by David and Solomon, the Israelite kingdom was already facing tensions that would threaten its short existence.

The ten northern tribes resented the power of the southern tribes of Judah and Benjamin, who had supplied the kingdom's rulers. (Saul was from the tribe of Benjamin, and David's dynasty was from the tribe of Judah). Establishment of the Temple in Jerusalem, in the land of Judah, only served to increase those tensions. But perhaps the most serious issue was the heavy tax burden, which the people of the north were no longer willing to bear.

Rehoboam did not have firm control over the situation, and his advisors suggested that he meet with the northern tribes in an effort to placate them. But Rehoboam lacked the sensitivity of his grandfather David and the shrewdness of his father Solomon. Instead, he was arrogant and intimidating. When asked for some relief from the tax burden and the need to provide labor, Rehoboam retorted, "My father made your yoke heavy, and I will add to your yoke."

The die was cast. The northern tribes seceded and established their own kingdom—the kingdom of Israel. The land to the south, inhabited by the tribes of Benjamin and Judah, became known as the kingdom of Judah. From that point forward, the twelve tribes of Israel would never be united again.

FACT

The two independent kingdoms were nothing but shadows of the former empire under David and Solomon. Soon, both kingdoms lost territory to foreign invaders as well as to internal revolts. One hundred years after the death of Solomon, Israel and Judah were small states, each no larger than the size of Connecticut.

The Kingdom of Judah

Rehoboam retained control of Judah, where he reigned for seventeen years, until 911 B.C.E. Up until the time of the Destruction of the First Temple in 586 B.C.E., the following kings would rule the kingdom of Judah:

- Abijah: 911–908 B.C.E.
- Asa: 908–867 B.C.E.
- Jehoshaphat: 867–846 B.C.E.
- Jehoram: 846–843 B.C.E.
- Ahaziah: 843–842 B.C.E.
- Athaliah: 842–836 B.C.E.
- Joash: 836–798 B.C.E.
- Amaziah: 798–769 B.C.E.
- Uzziah: 769–733 B.C.E.

- Ahaz: 733–727 B.C.E.
- Hezekiah: 727–698 B.C.E.
- Manasseh: 698–642 B.C.E.
- Amon: 641–640 B.C.E.
- Josiah: 639–609 B.C.E.
- Jehoahaz: 609 B.C.E.
- Jehoiakim: 608–598 B.C.E.
- Jehoiachin: 597 B.C.E.
- Zedekiah: 595–586 B.C.E.

The Northern Kingdom

The first king of the northern kingdom of Israel was Jeroboam, a scholar and leader, who made his capital in the city of Samaria. At first, the Northern Kingdom flourished. Israel had a much larger population than Judah, and its land was far more fertile. Moreover, it was situated close to trading routes.

During the major festivals of Passover, Shavuot, and Sukkot, some inhabitants of the kingdom of Israel continued to make pilgrimage to Jerusalem to worship and make sacrifices at the Temple. This disturbed Jeroboam, who wanted a complete break with the Southern tribes. Therefore, Jeroboam created two temples in the North—one in Bet El and the other in Dan. Once these temples were complete, the spiritual separation with Judah was complete as well.

After Jeroboam's death in 907 B.C.E., and until the fall of Samaria to the Assyrians 200 years later, eighteen different kings ruled the kingdom of Israel:

- Nadab: 907–906 B.C.E.
- Baasha: 906–883 B.C.E.
- Elah: 883–882 B.C.E.
- Zimri: 882 B.C.E.
- Omri: 882–871 B.C.E.
- Ahab: 871–852 B.C.E.
- Ahaziah: 852–851 B.C.E.
- Jehoram: 851–842 B.C.E.

- Jehu: 842–814 B.C.E.
- Jehoahaz: 814–800 B.C.E.
- Joash: 800–784 B.C.E.
- Jeroboam II: 784–748 B.C.E.
- Zechariah: 748–747 B.C.E.
- Shallum: 748–747 B.C.E.
- Menachem: 747–737 B.C.E
- Pekahiah: 737–735 B.C.E.
- Pekah: 735–733 B.C.E.
- Hoshea: 733–724 B.C.E.

The new kings were no longer the moral and religious leaders. That role fell to the prophets, who would try to steer their people toward moral and religious righteousness.

Chapter 7

The First Temple Period

The First Temple Period began with Solomon's construction of the Temple in Jerusalem. It continued with the division of the kingdom of Israel into Israel and Judah, and finally ended with the destruction of the Temple by the Babylonians in 586 B.C.E. During this time of political and military strife, the prophets emerged to inspire and guide the Israelites toward the path of righteousness and exclusive devotion to God.

Who Were the Prophets?

A prophet is a spokesperson for God and is therefore regarded as having been chosen by God. Indeed, the Hebrew word for prophet is *navi,* a term derived from the phrase *niv sefatayim* (fruit of the lips), clearly denoting the role of a prophet as someone who speaks for God. But despite their prominent roles, it seems they were an unkempt lot who frequently dressed in coarse animal skins and spent much of their time in the wilderness, where they brooded in silence like hermits.

FACT

The early prophets did not leave us any written work, and what we know of them comes from the Oral Tradition. However, beginning with Hosea and Amos around 750 B.C.E. (during the classical period), many of the prophets recorded their prophecies and lamentations or had personal scribes who would write down their message. The books of the prophets are now included in the Bible.

From what we know about the earliest prophets, it is likely that they went no further than stressing absolute monotheism and the "oneness" of God, reacting when the Israelites strayed from God's commandment to reject all other deities. (From time to time, the Israelites acknowledged the existence of other gods, although they always insisted upon the supremacy of Yahweh.)

Because the prophets vehemently condemned Israel whenever Israelites adopted some of the pagan ways of their neighbors, the Jews see the prophets as being chiefly responsible for Judaism's evolution into a religion of strict monotheism.

Prophets Throughout Jewish History

The Bible identifies fifty-five prophets beginning with Moses, who is considered to be the greatest of prophets because he saw the entire Torah that would be written hundreds of years after his death. Some Jews believe that nothing any of the subsequent prophets said could ever conflict with Moses because he saw everything. Of the fifty-five prophets, seven were women, most notably Sarah, whose prophetic vision the tradition holds to be superior to Abraham's; Miriam, Moses' sister; and Deborah, who was also a judge.

During the First Temple Period

As you know, the prophet Samuel played an important role in the creation of the kingdom of Israel under the reign of Saul and David. Later, the prophet Nathan provided moral and religious guidance for King David and his son Solomon. Once the kingdoms divided, four prophets preached in the northern kingdom of Israel:

- Elijah: 870–850 B.C.E.
- Elisha: 850–800 B.C.E.
- Amos: 750–745 B.C.E.
- Hosea: 750–745 B.C.E.

After the fall of the northern kingdom, the following prophets were active in the kingdom of Judah:

- Isaiah of Jerusalem: 742–700 B.C.E.
- Micah: 722–701 B.C.E.
- Zephaniah: 628–622 B.C.E.
- Jeremiah: 626–586 B.C.E.
- Nahum: 612 B.C.E.
- Habakkuk: 605 B.C.E.
- Ezekiel: 593–573 B.C.E.
- Obadiah: 586–585 B.C.E.
- Haggai: 520–515 B.C.E.
- Zechariah: 520–515 B.C.E.
- Isaiah (56–66): 515–500 B.C.E.

There is some controversy on whether the Book of Isaiah was written by one person. Isaiah 40–55 was most likely written two centuries after Isaiah's time, in 540 B.C.E.

During much of the First Temple Period, a time of turmoil and uncertainty, the prophets maintained that although the present was flawed with injustice and human suffering, the time will come when there will be a transformation ushering in an age when justice, peace, and harmony will prevail in the world.

Several themes can be discerned in the respective messages of the different prophets. Beginning with Elijah, there is a constant reminder that the people must hold fast to the belief that there is but one God, in order to avoid slipping into polytheism. Prophets like Amos insisted that God is best served by adhering to justice and having fair dealings with one's fellow humans. Hosea stressed the importance of love. Later, Jeremiah predicted that the Jewish people would be able to fulfill their covenant with God just as effectively in exile as they could in the Promised Land.

©Israel Ministry of Tourism. Courtesy of the Israel Ministry of Tourism.

▲ The Old City wall, Jerusalem.

Elijah, the Most Celebrated Prophet

Without doubt, one of the best known of the prophets is Elijah, who continues to be a part of several Jewish customs. Elijah is present with the

Jews at every Passover seder, where it is customary for Jews to pour and set aside a special cup of wine for Elijah. As someone opens the door of the home to invite Elijah inside, children sit with their eyes glued to Elijah's cup to see if there isn't just the slightest drop in the level of wine.

Similarly, Elijah is present at every ceremony of the *brit* or *bris* (circumcision), and one of the chairs is left empty for the prophet. And each week, at the conclusion of Shabbat, a song is sung expressing the hope that Elijah will soon arrive and usher in the age of the Messiah.

The Story of a Great Man

Not much is known about Elijah's past. Like many other prophets, he came from a poor family and appeared on the scene almost as if out of nowhere—coming from an obscure place called Tishbe in Gilead, east of the Jordan River.

FACT

Elijah was reputed to be a Rechabite, a member of a severe, fundamentalist sect that did not recognize the Temple and wished to adhere to the nomadic lifestyle of the Israelites before they had been influenced by the cultures of Canaan.

Denouncing Corrupt Leaders

Though charismatic, Elijah was a solitary person. For much of his life he was a fugitive, fleeing from the rulers he had antagonized with his denunciations. Elijah was critical of the House of Omri for both social and religious reasons. During Omri's reign, the gap between the rich and the poor widened significantly, and this injustice provoked Elijah, who believed that service to God and practice of Judaism is best done by practicing justice.

Elijah also condemned Omri's successor, King Ahab. When Ahab seized the vineyards of his poor subjects, Elijah was relentless in admonishing the king. But Elijah's disapproval of Ahab went beyond social and political issues; it struck to the heart of Jewish monotheism from which Ahab was dangerously deviating.

When Ahab married Jezebel, she convinced him to adopt her Canaanite deities and build a temple in honor of Baal. According to some interpretations, Jezebel was also responsible for persecuting the prophets of Yahweh. Needless to say, Elijah was incensed and challenged the 450 priests of Baal to prove whose god is the one and only God. A biblical passage narrates how a bull's carcass was prepared for a sacrifice, but no matter how much Baal's priests beseeched their god to accept their offering, the carcass did nothing but attract flies. When Elijah offered his sacrifice to the Lord, the offering was immediately set aflame and accepted.

Despite his great oratory talents and ability to arouse the masses, Elijah could not succeed in changing the ways of the northern kings, and he had to flee to the wilderness to avoid retribution from Jezebel. As other prophets both before and after him, he could not entirely prevent pagan practices from seeping into the religious customs of the Israelites.

Going Up in Flames

Elijah is also remembered for making a grand exit. The Bible tells us that when Elijah's days on earth were drawing to a close, he prepared Elisha to take over after him and anointed him as his successor. Then, a flaming chariot drawn by fiery steeds descended from the sky. Elijah boarded the chariot and was whisked up to the heavens—a fitting conclusion for a phenomenal life.

The Warnings of Amos and Hosea

Shortly before the northern kingdom of Israel's demise at the hands of the Assyrians, two prophets emerged to warn the Israelites of another danger that they saw as equally lethal—the corruption of their souls. Undaunted by the risk of incurring retaliation to their criticism, Amos and Hosea took every opportunity to convey their prophetic visions to the people of Israel.

Amos, a rude, powerfully built peasant, appeared suddenly in the town of Beth El. At first, he denounced the king, but then extended his reproach to all noblemen and even to the priests. God, Amos proclaimed, should be served through justice and mercy, not by hollow and meaningless religious ceremony.

Hosea is another prophetic figure who is shrouded in mystery—even his writings are mostly inscrutable. It seems that he was morose and generally pessimistic; some rabbis have suggested that perhaps his scathing criticism of overindulgence in alcohol and sexual misconduct stems from being a reformed drinker and philanderer himself.

Hosea was highly critical of the northern kingdom of Israel, which he felt never should have seceded in the first place. Like Amos, he lashed out at all organized groups and institutions including the priests and royal shrines. But perhaps he was most unique in elaborating on a theme that had been, up until then, only a subtle motif in the prophetic message.

Importance of Intent

In their criticism of the religious and secular establishment and their pretentious empty rituals, the prophets clearly were emphasizing the importance of intent. Indeed, this has come to be an essential ingredient in Jewish prayer and is called *kavanah*. Lacking proper intent, prayer is meaningless. This was inherent in the prophetic message up until then, but it was Hosea who said it explicitly.

FACT

Hosea was the last prophet to address the northern kingdom of Israel before it was destroyed by the Assyrians and its people dispersed. Although in his time Hosea's message fell on deaf ears, fortunately for us it has been kept alive throughout the ages and has influenced the way Jews practice their religion.

Hosea contended that all the material preparation that went into prayers before God do not matter at all. Sincerity and the love of God is by far the most important part of any prayer or ritual. With a religion composed of 613 specific laws and a body of Oral Law, what was in the heart had never received much attention. Hosea is credited with bringing this point to the attention of the Jews.

The Conquest of Israel

After the separation of Israel and Judah, the first to fall was the northern kingdom of Israel. The decline was military as well as spiritual. The weak state could not withstand the military might of the Assyrians, and the prophets told Israel that they no longer had God on their side.

Meanwhile, the power of the Assyrian empire continued to grow. By the ninth century B.C.E., it occupied the territories of what today are Syria, Iraq, and Turkey, and the Assyrian emperor looked south with the intent of acquiring additional land.

ALERT!

The fall of the kingdom of Israel is one of the first biblical events fully supported by archaeological findings. In Samaria, the entire royal quarters were demolished and leveled, and most of the cities were razed completely.

For a time, the Israelites were able to keep the Assyrians at bay, often by paying tribute. At other times, the kingdom of Israel established alliances with neighboring nations to halt the Assyrian advances. But beginning in 745 B.C.E., the Assyrian onslaught could no longer be prevented. The cruel Assyrian monarch, Tilgath-pileser, conquered Galilee and Transjordan, home to the tribes of Zebulun and Naphtali.

Tilgath-pileser's successor, Shalmanesar V, vanquished Samaria, the capital of the Northern Kingdom and the lands belonging to the tribes of Reuben, Gad, and Manasseh. The next Assyrian emperor, Sargan II, finished the job, and by 722 B.C.E., the kingdom of Israel ceased to exist.

A Policy of Exile

After the conquest of Israel, the Assyrians decided to uproot the local population and destroy the Israelites as a nation. The conquerors took the educated, professionals, and the upper echelons of the citizenry into captivity in Mesopotamia, the northern part of the Assyrian Empire, though the farmers and laborers were permitted to remain.

To fill the gap, Sargan II transferred some of the inhabitants of the northwestern section of Assyria to Israel. A good many of these people settled in Samaria. It was common for new arrivals, even those victorious in war, to fear the local gods who might wreak vengeance upon them. There-fore, the Assyrians in Samaria incorporated Yahweh into their religious prac-tices. Within a short time, Yahweh became the exclusive god of this cult.

Furthermore, the Assyrian arrivals and the remaining Israelites intermarried and merged into a distinct people, known as the Samaritans. Although this group practiced its own form of Judaism, the Jews of Judah to the south did not acknowledge any kinship with them, since they were not descendants of Abraham. This refusal to consider the Samaritans and their religion as part of Judaism and the Jewish people continued throughout history. Indeed, a small population of Samaritans still exists today near the city of Shechem (Nablus).

The Ten Lost Tribes

And what about the Israelites who were dispersed throughout the Assyrian Empire—whatever had become of them? Nothing is known about the fate of the ten lost tribes. Once they were deported to Assyria, they disappeared from history and into myth. We don't know why the Israelites lost their identity.

Although the Jews from the kingdom of Judah were also conquered and exiled to Babylon, they retained their culture and identity, and they later returned to Jerusalem to rebuild the Temple. And later still, when Jews were exiled from Palestine by the Romans, they would retain their identity throughout the Diaspora. So why didn't the Jews from the kingdom of Israel manage to survive in Assyria?

Perhaps the prophets were right when they railed against the Israel-ites' hollow and pretentious religious practices—it's possible that their lack of conviction could not survive the exile. Another explanation may have to do with the practice common to the northern tribes of fraternizing with their pagan neighbors. It is likely that when the Israelites found themselves in Assyria, they intermarried and assimilated Assyrian culture.

Explanations of the Mystery Abound

What became of the ten lost tribes has piqued the curiosity of many throughout the ages, and there have been numerous theories—some flimsy, others with some substance—but none have ever been proven. In the twelfth century, the Jewish traveler Benjamin of Tudela recorded that the ten lost tribes were living in Persia and in Arabia. In 1650, the Amsterdam rabbi Manasseh Ben-Israel published a book about the discovery of the missing Israelites in South America. The Pathans, a sect of five million Muslim fundamentalists living in Afghanistan and Pakistan, claim some of their populace is descended from the ten lost tribes. Others that have been linked to the vanished tribes are the Northern American Indians, the Eskimos, the British, and even the Japanese.

Isaiah's Preaching in Jerusalem

While the northern kingdom of Israel still existed, no prophets appeared in the kingdom of Judah. However, around the time of the northern kingdom's destruction, a prophet did appear in Jerusalem. The kingdom of Judah was in imminent danger. Seeing their northern neighbor destroyed by the Assyrians, many Judeans wondered if they would be next to fall.

Isaiah's appearance only added to the turmoil. Instead of mobilizing Judeans to a fight against the Assyrians, the prophet called on them to repent their sins and clear their souls, suggesting that Judah's downfall to the Assyrians would be God's punishment for sins committed by the Jews.

It is likely that Isaiah was born to a wealthy family. He had easy access to the palace, and he seemed comfortable among the ruling class. He was evidently well educated and developed a sophisticated linguistic style. Many Jews consider him one of the greatest writers in the Bible. But despite his aristocratic traits, Isaiah defended the common people against the corruption of the rulers and the priests.

Isaiah's Message

Isaiah's message incorporates four interrelated themes. First, he called on the people as individuals and on the community to reform and work toward social justice. Second, he proclaimed the importance of repentance and seeking God's forgiveness. Third, he advocated peace among the nations, promising that one day men "shall beat their swords into plough-shares, and their spears into pruning hooks; nation shall not lift up sword against nation, neither shall they learn war anymore." Finally, Isaiah predicted that the time would come when a "messiah" (anointed one) would appear, born of a virgin. This man, born of the House of David, would reunite all Jews once again in a kingdom of peace and devotion to God.

Though the Bible makes no mention of the circumstances of Isaiah's death, Talmudic tradition indicates that Isaiah was murdered during the reign of the idol-worshipping King Manasseh.

Jeremiah—A Belief Beyond the Land

Jeremiah was the last prophet before the end of the First Temple Period, and he was a witness to the destruction of the Temple. He came from a priestly family that lived in a village outside of Jerusalem. Totally dedicated to his work, Jeremiah never married.

Some have suggested that Jeremiah exhibited signs of paranoia, but this does not diminish the importance of what he had to say. We know a good deal about this prophet because he dictated his sermons to his scribe, Baruch.

A Promise of Return

Having witnessed the demise of the kingdom of Israel and with the imminent threat of the Babylonians, Jeremiah was convinced that Judah would be conquered as God's punishment. He considered the nation of Judah to be sinful and had no patience for the religious establishment, which he saw as corrupt and superficial.

And yet, Jeremiah's most important message for the Jewish people—a message that would continue to speak to generations of Jews yet to be born through the next two and a half millennia—was one of great optimism. Jeremiah told the people that one day the Jews would return to their land. In support of this conviction, Jeremiah purchased land in Palestine just before the Jews were exiled.

However, the crux of Jeremiah's message was that it really didn't matter where the Jews lived—whether in Jerusalem or greater Israel or elsewhere. Jeremiah taught that the Jewish people would be able to survive in exile and maintain their covenant with God, and that they did not need to have land in order to be a nation. Jeremiah's message gave comfort to the Jewish people as they left for the Babylonian exile, and it would continue to provide comfort during the 2,000-year Diaspora. Ⓔ

Chapter 8

Judah's Defeat and Babylonian Exile

For a time, it seemed that Judah would survive the fate of the kingdom of Israel. They had withstood the advances of the Assyrians, and they managed to stay afloat among the vicious politics of Egypt and Babylon. But freedom was not to be. In 597 B.C.E., the Babylonians marched into Jerusalem and much of the population of Judah was sent into exile. And yet, despite the defeat, the Babylonian exile turned out to be a time of great Jewish revival that saw the growth of Judaism into a religion as we know it today.

Jerusalem Survives the Assyrian Onslaught

Shortly after Israel fell to the Assyrians, the king of Judah, Hezekiah, began to fortify Jerusalem. The Bible tells us that Hezekiah was a righteous man and the son-in-law of the prophet Isaiah. This king was a man of great foresight; in fact, he is credited with saving Jerusalem from the same fate that befell Samaria.

By the time Hezekiah assumed the throne, Jerusalem had expanded well beyond the inner city walls, leaving the new neighborhoods practically defenseless. To remedy this situation, Hezekiah constructed the Broad Wall; its remnants still surround Jerusalem's Old City today. In addition, Hezekiah made plans to build a tunnel from the Gihon Spring, located a third of a mile away, into the city, a strategic move that provided Jerusalem with fresh water.

©Israel Ministry of Tourism. Courtesy of the Israel Ministry of Tourism.

▲ The Citadel and David's Tower, Jerusalem.

When the Assyrians, led by Sennacherib, made their way to Jerusalem and placed it under siege, the city was well fortified and assured of a regular water supply. Although the situation was grim, the Jerusalemites did not lose hope. According to the biblical narrative, their trust in God was strong. Sure enough, a plague struck the Assyrian encampment, and 185,000 soldiers died. What remained of Sennacherib's forces scurried back to Assyria.

Hezekiah had saved Jerusalem from conquest by Assyria. After his death, the kingdom of Judah remained independent. Unfortunately, the kings who followed Hezekiah were not of his caliber. Indeed, the throne of Judah found itself occupied by some rather ignominious characters. One especially despicable monarch, Manasseh, executed his own grandfather, the prophet Isaiah. Soon, it became clear that Judah's days were numbered.

The Rise of the Babylonian Empire

Around 1000 B.C.E., a Semitic people called the Chaldeans entered Southern Mesopotamia. After the death of King Assurbanipal in 626 B.C.E., the Chaldean leader Nabopolassar seized the throne in Babylon, establishing a new Chaldean Empire that would be known as the Babylonian Empire. By this time, Assyrian power had waned, and Babylon's only rival was Egypt. Unfortunately, the kingdom of Judah was caught in the middle of this rivalry.

FACT

The Babylonian Empire was expanded further by Nabopolassar's son and successor, Nebuchadnezzar II (605–562 B.C.E.), who pushed farther east and north, conquering all of Mesopotamia.

In fact, the Egyptian Empire was a force to be reckoned with. The Egyptians had expanded all the way to Palestine and Syria. In 608 B.C.E., they deposed the Judean King Jehoahaz and Judah became a tribute state of Egypt. Three years later, when Nebuchadnezzar came to power, the Babylonians crushed the Egyptians at the battle of Karchemish, and Judah became a tribute state to Babylon. Jehoiakim, who had aligned himself with the Babylonians, was crowned as king.

Four more years passed, and Egypt returned to wage battle against

Babylon, now led by Nebuchadnezzar. When Jehoiakim saw that Egypt was gaining the upper hand, he switched his allegiance to Egypt. History would show that it was a big mistake.

Judah Is Vanquished

Jehoiakim's disloyalty provoked the wrath of Nebuchadnezzar, who raised an army and dispatched it to Judah in 597 B.C.E. As a result, cowardly Jehoiakim defected to the Egyptians and the Judeans crowned Jehoiachin as their new king, but it was too late. Judah was certainly no match for the forces of the Babylonian Empire. According to the Babylonian Chronicle, Jerusalem surrendered that same year, in 597.

QUESTION?

What is the Babylonian Chronicle?
The Babylonian Chronicle is a clay tablet dating back to 550–400 B.C.E. The Chronicle describes historical events that occurred around the time of Nebuchadnezzar's reign—the siege of Jerusalem in 597 B.C.E. and the exile of its king, Jehoiachin, among others.

In accordance with Nebuchadnezzar's decree, the king of Judah, all royalty, and tens of thousands of captives were taken to Babylon. It is believed that most of the deportees came from the upper class or were professionals, merchants, and craftsmen. A puppet governor, Zedekiah, was installed as the new monarch of Judah. The land that had belonged to the exiled was redistributed among the poor that were able to remain.

Jerusalem Under Siege

Unfortunately, Zedekiah was a poor choice to rule from the standpoint of both the Babylonians and the Jews. In 588 B.C.E., he broke his oath of allegiance to Babylon and led Judah in a revolt. In response, Nebuchadnezzar sent expeditionary forces to Judah that laid Jerusalem under a siege.

The siege lasted for two years. During this period, the prophet Jeremiah was tenacious in repeatedly calling upon all those who would listen that it was time to repent and that resistance was pointless. Jeremiah declared it was God's will whether Jerusalem would survive the siege.

Eventually, his ranting and raving landed Jeremiah in jail. While in confinement, Jeremiah put his time to good use, writing the Book of Lamentations. Given the circumstances in which it was written, it is not surprising that the tone of this work possesses a despairing quality. In one of the darker passages, Jeremiah predicted the fall of Jerusalem and the destruction of the Temple.

The Temple Is Destroyed

On the seventh day of Av in the year 586 B.C.E., the Babylonians breached the walls of Jerusalem, and a vicious slaughter followed. The rebellious Zedekiah was captured trying to escape and he was forced to watch while his children were murdered in front of him. Zedekiah's eyes were then gouged out and the Babylonians carted him off to Babylon.

On the ninth day of Av, the Temple was destroyed, its walls demolished. Many magnificent structures in the city were devastated. Many prominent citizens were deported to Babylon, though this was a far smaller exile than the one in 597.

FACT

Up to this day, the Jewish people mourn the destruction of the Temple on Tisha B'av (the ninth of Av), which also commemorates the destruction of the Second Temple in 70 C.E. as well as other tragedies that befell the Jews on this day.

The New Jewish Communities

Although the Babylonians did not resettle any other nation in the land of Judah, the small Jewish community that remained there lacked any kind of infrastructure—they had no king and no leaders, and they were left to fend for themselves.

The educated and the literate left for Babylon, where they continued to practice Judaism and maintain their traditions, and so practically nothing is known regarding those Jews who remained in Judah. Nor do we know what became of those from the tribe of Benjamin, except for the fact that they were allowed to stay in their villages and cities after they surrendered in 588 B.C.E. Unlike Judah, the Benjaminite cities of Gibeon, Mizpah, and Beth El were left intact.

The Dispersal of Jews Begins

While some Jews were deported to Babylon, others were scattered to places far and wide. Many of the Jews fled north to Samaria, where they may have mingled with the Samaritans. Other Jews escaped to Edom, Moab, or Egypt.

After the fall of Jerusalem, Jeremiah's supporters took him to Egypt, where he lived to be an old man and continued to preach about repentance and the retribution God would inflict upon those who stray from the covenant.

The Jews in Babylon

Unlike the ten lost tribes of Israel, the Jews of Babylon managed to preserve their religion and distinct identity in exile, thanks to several important factors. First of all, they were resettled as a community, in a single location. And while some did adopt the Chaldean religion, most Jews held fast to Judaism. These Jews living in Babylon began to refer to themselves as *gola* (exiles), or the *bene gola* (the children of exiles).

As you may recall, most of the resettled Jews were from the ranks of the upper class, so it wasn't long before they developed a thriving community. Moreover, the Babylonian policy was innocuous to the exiles. Under the Babylonian regime, the Jews were permitted to appoint a leader who would represent them before the Babylonian authorities. The first leader was Jehoiachin, the deposed king of Judah, who was given the title of *Resh Galusa,* an Aramaic term equivalent to the Hebrew *Rosh Galut* and the English "Head of the Diaspora."

QUESTION?

What is the Diaspora?
Any place other than Israel where Jews live. Although the Jews of Babylon lived in the Diaspora, the term often refers to the time period following the destruction of the Second Temple in 70 C.E. until the establishment of the modern State of Israel in 1948. The term itself has come to us from the Greek *diaspora,* or "dispersion."

A New Wave of Exiles

By the time the second wave of Jewish exiles arrived in Babylon, bearing news of the destruction of Jerusalem and Solomon's Temple, they found an established Jewish community and an existing Jewish infrastructure that was more than capable of absorbing them. But this is not to say the new arrivals from Judah brought nothing with them to Babylon. While the Babylonians had been preoccupied looting the Temple of its gold and silver, the Judeans salvaged religious scriptures, which they took with them into exile. The inscribed laws that made the journey from Jerusalem to Babylon would help form the basis for a spiritual reawakening of the Jewish people.

The Jewish community of Babylon survived the exile and continued to exist—and thrive—even after many Jews were able to return to Palestine. It survived many centuries, and has remained the oldest Diaspora community, though the land is no longer known as Babylon but as Iraq. Indeed, when the Iraqi Jews returned to the modern state of Israel, they were called *Bavli* and were still identifiable as descendants of the Judeans exiled by Nebuchadnezzar from the kingdom of Judah.

Judaism Evolves in Babylon

It would be logical to assume that when the Jews saw the Temple destroyed, their nation vanquished, and their communities in ruins, they lost faith in God and gave up their tradition. Astonishingly, they did the exact opposite. Instead of questioning the validity of their covenant with God, Who seemed to have abandoned them, they repented of their sins, and the Babylonian exile brought forth a resurgence of the Jewish faith.

Judaism Without the Temple

One of the most important changes that Jewish religion underwent during the Babylonian exile was the movement from Temple Judaism to a religion practiced within the community. Previously, the Temple had been the spiritual and geographical center of Judaism. Temple priests carried the responsibility for all the sacrifices made to God throughout the year and during holidays, when pilgrims would arrive from Israel and Judah to give their thanks to God.

The Jews of Babylon remembered the warnings of the prophet Jeremiah, who had told them that God would punish them for their sinful ways, and they accepted their responsibility for what had befallen them.

In Babylon, community leaders like the priest Ezekiel realized that without the Temple, it was now up to each and every individual to be accountable to God. The Jews no longer had their priests as intermediaries. Thus, Jews continued to practice the traditions that were not related to the Temple—including circumcision, the Sabbath, and the recurrent feasts of Passover and Yom Kippur. These traditions reinforced the Jews' identity as a distinct people and made each individual personally responsible for upholding Jewish customs and rituals.

This shift of responsibility would come to play a crucial role in the survival of Judaism throughout the millennia, among people who were not as open to their religious practices as the Babylonians. Because each and every Jew had a primary obligation to obey God's laws over those of men and monarchs, the Jews maintained their identity no matter where in the Diaspora they found themselves.

Religion of a Community

Despite this emphasis on the individual, the Jewish faith had its communal component as well. Although they no longer had the Temple, people would still congregate in order to pray, study, and celebrate holidays and special events. These meeting places were in a sense the first synagogues.

In these centers of study, learned men began to write down the Oral Law and Tradition, much of which had only been passed on by word of mouth from generation to generation. The compilation of the Oral Law and Tradition became a matter of the utmost importance to help ensure that the *mitzvot* from God and the traditions of the people would not be lost. Ezekiel and Ezra, as well as other learned scribes, not only copied but also edited and scrutinized the holy texts rescued from the ruins of Jerusalem. In fact, many Jews believe that the Torah took its final shape during the period of Babylonian exile. According to the Bible, about 150 years after the Jews were sent into exile in Babylon, Ezra the scribe returned to Jerusalem bearing the book of the Law of Moses that he read aloud to the entire community.

FACT

Although for the most part the Jews in Babylon were allowed to practice their religion and abide by its rules, tensions occasionally rose. In the biblical Book of Daniel, the narrator recounts how Daniel chose to be thrown into the lion's den rather than give up his belief and allegiance to Yahweh.

A New Hope

The changes in religious practices and the formation of the new Jewish identity were fundamental to the survival of Judaism in the much longer and more difficult exile of the Diaspora. But perhaps the most significant factor was the renewal of hope. Without faith in God and hope in a better future, it is doubtful the Jewish community would have survived the Babylonian exile.

The hope came from the prophets. Even before Babylon, prophets like Isaiah and Jeremiah talked about the future messianic age when all Jewish people would once again gather in the Promised Land. In exile, the Jews remembered these prophecies, and prophets like Ezekiel reaffirmed them. The Babylonian Jews fervently believed that they would soon return to Jerusalem, re-establish the unified kingdom of David, and rebuild the Temple. By keeping the dream alive, the Jewish community refused to assimilate, and it survived. Ⓔ

Chapter 9

Purim— A Celebration of Deliverance

In the year 538 B.C.E., the Babylonian Empire fell to Cyrus the Great, and the Jews found themselves under the rule of Persia. Cyrus permitted the Jews to return to Jerusalem, and many of them did leave for the Promised Land (see Chapter 11). However, many Jews remained in the Persian Empire. Purim is a celebration of survival of the Jews in Persia, who were saved from annihilation thanks to their queen, Esther.

The Book of Esther

The Jewish festival of Purim is one of the most joyous holidays of the year. Purim commemorates a historical episode in Jewish history filled with intrigue, treacherous plots, courage, revelry, insobriety, and a beautiful woman who saves her people from annihilation. However, although the events recounted in the Purim make for a great story, it must be admitted that the Purim narrative may or may not be authentic.

The chief source for the Purim chronicle comes to us from the Book of Esther, a biblical account attributed to Esther and Mordecai, the tale's chief characters. Traditionally, it is known as the *Megillah*, or scroll, perhaps because the Jewish tradition says the Book of Esther is most likely based on letters between Mordecai and Esther. Later (between the fifth and fourth centuries B.C.E.) the Men of the Great Assembly, of which Mordecai was a member, edited these letters to produce the Book of Esther as we know it today.

Other Possible Origins

The story of Purim has other explanations as well. One alternative version proposes that Purim is a carryover from a pagan carnival held during the Babylonian celebration of the New Year. The carnival was an occasion filled with dancing and merrymaking, and many Jews could not restrain themselves from joining in the fun. Realizing that any prohibition to participate would be fruitless, the rabbis added a Jewish flavor to the affair and rewrote it as the Esther-Mordecai-Haman legend.

ALERT!

Some secular scholars have suggested the possibility that the Purim story may have a historical basis. Indeed, there might have been an attempt to murder the Jewish population during the reign of Xerxes (485–465 B.C.E.) or Artaxerxes (403–358 B.C.E.).

These conjectures are no more or less likely than the possibility that the story of Purim (or some variation thereof) did in fact occur. Either way, Purim has become an integral part of the heritage and culture of the

Jewish people, and Jews have been observing the festival for more than two millennia.

Ahasuerus Makes Esther His Queen

Following the death of Cyrus the Great in 529 B.C.E., Xerxes I took over the rule of the Persian Empire. It is likely that King Ahasuerus, as he is called in the Book of Esther, is Xerxes I—the name Ahasuerus is the Hebrew form of Xerxes.

The Bible tells us that after a series of victories that expanded the Persian Empire and brought fame to its king, Ahasuerus held a six-month feast that celebrated his achievements. Although the rabbis forbade the Jews from participating, most Jews joined in the festivities.

During one of the many feasts, an intoxicated Ahasuerus sent for his queen, Vashti, to appear at the party. Vashti had royal blood flowing through her veins. She was the granddaughter of Nebuchadnezzar and the sole survivor of the slaughter in the royal palace of Belshazzar, the last king of Babylon, during the Persian invasion.

For whatever reason—one version has it that she was too modest to dance in front of the king and his company, while another suggests she was vain and didn't want to appear because of a blemish on her face—Vashti refused to oblige the king. The refusal cost Vashti her life.

FACT

Esther's Hebrew name was Hadassah. According to the Purim tradition, Persians called her Esther because her beauty was compared to the beauty of the Persian goddess Ishtar/Astarte/Easter. But in Hebrew, the name Esther has the same root as the word "hidden," and being hidden is one of the central motifs in the Purim narrative.

The New Queen

Ahasuerus needed a new queen, and so he staged a beauty contest and proclaimed that he would pick the winner as his wife. Among the women of Persia, the most beautiful one of all was Esther, a Jewish woman. When Ahasuerus picked her, she consented to marry him. Following the advice of her uncle and guardian, Mordecai, Esther kept the fact she was Jewish to herself, hiding her Jewish identity. Ahasuerus married Esther, and that may have been the end of the story, if it wasn't for Haman, an ambitious and ruthless advisor of the king.

Haman's Plot to Annihilate the Jews

According to the Jewish tradition, Haman Ha-Agagi was a direct descendant of Agag, the king of the Amaleks. As you may recall from Chapter 6, God had commanded the Jewish king Saul to conquer the Amalekites and kill all of them, including their king, Agag. Despite Saul's victory, he didn't follow through with God's orders. Instead, he pardoned Agag, providing an opportunity for the ruthless monarch to sire a son and continue his bloodline. Haman, being an Amalekite and descended from Agag, hated the Jews, and he was waiting for the right opportunity to exact revenge.

When King Ahasuerus appointed him as his chief minister, Haman issued a proclamation that all must bow before him; to bolster the legitimacy of his edict, he wore a small idol around his neck. Mordecai's refusal to prostrate himself before the king's chief minister (because Jews are forbidden to bow to any person or idol) enraged Haman. The Book of Esther suggests that this incident served as the impetus for Haman's plot to get rid of Mordecai as well as the entire Jewish race. Convincing Ahasuerus that the Jews were strangers among the Persians and that they posed an internal threat, Haman obtained the king's permission to have them slaughtered.

The Lots Are Cast

Following Haman's advice, King Ahasuerus issued a secret decree that empowered the Persians to rise up and murder their Jewish neighbors. The day of the slaughter was established by the casting of lots, which pointed to the thirteenth day of *Adar* as the day of the massacre of Persia's Jews.

What is the origin of the term "Purim"?
Purim is the Hebrew term for "lots," which were cast to determine the date of the slaughter. Thanks to the heroic efforts of Esther and Mordecai, the tables were turned against Haman, and the thirteenth day of *Adar* became a day of joy and celebration for the Jews.

Esther and Mordecai Thwart the Plot

Luckily, Mordecai learned of the plot against the Jews, and he went to Esther to ask her to intercede with the king. Esther knew that she was risking her life. No Persian queen ever interfered in affairs of state, and Ahasuerus was a dangerous husband—everyone knew of the fate of his previous wife, Vashti. But after some vacillation, Esther accepted her mission. She fasted and prayed for three days, and then went to pay a visit to the king.

The purpose of the visit was to invite both Ahasuerus and Haman to a special banquet. Haman construed the invitation as a sign of royal favor. Sure of his power, and thinking that revenge was close at hand, Haman ordered his men to construct the gallows where Mordecai would soon be hanged.

Mordecai's Reward

Just before the banquet, King Ahasuerus remembered how the Jew named Mordecai had uncovered a plot to assassinate Ahasuerus and had thwarted the conspiracy. He inquired about Mordecai and learned that this man was never rewarded.

At the banquet, Ahasuerus asked Haman how a man who saved the king's life should be compensated. Haman assumed that the king was hinting at none other than himself, and so he quickly suggested lavish gifts and honors. The king agreed, and told Haman to reward Mordecai just as he had proposed.

Ahasuerus also wanted to reward Esther for the wonderful banquet, and so he told her to ask him for anything she wanted. Esther's response baffled the king—the queen asked him to spare her life and the lives of her people. She told him that she was Jewish, and that the edict that called for the death of the Jewish people would also apply to her.

The Jews Are Saved

Ahasuerus was furious with Haman. As a punishment, he issued an order to hang Haman and his sons on the very same gallows Haman had erected for Mordecai. Then, Ahasuerus appointed Mordecai to Haman's former position of chief minister. Although Ahasuerus' original decree could not be rescinded, the king authorized Mordecai to send out another order that allowed the Jews to defend themselves.

On the day of the attack, those who chose to rise up against the Jews were met with fierce resistance. The mobs were vanquished, and the Jews prevailed. What would have been a day of tragedy in Jewish history instead turned into a day of jubilation. The next day, the Jews rejoiced and celebrated their deliverance.

FACT

In cities that were enclosed by a wall during the time of these events, Purim is celebrated a day later. This is because, according to the Book of Esther, the Jews of Shushan (an enclosed city) fought for an extra day, and did not celebrate until a day later.

Purim's Customs and Traditions

Purim marks the deliverance from death of the Jewish community that lived in Persia 2,500 years ago, and its celebration is similarly communal in nature. Much of the holiday's celebrations take place in the synagogue.

Celebrations begin even before the actual day of Purim arrives. On the Saturday preceding the month of *Adar* and on the Saturday immediately before Purim, religious Jews include special readings in the Shabbat service. The day before Purim, many Jews also observe the Fast of Esther, in commemoration of Esther's three-day fast before she went to see Ahasuerus. This fast lasts from dawn until nightfall, and it reminds the Jews of the fighting that occurred on the day before the celebrations.

Reading the Book of Esther

On Purim, each congregation hears the reading of the Book of Esther. The *Megillah* is chanted with a special melody. During the reading, it is customary to boo, hiss, or rattle noisemakers each time the reader pronounces the name of Haman. The purpose of this practice is to blot out Haman's name.

Though Purim practices vary among different Jewish communities, the common thread is the emphasis on the celebration of Purim as a day to rejoice and commemorate the deliverance of the Jews from the hands of Haman.

Purim Carnivals

On Purim, many people arrive at the synagogue in costume, and many synagogues organize Purim parades or carnivals. Most often, people dress in costumes that represent one of the characters in the Purim story, but other political and historical figures appear as well.

While there are several explanations for dressing in disguises or costumes, probably the best answer is that this custom recalls how God saved the Jews while remaining hidden. Dressing in disguise is a reminder of how, behind the scenes, God delivered the Jews from annihilation (more on that later).

Many synagogues also stage humorous plays called *Purimspiels*. Anything goes in such plays—and the sillier the better! Children enjoy these activities, especially after having sat through the lengthy reading of the *Megillah*.

A Day of Feasting

It is a *mitzvah* to eat, drink, and be merry on Purim. In fact, tradition encourages Purim partiers to keep drinking until they can no longer distinguish between "blessed be Mordecai" and "cursed be Haman"! Of course, nobody needs to drink so much as to become seriously ill or violate other *mitzvot*.

Many Jewish holidays boast special and sumptuous foods prepared for a particular historical or symbolic reason, and in this regard Purim is no different. The primary holiday meal is served late in the afternoon, following *Mincha* (the afternoon service). At this meal, called *Purim Seudah,* observant Jews eat bread and at least one cooked food, drink at least one cup of wine, and dine on anything else they desire.

Traditionally, Jewish people also eat a delectable Purim pastry called *hamentaschen* (Yiddish for "Haman's pockets") or *oznei Haman* (Hebrew for "Haman's ears"). These are triangular cookies usually filled with fruit jam or poppy seeds. The three-corner shape of these cookies carries different interpretations. Some say it represents the type of hat Haman is said to have worn; others claim that they are meant to make fun of his funny-shaped ears.

Purim Tzedakah

Tzedakah is the Hebrew word for "justice" or "righteousness" and refers to acts of charity and kindness. Performing *tzedakah* is a *mitzvah* and an integral part of the Jewish heritage.

Jews practice *tzedakah* throughout the year, but several traditions are practiced specifically during Purim. One such tradition stems from the Book of Esther, which quotes Mordecai's declaration that Purim is a time "of feasting and gladness and of sending food to one another, as well as gifts to the poor." As a result, it is now a Purim tradition to send baskets or packages of food to friends and relatives.

Purim food baskets are called *mishloach manot* in Hebrew and *shalach-manos* in Yiddish (in both cases, a literal translation is "sending out portions"). These packages may be simple or elegant, but they must contain at least two different types of food that are prepared and ready to be eaten.

Mordecai also instituted the practice of *matanot l'evyonim* (gifts for those in need), which requires making gifts to the poor and donations to charitable organizations. In fact, the Jewish tradition holds that on Purim, you should give to anyone who asks, so that likewise, God will respond to your prayers.

A Holiday Full of Meaning

A recurring motif of Jewish history is a story of the Jews living in a foreign country as a distinct people set apart. For whatever reason, the government takes a hostile position to the Jews and sanctions anti-Semitic laws or even promotes violence against the Jewish people. The native population's latent (or not-so-latent) anti-Semitism is unleashed, and the Jews find themselves in grave danger. Would a miracle happen this time? Would the Jews find a way to save themselves? Purim marks one occasion when the Jews did survive and emerged victorious. Its message of hope and joy assures this holiday a prominent place in the hearts and minds of the Jewish people.

Other occasions when the Jews have been delivered from mass destruction sometimes get the title *Purim Katan* (small Purim). One well-known *Purim Katan* was the Wintz Purim of 1614, when the Jews of Frankfurt-am-Main were driven from the city by a mob led by Wintz Fettmilch. When the emperor intervened, the Jews were allowed to return to their homes.

Purim is important because it is a story of survival. When Mordecai learned of Haman's plot and the king's decree, he immediately took action and approached Esther. Despite her fears, Esther gathered her strength and courage, and went to Ahasuerus, doing all that she could to change the course of events and to save her people. Esther, Mordecai, and their fellow Jews serve as models that modern Jews can certainly strive to emulate if they should ever find themselves in similar circumstances.

The Hidden Presence of God

Purim also carries special meaning in terms of the Jews' relationship with God. Even though the tradition credits God with saving the Jews from Haman's plot of annihilation, God is never mentioned in the *Megillah*. How can this be?

As you might recall, Esther's name contains the root of the word "hidden." Even though God remains hidden in the story of Purim, it is believed that He engineered the events that the story describes. Purim is a celebration of *hester panim* (the hidden face of God). The message here is that although it may appear that humans control their own destinies, God is the designer of all that goes on, manipulating events in ways that are not often apparent.

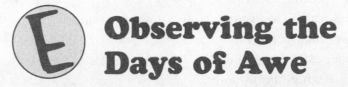

Chapter 10

Observing the Days of Awe

At this juncture in the history of the Jewish people, it is appropriate to introduce the Days of Awe, a ten-day period that begins on the first of *Tishri* with the celebration of Rosh Hashanah (the Jewish New Year's Day) and ends with Yom Kippur (the Day of Atonement), the holiest day of the year—except, of course, for the Shabbat. The traditions associated with the Days of Awe go back to the sixth century B.C.E., and yet they remain central in our lives today.

A Time of Repentance

The Days of Awe, also known as *Yamin Noraim* (Days of Repentance), are a special time in the Jewish calendar. During those ten days, each person has a chance to reflect on the past year and amend for the mistakes and transgressions he or she had made through a process known as *teshuvah* (turning or returning to God), which begins with an intense examination of one's actions and the desire and intent to strive toward being a better person.

Teshuvah is based on the Jewish belief that humans have within them the capacity to do both good and evil, and that every day each person chooses between right and wrong. Judaism recognizes that people are not perfect and that they make mistakes. Even the heroes of Jewish history have had the faults and frailties that make them human—just think of David's affair with Bathsheba.

FACT

Observance of Jewish holidays and festivals is determined by the Hebrew calendar, which is based on the lunar cycle and adjusted to the solar year by the device of the leap year. Unlike the Gregorian calendar's leap year, which contains February 29, the Hebrew leap year has an extra month, and there are seven leap years in every nineteen-year cycle.

During the Days of Awe, Jews make an effort to become better people and seek forgiveness for the sins they committed. The Jewish tradition makes it clear that we need to seek forgiveness from those we had wronged. God will only absolve sins committed against Him, so a person who acted unjustly toward another person must seek forgiveness and reconciliation from that person.

The Book of Life

According to Jewish tradition, God has a heavenly ledger known as *Sefer Ha-Chayyim* (The Book of Life). During the Days of Awe, God writes down the names of those who will have a good life and those who will not, those who will live and those who will die in the ensuing year. God opens the Book of Life on Rosh Hashanah and closes it at the conclusion of Yom Kippur.

Traditional Jews believe that each person's actions during this ten-day period can alter the initial determination. This can be accomplished with the proper combination of *tefilah* (prayer), performing acts of *tzedakah* (good deeds and charity), and the process of *teshuvah*.

Tsom Gedaliah and *Shabbat Shuvah*

In addition to Rosh Hashanah and Yom Kippur, the period of the Days of Awe contains other special days. On the third day, observant Jews participate in a minor fast known as *Tzom Gedaliah* (the fast of Gedaliah). This fast marks the execution of Zedekiah (Gedaliah), the last governor of Judea before the destruction of the First Temple.

The Sabbath that occurs during the Ten Days of Repentance is known as *Shabbat Shuvah*, the Sabbath of Return. It is customary that at this service the rabbi reads a rather lengthy sermon about repentance that includes excerpts from the Books of Hosea, Micah, and Joel.

ALERT!

During this season, many people visit the graves of their loved ones. This custom likely originated with the belief that the thoughts or prayers of the deceased can intercede in heaven on behalf of the living. Obviously, such assistance would be particularly welcome during the Days of Awe.

The Jewish New Year

The Days of Awe begin with Rosh Hashanah ("head of the year"), a holiday commonly known as the Jewish New Year. Rosh Hashanah is a joyous day, perhaps because it commemorates the creation of the world. Most Reform Jews and Jews living in Israel celebrate Rosh Hashanah for one day; other Jews in the Diaspora observe Rosh Hashanah (and many other one-day holidays) for two days, a practice that acknowledges their distance from Israel and their inability to celebrate the holiday during the proper times (because of time difference).

FACT

The Jewish calendar contains three other "new year" celebrations: the first day of *Nisan*, the springtime month of Passover, which begins the counting of the calendar months and the reign of kings; the first day of *Elul*, the month preceding Rosh Hashanah, because it's the symbolic new year for tithing animals, a form of charity; and *Tu B'Shevat*, the fifteenth day of *Shevat*, which marks the new year for trees.

Origins of the Holiday

The Torah contains two distinct commandments to observe Rosh Hashanah. In Leviticus 23:24–25, it is written that on the first day of the seventh month, there "shall be a solemn rest unto you, a memorial proclaimed with the blast of horns, a holy convocation." Later, in Numbers 29:1, it is proclaimed that this day shall be a "holy day," a day when Jews should not work, and a day when "the *shofar* is trumpeted."

In fact, the Torah only refers to Rosh Hashanah as *Yom Teruah* (the day of the sounding of the *shofar*) or *Yom Ha-Zikaron* (the day of remembrance). The latter term is a reference to Abraham's willingness to sacrifice his son Isaac in demonstration of his unswerving obedience to God, which is said to have occurred on the first of *Tishri*.

One explanation for avoiding the term Rosh Hashanah (head of the year) may have had to do with similar New Year celebrations and moon festivals practiced by pagans around the same time, in the early fall. The term Rosh Hashanah emerged much later, sometime during the Talmudic period (the first five centuries of the Common Era). However, we know that the holiday itself was well established by the fourth century B.C.E., when some of the Jews had returned from the Babylonian exile to construct the Second Temple in Jerusalem.

©2001 Brand X Pictures

▲ The Western Wall is the only surviving wall of the Second Temple.

Observances and Customs of Rosh Hashanah

During the Days of Awe, or even sometime before the holidays begin, it is customary for Jews to send greeting cards to friends and family, wishing them a *Shanah Tovah* (good year). Jews also have a special way of greeting each other during this time of the year. They may say *L'shanah tovah!* (for a good year) or *L'shanah tovah tikatevu v'taihatemu!* (may you be inscribed and sealed for a good year), which is a more formal greeting.

On the last Saturday before Rosh Hashanah, observant Jews attend a special nighttime service known as *Selichot* (forgiveness), which includes a series of important prayers. Around midnight, the congregation reviews the thirteen attributes of God, a ceremony that helps prepare everyone for the approaching holy days.

Welcoming the New Year

Rosh Hashanah is announced by the sounding of the *shofar,* a trumpet made of a ram's horn. During biblical times, people used the *shofar* as a method of communication, sending signals from one mountain peak to another. Blowing the *shofar* also heralded important events such as holidays, the new moon, or preparation for war.

According to Jewish tradition, the *shofar* is symbolic of Abraham's aborted sacrifice of Isaac, when a ram was offered in Isaac's stead. Today, its plaintive and evoking tone is designed to stir the heart of every Jew to repentance and toward a closer relationship with God.

It is customary during any holiday to follow the Torah principle of *hiddur mitzvah* (beautification of the commandment), which requires taking additional time and effort to observe rituals in a more beautiful and exceptional manner. This is why during this time of year, Shabbat and holiday dinners are served upon the best dishes, glassware, and fine linen. Frequently, people will adorn their home with fresh flowers.

The *shofar* is not just a plain ram's horn. The horn needs to be treated with a special cleaning process that hollows it out to produce three basic sounds: *teki'yah*, a single blast; *teru'ah*, a series of three short blasts; and *shevarim*, a series of nine short staccato blasts. It is considered a great honor to blow the *shofar*, and it is no easy task. Though it works a little like a trumpet or bugle, it's more difficult to blow the *shofar* and produce the right sounds.

The ceremony of blowing the *shofar* is generally conducted in the synagogue. At home, Rosh Hashanah is welcomed by the lighting of two candles, over which the mother of the family recites two special blessings. Then, the father recites the *Kiddush* (blessing over the wine) and the *motzi* (blessing over bread), which is made over two loaves of specially prepared *challah*.

FACT

Challah prepared for Rosh Hashanah is baked in a round shape, to symbolize a crown and remind the Jewish people of the sovereignty of God. Another explanation is that the round *challah* represents the circle of life and the hope that it will continue for eternity.

The Holiday Dinner

There are no special menus designated for the Rosh Hashanah dinner; traditionally, the meal is similar to a Shabbat dinner. However, there is one special dish that is customarily served on Rosh Hashanah—apples and honey. That's because dipping apples in honey is symbolic of having a sweet new year. Honey is also spread over bread or included in recipes such as honey cakes or *tzimmes,* a sweet stew made of carrots, cinnamon, yams, and/or prunes (the recipes vary). Other symbolic foods include carrots, leeks, cabbage, beets, dates, gourds, pomegranates, and fish.

A Ceremony of Purification

Even though Rosh Hashanah is a happy, festive holiday, we should remember the somber nature of the Days of Repentance. On the afternoon of the first day of Rosh Hashanah, observant Jews perform the ritual of *Tashlikh* (casting off). The ceremony involves walking to a body of water, reciting designated prayers, and then emptying one's pockets or tossing bread crumbs into the water. These actions symbolize casting off sins of the last year in order to be pure in the eyes of God.

The Day of Atonement

Yom Kippur concludes the ten-day period of the Days of Awe and is designated to atone for sins of the prior year. It is arguably the most important day of the year and has been an integral part of Judaism for thousands of years. Although it is not holier than the Shabbat, it does occur only once a year and so is a special and solemn occasion, sometimes referred to as the "Sabbath of Sabbaths." Many Jews who never attend Shabbat services during the rest of the year go to synagogue on

Yom Kippur. And even those who do not attend Yom Kippur services will likely take off from work, stay at home, and observe the day in other ways.

Biblical Origins

The first Yom Kippur was celebrated at Mount Sinai. Recall that when Moses returned to the base of the mountain and saw some of the Israelites worshipping a golden calf, he destroyed the original Ten Statements. After the idolaters were punished and Moses asked God for forgiveness, He relented and Moses ascended the mountain once again.

During his absence, the Israelites fasted from sunrise to sunset, praying for forgiveness. On the tenth day of *Tishri*, Moses returned with the second set of the Ten Statements. When he saw that the Israelites were truly repentant, he announced that God had forgiven them.

In Leviticus 16:29–31, it is written that every year on the tenth day of *Tishri,* "you must fast and do no work . . . This is because on this day you shall have your sins atoned . . . It is a Sabbath of Sabbaths to you . . . This is a law for all time."

Observances and Customs of Yom Kippur

Jewish people have been observing Yom Kippur for thousands of years, often going against great odds to fulfill the obligations of this special day. The customs of observing Yom Kippur have changed over centuries. When the Jews had the Temple in Jerusalem, the High Priest would make sacrifices in order to seek God's forgiveness of all Jews. One custom was to place all of Israel's sins on two goats—one to be sacrificed and the other sent to its death in the wilderness. (It is said that this is the origin for the word "scapegoat.")

As you may recall, Yom Kippur was the only time the high priest was allowed to enter the inner chamber of the Temple, known as the Holy of Holies. There, in a sacred place said to be inhabited by the spirit of God, the high priest would utter a special prayer on behalf of the people of Israel.

Another ancient practice, still observed by very observant Jews and many of the Sephardim (both religious and secular) living in Israel, is *Kapparot* (atonements). The person performing *Kapparot* swings a live chicken around his head while reciting a special prayer. The chicken is then slaughtered and the meat is given to the poor (or a donation is made to a charity).

Today, forgiveness from God is sought through prayers of penitence and by fasting. In addition, people pursue other activities, mostly of an introspective nature, to help them accomplish *teshuvah* and lead a better life.

A Day of Fasting

Almost everyone—even non-Jews—knows that Yom Kippur is a day when Jews are forbidden to eat and drink. But fasting is only one of five prohibitions that must be obeyed. The other four forbid the following:

- Washing or bathing.
- Using creams and oils (a prohibition that extends to deodorants and cosmetics).
- Sexual relations.
- Wearing leather shoes.

One reason for not wearing leather shoes is the incongruity of deriving a benefit from the slaying of one of God's creatures while praying and beseeching God for a long life. This proscription might explain why it's not uncommon to see men wearing formal suits and canvas sneakers on Yom Kippur.

Unlike most religious fasts, which begin at sunrise and end at sunset, on Yom Kippur the fast commences before sunset on the evening of Yom Kippur and ends after nightfall the next day.

Since the fast lasts twenty-five hours, you can imagine the extensive preparations that go into the final meal before the fast, known as *seudah ha-mafseket* (the final meal). While there are no absolute requirements governing what is eaten, the meal is traditionally very similar to what is served on Shabbat.

ALERT!

Families traditionally light candles that will burn throughout Yom Kippur. Customarily, candles are lit before the holiday meal, but on Yom Kippur, the Jews will eat first and then light the candles, an act that symbolizes the beginning of Yom Kippur.

Why do the Jews fast on Yom Kippur? The best answer is that the Torah tells us God commanded the Jews to fast on this day, but there are other explanations as well. For one, refraining from consuming food or liquid is a concrete, physical expression of the gravity of the day. It helps each person attain the state of mind necessary to focus on the spiritual. Furthermore, fasting manifests a form of self-mastery over bodily needs. Another more socially conscious justification states that by fasting, people can identify more readily with the poor and hungry. But regardless of the reason, fasting is fundamental to the observance of Yom Kippur.

Of course, there are exceptions to every rule. Jews are allowed to break the fast if it poses a physical threat. Thus, children under the age of nine and women in childbirth (that is, from the time the labor commences to three days following the birth) are absolutely forbidden to fast. Older children, not yet bar or bat mitzvah (thirteen years old for boys and twelve years old for girls), and women from the third to the seventh day after childbirth, are permitted to fast, but should resume eating or drinking if they feel the need.

Yom Kippur Services

Though Yom Kippur is a day of personal repentance, its customs and practices are conducted as a community. In the Yom Kippur liturgy, all sins are confessed in the plural, using "we" and "us." This is because Judaism sees the individual in terms of a greater group and holds the belief that each person carries responsibility for the entire community.

The liturgy of both Yom Kippur and Rosh Hashanah is so special, a special prayer book (the *machzor*) is published for these services. (The *machzor* also contains the liturgy of Rosh Hashanah.) The services begin even before Yom Kippur commences at sundown, with the *viddui* (confessional) performed during afternoon prayers. Then, Yom Kippur services begin in the evening, with a special service known as the *Kol Nidre* (all vows), named for the prayer with which it begins—a chant that is likely to stir the soul of even the staunchest stoic.

The *Kol Nidre* prayer is a legal formula written in Aramaic, and it renders null and void all promises that are made to God but will not be kept in the ensuing year. However, in keeping with the principle that absolution is rendered only for sins committed against God, the *Kol Nidre* does not apply to promises made to people. It is also considered to be a declaration by worshippers that they should not be held liable for oaths made either in anger or under duress.

Following the *Kol Nidre* service is the customary *Ma'ariv* (evening) service with a special *Amidah* confessional. (The *Amidah* is one of the central prayers of synagogue services, performed three times a day and during all holiday services.) The next day, Jews spend most of the day in the synagogue, though people who are exhausted by the fast go to rest at home and then return. Among the many readings and prayers, the Yom Kippur service includes reading a passage from the Book of Isaiah (57:14–58:14). This passage is appropriate for Yom Kippur because it denounces those who fast without having a true understanding of the day and reminds the Jews that the meaning of Yom Kippur does not lie in fasting, but in repentance. There is also an opportunity to say a special memorial prayer, called *Yizkor,* for deceased relatives, particularly parents.

FACT

The mood of Yom Kippur is enhanced by the prevalence of white, which represents purity. More observant men often wear a *kittel,* a white ankle-length robe, over their clothes. The rabbi and cantor wear white robes. The Torah scrolls are dressed in white, and the table on which the Torah is read is covered with a white cloth.

The services are concluded with *Neilah* (literally, "locked"), a ceremony that symbolizes the closing of the gates of heaven. *Neilah* ends with a very long blast from the *shofar*. With Yom Kippur now concluded, families hasten home for the break-the-fast meal.

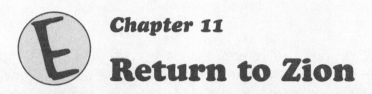

Chapter 11

Return to Zion

When Cyrus the Great conquered the Babylonian Empire in 538 B.C.E., he issued an edict that encouraged the Jews in Mesopotamia to return to Judah, and many Jews did in fact set forth, anxious to reclaim their land and rebuild the Temple in Jerusalem. Their new nation, sometimes referred to as the Second Commonwealth (the First Commonwealth being the two kingdoms of Israel and Judah before the Babylonian exile) would survive as a tributary state to Persia until the arrival of Alexander the Great in 332 B.C.E.

Emergence of the Persian Empire

In the middle of the sixth century B.C.E., while the Jews in Babylon were making themselves comfortable and establishing what would become a great center for Jewish culture, not far on the horizon a new world order was in the making. For the most part, this was the work of one man—Cyrus the Great, the ruler of the Persian Empire.

FACT

Before Cyrus, the Persians were a crude assortment of Indo-European tribes that inhabited areas north of Mesopotamia. But sometime between 559 and 549 B.C.E., Cyrus led the Persians to victory over Astyages, king of the Medes. Subsequently, he conquered the Median kingdom, thereby launching the expansion of the Persian Empire.

Despite his fame, Cyrus's origins and life are shrouded in mystery and legend. Some scholars suggest that Cyrus was the son of an Iranian noble and a Median princess, but the claim to the royal bloodline is disputed. But irrespective of who he was or where he came from, Cyrus was undoubtedly a great man, credited with building up the Persian Empire's dominions to be the largest land mass under one rule up to that point in history.

According to Zarathustra

What made Cyrus unique for his time is that he desired much more than land. To understand what motivated him, you must know a little bit about his religion that, at least indirectly, would prove beneficial for the Jews.

Cyrus was a Zoroastrian, a religion named after the seventh-century B.C.E. Persian prophet, Zarathustra, who had proclaimed the existence of one eternal beneficent god, Marduk, the creator of all things. But opposing this one great god, Zarathustra warned, was another malevolent deity. From the Zoroastrian viewpoint, the universe was a duality of two forces—one of goodness and light and the other of evil and darkness. In the Zoroastrian universe, there was room for other gods as well, but these were minor deities that were either on the side of good or evil. Fortunately for the Jews, Cyrus believed that their god, Yahweh, was on the side of goodness.

Zarathustra had predicted that one day there would be a cosmic battle between these forces of good and evil. Cyrus believed that this time was fast approaching, and his mission was to conquer the entire world on behalf of the side of righteousness.

According to Jewish tradition, what motivated Cyrus to make this decree was a vision he had of Yahweh commanding him to re-establish the worship of Yahweh in Jerusalem.

The Option to Return

In fact, Jews weren't the only nation that benefited from Cyrus's benevolence in this regard. The Cyrus-cylinder, discovered by archaeologists in the nineteenth century, indicates that he had given many other people permission to return to their native lands so that they could worship their local deities. In part, the decree states: "I am Cyrus, the King of the world . . . I gathered all their people and led them back to their abode . . . installed in joy in their sanctuaries."

Consequently, some people believe that Cyrus allowed the Jews to return to their homes in Judah for the specific purpose of rebuilding the Temple and worshipping Yahweh. While it would take some time, the Jews eventually achieved this objective.

The Migration from Babylon

The Jews returned to Jerusalem in four distinct waves. Immediately upon the issuance of the decree by Cyrus, a contingent of Jews set off under the leadership of Shenazar, the son of the former king of Judah, Jehoiakim. Unfortunately, this expedition was an abject failure. Upon reaching their destination, the newcomers faced a hostile reception.

The indigent Jews who had been left behind at the time of the exile had joined with the Samaritans, Edomites, and Arabs to prevent the settlers from erecting walls to secure safe abodes.

In 520 B.C.E., a decade after Cyrus had died, a second effort was authorized by King Darius, whom some believe was the son of Esther of the Purim legend. It has been estimated that as many as 50,000 Jews embarked from Babylon under the leadership of Zerubabel, a descendant of the House of David. To bolster Zerubabel's authority even further, Darius appointed him governor of Judah. This wave of immigration, which included many scribes and priests, was much more successful, and soon efforts commenced to rebuild the Temple.

A New Leader Emerges

More than six decades would pass before the third group of Jews, led by a man named Ezra, made the journey from Babylon to Jerusalem, in 458 B.C.E. According to the biblical Book of Ezra, Ezra was an inspirational and effective leader who had been a scribe, scholar, and a prominent figure in the Jewish community in Persia. Hearing that the settlement in Jerusalem was floundering, Ezra decided to go there and make things better; he selected about 1,500 men with leadership abilities to join him.

Ezra's major achievement was to strengthen Judaism in Jerusalem. When he arrived, he brought with him the written Torah, as it had been written down in Babylon. Upon entering the city of David, he called the people together and read to them from the holy scrolls.

Ezra's concern for the spiritual lives of the Jews inspired him to preach to the people and instigate the Jews to keep the Sabbath, donate funds for the construction of the Temple, and so forth. Fearing that the settlers would mix too freely with their pagan neighbors and the community would lose its identity—as had happened in the case of the Samaritans—Ezra spoke out against intermarriage between Jewish men and gentile women (for the offspring of these marriages would not be Jewish), and all such marriages were dissolved.

Arrival of Nehemiah

Three years later, in 445 B.C.E., a Jewish leader and prominent Persian official by the name of Nehemiah was appointed governor of Judah by the Persian King Artaxerxes. (It was Artaxerxes' intention to turn Judea into an independent political unit within the Persian Empire.) That same year, Nehemiah led the fourth and final group of migrating Jews to Jerusalem.

Upon arrival, Nehemiah stabilized the settlement by rebuilding the walls of Jerusalem and creating a secure enclave. His achievements are described in the Bible, in the Book of Nehemiah.

Construction of the Second Temple

The most important reason for leaving Babylon and returning to Jerusalem was to rebuild the Temple. Work began as soon as the first group of settlers had arrived. Unfortunately, the job would take a long time to complete, because the Samaritans and other Jews regarded as heretical were excluded from participating in the project. Moreover, the first group of migrants wasn't very large. As a result, very little was accomplished until the arrival of the second wave of immigrants eighteen years later. Then, work began in earnest.

When Ezra reached Jerusalem in 458 B.C.E., he saw to it that construction of the Temple was completed and that it was rededicated. But the Second Temple was merely a shadow of its former self, both in physical appearance and in its spiritual attributes. It was a humble edifice and would remain so until more than 400 years later, when Herod the Great rebuilt it into a spectacular structure.

FACT

The Jews believe that the presence of God, *Shekinah,* dwelt in the Holy of Holies. Even after the destruction of the Second Temple, the platform upon which the Temple stood remains holy, for the spirit of God had never departed. During the Middle Ages, the great Jewish scholar Maimonides ruled that the site was sanctified for all time.

The Second Temple lacked something else as well. Although the Jews rebuilt the inner chamber known as the Holy of Holies, it remained empty. The Ark of the Covenant had disappeared after the destruction of the First Temple by the Babylonians.

The High Priests

Once again, the caste of priests *(kohanim)* began to work in the Temple, making offerings and performing other rituals on behalf of the Jewish people. The chief among the priests was the high priest, whose role was to preside over Temple services and be a moral and religious representative of the Jewish people—the high priest's sins were considered the sins of the entire Jewish nation, and, likewise, his purity was said to extend to that of his people.

Originally, the role of the high priest was hereditary. The first high priest was Aaron, the brother of Moses. After his death, Aaron's son assumed this role. However, during the Second Temple period, this practice changed, and the position would go to the highest bidder. Later still, during the times of Roman rule in Judea, the government would have the power to appoint the high priest.

What we know of the high priests of the Second Temple period comes to us from the Bible and the Talmud, a collection of the Jewish oral tradition that interpret the Torah, edited around 500 C.E. The Talmud informs us that during the First Temple period (about four centuries), there were only eighteen high priests. The institution was stable and the caliber and integrity of the high priests was impressive. But this was not the situation during the years of the Second Temple.

Corruption among the High Priests

Although the Second Temple did not survive for a much longer period than had the First Temple, instead of eighteen high priests, it is believed that there were as many as 300! If we take out Yochanan, Shimon, and Yishmael, the three high priests who served a total of 110 years, we have one high priest per year. How can this be? The Talmud offers one explanation.

Recall that once a year, on Yom Kippur, the high priest may enter the Holy of Holies to perform specific rituals, seeking forgiveness on behalf of the entire Jewish people. (According to one Talmudic legend, it was the high priest's responsibility to enter the Holy of Holies in order to pronounce the Name of God.) Since the Holy of Holies was the dwelling place of the *Shekinah,* the spirit of God, only a high priest who was spiritually and ritually pure could withstand God's presence without dying on the spot.

The Talmud narrates that in order to solve the potential problem of retrieving the body from the Holy of Holies, should the high priest lack sufficient virtue, other priests would tie a rope around the high priest so that, if needed, they could haul him out. Unfortunately, during the period of the Second Temple, the high priests were so corrupt, one Talmud commentator notes that they died just about every year.

Emergence of a Theocracy

Despite the difficulties among the priesthood, the Jews persevered as a nation and established what is known as the Second Commonwealth. But unlike its predecessor states, the kingdoms of Israel and Judah, this new nation was a theocracy, under the mandate of the Persian Empire to occupy the land of Israel in order to worship Yahweh.

To keep their community pure, non-Jews could not be tolerated, and those expressing belief in a foreign religion were expelled. In the new state of Judah, only those worshipping Yahweh were welcome.

During the Babylonian exile, many Jews had come to believe that their defeat at the hands of the Babylonian Empire came about because they had been untrue to the covenant with God. In Babylon, the Jews had decided to purify their religion—to return to the ways of Moses and restore a dimension of spirituality that had somehow been lost over the centuries. When the news came that they could return to Jerusalem, the Jews who did make the effort to go back were very concerned with religious matters, and so it is natural that the nation they established in Israel was a theocracy.

The Great Assembly

The leaders of the Second Commonwealth formed the Great Assembly *(Knesset Ha-Gadol)*. The first convocation of the 120 members of the Great Assembly is attributed to Ezra, who wished to strengthen Judaism and heighten the spirituality of the Jewish people. The Great Assembly would continue to lead the Jewish people until the arrival of Alexander the Great.

Who made up the composition of the Great Assembly and what did they accomplish? Included in the membership of this esteemed body were the last of the prophets: Haggai, Zechariah, and Malachi. Mordecai of the Purim story was also a member. Other luminaries included the High Priest Yehoshua, Nehemiah, and the High Priest Shimon Ha-Tzaddik.

Compiling the Jewish Bible

One of the Assembly's greatest accomplishments was the creation of the Hebrew Bible, or Tanach, which comes from the acronym T(a)N(a)Kh, formed from the first letter of its three sections:

1. Torah: Also known as the Pentateuch or the five books of Moses.
2. *Nevi'im* (Prophets): Eight books of the prophets, the last of which contains twelve short books.
3. *Ketuvim* (Writings): Eleven books of various writings.

The Great Assembly was involved in much more than mere compilation. Its members edited the books of Ezekiel, the twelve minor prophets, and the books of Daniel and Esther. By making these books available to all the literate, the Great Assembly took an important step toward democratizing the Jewish religion and education, which was no longer in the exclusive domain of the priestly class.

©Israel, Ministry of Tourism. Courtesy of the Israel Ministry of Tourism.

▲ When the Zionist Congress convened in 1948 to set up a parliamentary body, now known as the Knesset (pictured here), they drew inspiration from the *Knesset Ha-Gadol* of the Second Temple Period.

Formalizing the Prayers

As you may recall, the destruction of the First Temple made it practically impossible to conduct sacrifices and certain rituals, and the exiled Jews had turned to prayer as a way to connect with God. When the Second Temple was constructed, the Temple services resumed, but some Jews still desired to pray. Moreover, many Jews remained in Babylon or lived somewhere other than Jerusalem; for them, prayer was the chief mode by which to commune with God.

ALERT!

The work of the Great Assembly did nothing less than help define and provide uniformity for the religious practice of the Jewish people. Without the efforts of this esteemed body, it is possible that the Jews would not have survived their 2,000-year Diaspora intact.

The Great Assembly is credited with composing what has become the centerpiece of the Jewish litany—the *Shemoneh Esrei,* or the Eighteen Blessings, a prayer that is recited three times every day. Because you must rise to say *Shemoneh Esrei,* this prayer is also called the *Amidah.*

Arrival of Alexander the Great

For 200 years after the return of the Jews from exile, Judah remained a tribute state to Persia. However, the maps were to be redrawn once again. Although the Persian Empire remained strong, it nonetheless became a tempting target to Philip II of Macedon, who had successfully invaded Greece and was looking to expand to the east. Philip didn't realize his dream of conquering Persia before he was murdered, in 336 B.C.E. Upon Philip's death, his son Alexander III, who would be known as Alexander the Great, ascended to the throne at the age of twenty.

Like Cyrus the Great, who established the Persian Empire, Alexander also had a vision. But his was not a crusade on behalf of his god and of righteousness. Alexander was a student of Aristotle's, and he saw himself as the disseminator of Pan-Hellenic ideals. At the head of a united Greek army, Alexander marched on what is now Syria, then to Egypt, and finally Babylon proper. By 331 B.C.E., Alexander had accomplished his goal of conquering the Persian Empire.

The Fate of Judah

The Jewish state fell to Alexander's control in 332 B.C.E. and became a Greek state. The Jews did not resist the army of Alexander when it arrived in Jerusalem. They saw in Alexander a benevolent ruler who spoke of a universal culture that blended Greek religions and Eastern philosophy. This culture, known as Hellenism, would prove an insidious threat to Judaism and a cause for divisiveness among the Jewish people. (E)

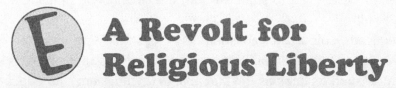 A Revolt for Religious Liberty

The arrival of Alexander the Great and Greek culture (Hellenism) to Judah brought many changes—improvements as well as problems. Eventually, the tension between Greek and Jewish culture would lead to a revolt and a bloody war that would end with Jewish victory and the miracle of the burning oil in the Temple candelabra (menorah), celebrated by Jews to this day during the eight-day festival of Chanukah.

The Invasion of Greek Culture

Alexander the Great had created a mighty empire, and the Greeks were eager to colonize many of the new territories. Once lands were conquered and stabilized, colonists poured into the subjugated regions. But instead of facing a hostile reception, many if not most of the local population were eager to share in both the Greek style of living and Greek wealth.

Frequently, colonists established new cities that were modeled on those in Greece; in addition, they revamped existing municipalities to include such features as the *gumnasion* (gymnasium), an educational/athletic center; elected assemblies and magistrates; and temples for Greek gods and local deities. The Greek language soon became the international language for commerce and diplomacy. Greek culture, dress, and modes of thought quickly spread throughout the conquered lands.

The Situation in Judah

Soon after Alexander's troops marched through Jerusalem, the city found itself encircled by a ring of "Greek" cities, which sprang up throughout Jewish Samaria and Judah. Like most of the vanquished peoples who fell under Greek rule, many Jews eagerly embraced Hellenism—indeed, the Greek culture permeated myriad levels of the Jewish community.

ALERT!

Not all Jews adopted the Greek way of life, and many others only accepted it partially. These varying attitudes toward Greek and Jewish culture soon developed into profound divisions within Jewish society.

Jewish Reaction to Hellenism

Exposure to Greek ideas provoked many different reactions among the Jews. A few Jews chose to embrace Greek culture so completely that they became entirely Hellenized and lost their Jewish identity. Other Jews were so antagonized by Greek ideas and their prevalence among the Jews, they left their communities and moved to the desert, joining fundamentalist groups that practiced the Rechabite tradition. The Rechabites had always believed that Jerusalem was corrupt and that the Temple hindered the true practice of Judaism. These Jews believed that the spirituality in which Judaism arose could best be experienced in nomadic living and was inhibited within the confines of a temple or walled city like Jerusalem.

A Schism Within the Jewish Community

Even within the Jewish community, there was a deep divide between the Hellenists—those Jews who accepted Hellenist ideas without giving up their Jewish identity, and the reactionary Jews, who viewed Hellenism as a threat to Jewish religion, culture, and traditions.

The Hellenists were generally from the upper class; they were educated, and many were from the caste of priests. To these people, Greek culture represented the future and the road to success. Many Hellenists assumed Greek names, though some used these new names only in business dealings, retaining their Hebrew names at home and for the purpose of religious services.

The Hellenists' delight with all things Greek was not shared by all. Many pious Jews viewed Hellenism as anathema. While acknowledging the beauty and accomplishments of the Greek religion and culture, these Jews believed Greek values were superficial and inconsistent with Judaism. Consequently, they argued, Judaism and Hellenism were mutually exclusive. While they were willing to pay the taxes to the secular Greek authority, they wanted to be left alone to practice Judaism in peace.

Gradually, a schism developed within the Jewish population between the Hellenists, who would later become known as the Sadducees, and the reactionary rabbis and some of the priests, later known as the Pharisees (see Chapter 13).

Because of their high social status as well as easy dealings with the Greeks, the Sadducees managed to gain influence with the Greek rulers. Because most of the priests were Sadducees, this group secured control of the position of high priest and the *Sanhedrin* (the highest Jewish court).

The Reform Movement

Hellenists also made changes in the way they practiced Judaism. Hellenist reformers (not to be confused with Judaism's Reform Movement that began in the nineteenth century) wanted to expedite the process of Hellenization and had no problem modifying their religion to fit with the new culture. Because many Hellenists spoke Greek, the reformers translated the Hebrew Bible into Greek. Furthermore, they rejected the Oral Law, which they saw as nonbinding interpretation of the Bible. This reform movement soon found an ally in the new Seleucid monarchy that came to rule the Jews.

Fertile Soil for Rebellion

When Alexander the Great died in 323 B.C.E., his empire was divided among three of his generals: Antigonus, Seleucus, and Ptolemy. Ptolemy and his successors, proponents of Hellenism, ruled Egypt and Israel. However, the Ptolemaic dynasty was relatively weak. In 199 B.C.E., Israel found itself under the control of the Seleucid dynasty, which controlled Syria. The new government issued decrees that limited the practice of Judaism, including prohibitions on Sabbath observance, the study of Torah, and male circumcision. In addition, symbols of the Greek religion and gods were placed inside the Temple.

In 175 B.C.E., after Seleucus was murdered, his brother Antiochus IV Epiphanes ("god manifest") assumed the throne. Antiochus was anxious to expedite the Hellenization process because he felt it would increase his tax base and help finance his war efforts. He replaced the orthodox High Priest Onias III with his brother Jason (the name "Jason" is the Hellenic equivalent of "Joshua"). Jason immediately began the transformation of

Jerusalem into a *polis* (Greek city) by renaming it Antiocha. He constructed a gymnasium at the foot of the Temple Mount and diverted Temple funds away from the sacrifices and toward athletic games and theater productions.

However, despite Jason's tilt toward Hellenism, he was not moving fast enough for Antiochus. In 171 B.C.E., the king replaced Jason with Menelaus, an even more Hellenized high priest, who built a citadel overlooking the Temple. More stringent laws were enacted—even the refusal to eat swine's flesh or desecrate the Sabbath became illegal. The punishment for breaking these laws was death, and many Jewish parents were executed for circumcising their male babies.

FACT

Those who were willing to accept death rather than violate their religious beliefs are still remembered as martyrs. Ironically, the word "martyr" comes from the Greek *martus,* "to witness."

Meanwhile, Antiochus was busy in his campaign to conquer Egypt. When he was finally forced to withdraw, sometime between 171 and 169 B.C.E., a rumor spread that he had been killed in battle. Believing Antiochus to be dead, the deposed High Priest Jason led a rebellion against Menelaus. Antiochus ordered the insurrection crushed and in 167 B.C.E., he issued an edict that abolished Mosaic Law and replaced it with a secular system. A statue of Zeus was installed in the Temple, which became an ecumenical place of worship.

Discontent of the Populace

Even those Jews who were Hellenized were appalled at what was going on in Judah and the brutality of the persecution of religious Jews. As a result of the oppressive measures instituted by Antiochus, the reformers lost the support of the population. Soon, the Jewish fundamentalists would succeed in transforming the religious dispute into a revolt against the occupying power. The time was ripe for a full uprising.

The Maccabean Revolt

The story of the Maccabean revolt begins in the Judean foothills just northwest of Jerusalem, in the village of Modin. In 166 B.C.E., when the Syrian general Appolorius sacked Modin, he commanded the construction of a religious altar. When a Jewish reformer stepped forward to comply with the order to burn incense and sacrifice forbidden animals, he provoked the wrath of Mattathias (Mattityahu) Hasman, an elder and religious leader of the distinguished Hasmonean family. Mattathias killed the Jewish reformer; then, turning his fury upon the Greeks, he attacked the soldiers. Thus, the action of one man sparked the rebellion of the Jews, who fought for religious liberty.

Mattathias and his five sons became the leaders of the Maccabees, "men who are strong as hammers." The Maccabees would ultimately fight on three fronts: against the Seleucid troops that had been sent to restore calm to the region; against the Jewish Hellenizers, some of whom aligned themselves with the Greek forces; and against non-Jews who attacked the Jews living in northern Trans-Jordan, western Galilee, the coastal plain, and the Idumean district of Jerusalem.

Soon after the struggle began, Mattathias died, and his son Judah led the Jews in a guerrilla campaign against the Seleucid garrisons. Judah was a great military strategist, and he defeated the enemy in the narrow passes of his native mountains at Beth Horon. In two years, the Jewish forces under Judah's command drove the Greeks out of the area around Jerusalem and succeeded in cutting off the main road connecting the seacoast to the city. On the twenty-fifth day of *Kislev* (sometime in December of 164 B.C.E.), the Maccabees and their followers reclaimed the Temple from the Greeks.

The Miracle of the Oil

When the Jewish forces recaptured the Temple Mount, they wanted to rededicate the Temple. Part of the rededication ceremony required lighting the Temple menorah, but the Jews could find nothing more than one sealed jar with the oil suitable to burn in the Temple, enough to last for one day.

The day after the battle for the Temple Mount, a rider was dispatched to Mount Ephraim, where the olive trees grew that provided oil for the menorah. It would take three days to get there, three days to return, plus the day needed to press the oil. There was no way the oil found in the Temple would last that long—but it did. The small quantity of oil burned for eight days, until the messenger returned with new oil appropriate for the Menorah.

The Hebrew word for "dedication" is *chanukah*. The Jewish holiday of Chanukah is a holiday that emphasizes the importance of the rededication of the Temple and the miracle of the oil, not the military victory of the Maccabees. The Maccabean Revolt was fought over religious freedom—not over territory or political sovereignty.

Interestingly enough, the episode of the oil that burned for eight days is not even mentioned in the Book of the Maccabees. Instead, the narrative of the miracle of the oil is recounted in the Talmud. While some believe that the miracle was God's work, there are those who feel that it is merely a lovely legend.

The Meaning of Chanukah

The religious leaders, consisting of judges and rabbis who comprised the *Sanhedrin,* realized at once that something very important had occurred when the Jews reclaimed the Temple Mount, and they began Chanukah celebrations the very next year. However, it remained a minor holiday. In the *Mishna,* there are few references to Chanukah, perhaps because it was written at a time when Rome governed Jerusalem and rebellions were not tolerated. This explanation also supports the contention that the rabbis added the miracle of the oil to the *Gemara* to emphasize God's involvement and discourage political activism.

It was not until the first century of the Common Era that the Jewish historian Josephus retold the Chanukah story, which subsequently became popular in the Middle Ages. Indeed, it was Josephus who first referred to Chanukah as "the feast of lights."

What are _Mishna_ and _Gemara_?
Mishna is the code of Jewish law, edited by Rabbi Judah Ha-Nasi around 200 c.e. and based upon oral tradition. _Gemara_ is a collection of commentaries on the _Mishna_ made by the rabbis of the third through the fifth centuries of the Common Era. Taken together, the _Gemara_ and _Mishna_ comprise the Talmud.

Celebration of Religion Freedom

Regardless of how the Chanukah story made its way down through the ages or how much of it is fact (and there is indeed much fact) and how much of it is legend, Chanukah is imbued with a great deal of meaning.

First and foremost, Chanukah is a religious holiday that celebrates the rededication of the Temple. It commemorates a battle for religious liberty and the people who fought valiantly to gain the freedom to practice Judaism. Numerous scholars, rabbis, and historians have postulated that Chanukah was the first organized rebellion ever undertaken for the sole sake of religious freedom.

The Maccabean insurrection also serves as an inspiration for all people who find their freedoms curtailed by dictatorial rule. A tiny, ill-equipped, poorly trained force led by a family of priests overcoming the awesome might of the Greek Empire is surely a miracle that shows the power behind fighting for what is right.

Celebrating the Festival of Lights

The most significant rite of Chanukah is the lighting of the menorah, a ceremony performed in memory of the menorah used in the Temple. The Chanukah menorah, also called _chanukiah_, has spaces for eight candles all in a row, plus an additional ninth space above the other branches. This last space houses the _shamash_ (the "servant" candle), which is used to ignite the other candles.

Lighting the Chanukah Menorah

There is a specific order for lighting the Chanukah candles. On the first night, you light the *shamash* and then use it to light the candle at the far right of the menorah. On each subsequent night, an additional candle is set to the left of the candles lit the previous night. On the eighth and final day of Chanukah, the *shamash* will ignite all eight candles.

Everyone in the home participates in lighting the menorah—ideally, every person has one's own Chanukah menorah. Before lighting the menorah, the observant Jews recite two blessings. An additional blessing, the *Sheheheyanu*, is recited on the first night.

Part of the purpose of lighting the Chanukah menorah is to publicize the miracle of Chanukah and share it with the world. Therefore, it is customary for menorahs to be placed in front of a visible window or even set outside the front door. In Israel, some homes are constructed with cut-outs in the wall next to the front door for the Chanukah menorah to be displayed.

A Time of Joy and Playfulness

Following the lighting of the menorah, families sing songs that celebrate the Chanukah story. Perhaps the most well known of these songs is *Ma'oz Tzur*, or "Rock of Ages" (literally, "Mighty Rock"). At this time, children receive Chanukah *gelt* (a Yiddish term for "money") or candy money. Giving other types of gifts, often one on each night of the festival, is a relatively new tradition practiced by American Jews, a likely reaction to Christmas celebrations, which occur about the same time of the year.

FACT

Popular food dishes that appear during Chanukah are *latkes* (potato pancakes) and *sofganiot* (fried jelly doughnuts). Both of these treats are fried in oil, as a reminder of the miracle of the oil that lasted for eight days.

Chanukah Gambling

During Chanukah, people also play the *dreidel* game, gambling with pennies, candy coins, or other small stakes—and children love to participate. The *dreidel* is a four-sided spinning top; each side displays a Hebrew letter:

- נ *(nun)* for *nes*
- ג *(gimmel)* for *gadol*
- ה *(heh)* for *hayah*
- ש *(shin)* for *sham*

Together, these four words make up the phrase *nes gadol hayah sham* ("a great miracle happened there"). In Israel, *dreidels* substitute the Hebrew letter פ *(pei)* in place of *shin,* because *pei* denotes *po* (here).

©2001 Brand X Pictures

▲ During Chanukah, children play with the *dreidel* (a special spinning top).

Another way of looking at these letters is that they stand for the Yiddish words *nit* (nothing), *gantz* (all), *halb* (half), and *shtell* (put), which are the rules of the game and determine what happens to the "pot" after a person spins the *dreidel*.

Synagogue Services

Most of the Chanukah observances are conducted in the home, but this holiday does make its presence known in the synagogue. Special psalms and prayers are recited on each day of Chanukah and some congregations may read from the Book of Maccabees or other works that express Chanukah themes. On the Sabbath that falls during Chanukah, there is a special reading from Zechariah that includes the following phrase: "Not by might, not by power, but by My spirit says the Lord of Hosts" (Zechariah 4:6), reminding the Jews that the Maccabees persevered because of their faith in God.

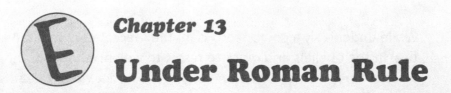

Chapter 13

Under Roman Rule

The victory over the Greeks proved to be short-lived. Soon, the failures of the Hasmonean dynasty led to loss of power, as the Roman Empire assumed control over its new province of Judea. Unable to accept the rule of the pagans, the Jews staged several rebellions, which culminated in the Roman Jewish War and the destruction of the Second Temple.

The Hasmonean Monarchs

For several years following the rededication of the Temple, an environment of tranquility prevailed in Judah. However, further conflict broke out in 161 B.C.E., when the Maccabees voiced disapproval over the appointment of a new high priest.

> While undeniably a courageous clan, the Maccabees were fanatical in their beliefs and quick to resort to violence. Indeed, they were often brutal to their enemies and most met violent deaths.

Despite Judah Maccabee's sweeping victory over the Seleucid general Nicanor, the Jews were doomed. The Seleucids sent another army led by a general named Bacchides, who defeated the Jewish troops and killed Judah. Judah's brother Jonathan then assumed command.

Peace with Rome

Eventually, an arrangement was made with Rome that in effect established Judah as a state independent of the Seleucids in Syria and ruled by the Hasmonean family. As a result, not only did the Hasmoneans govern the religious establishment but they controlled the military as well. In 152 B.C.E., Jonathan Maccabee was recognized as the high priest, a post that would belong to the Hasmoneans for more than a century. When Jonathan died later that year, his brother Simon, the last of the famous five Maccabee brothers still alive, became both high priest and ruler—until he was treacherously murdered, along with two of his sons, by the Ptolemies in 134 B.C.E.

Corruption of the Monarchy

The Hasmoneans embodied the reactionary spirit within Judaism. During their reign, they expelled pagans and conducted forced conversions. They were intolerant of those who did not adhere to their religious views. Nor were they content to merely govern what land they possessed. Simon's surviving son, John Hyrcanus, who assumed power after his father's death and who would rule Judah until 104 B.C.E., believed it was his destiny to restore the kingdom of David. At the head of a mercenary army, he went to war and crushed the Samaritans.

After John Hyrcanus' death, matters degenerated even further. His son Aristobulus received the post of high priest, but it was his mother who retained the power of the throne. Unhappy with this arrangement, Aristobulus threw his mother in jail, until she starved to death and he assumed the throne. Aristobulus died a year later, under mysterious circumstances, and his brother, Alexander Jannaeus, assumed control. During his reign, this tyrant had to fend off a six-year rebellion that may have cost as many as 50,000 Jewish lives. When he prevailed, he ordered the crucifixion of 800 of his Jewish captives and watched the executions while feasting with his concubines.

Loss of Sovereignty to Rome

When Alexander Jannaeus died in 76 B.C.E., he was succeeded by his widow, Salome Alexandra, who made peace with the Pharisees. Calm was restored temporarily, but when she died in 67 B.C.E., her three sons fought for succession, and the internal strife resulted in the loss of Palestine's sovereignty and the end of the Hasmonean monarchy. Emerging victorious from the struggle was Antipater, an Idumean whose family had been forcibly converted to Judaism by the Hasmoneans.

In 63 B.C.E., Antipater was appointed ruler of the province of Judea, which would become a client state of Rome. However, because his family had been Idumean and forcibly converted to Judaism, he was unable to assume the position of high priest. When Antipater died, his son Herod ascended the throne.

The Reign of Herod the Great

Herod, also known as Herod the Great, ruled in Judea from 37 B.C.E. to 4 C.E. Through his friendship with Marc Antony, the Roman politician and soldier who is most well known for his affair with Cleopatra, Herod secured the title of king of Judea. Though Herod could not assume the role of high priest, he had the power to appoint and dismiss others for this role. In Judea, Herod's control over matters both secular and religious was practically absolute.

The Golden Age of the Second Temple

Generally, Herod made efforts to mollify the Jews. He publicly observed *Halakhah* and re-established the Jewish religious court known as the *Sanhedrin.* One of his greatest achievements was the improvements he made in the construction of the Second Temple. Under Herod's guidance, the Temple was transformed into a magnificent structure known throughout the Roman Empire. The Western (Wailing) Wall that remains standing in the Old City of Jerusalem is merely the platform upon which the Herodian Temple stood.

FACT

During Herod's reign, the Temple was a hub of activity with thousands of priests, scribes, Levites, and pious Jews conducting religious ceremonies. Each morning and again at sunset, two lambs were slaughtered as sacrificial offerings. The services ended with the ritual drinking of wine, reading of scriptures, and singing of hymns and psalms.

Herod's architectural projects extended far beyond the improvements of the Temple. Herod erected several imposing edifices throughout Judea and established several new cities, the most famous of which is Caesarea, a seaport built on the Mediterranean coast. He also built a string of fortresses, most notably the citadel on top of a mountain in the Judean desert, known as Masada.

A Brutal Leader

Herod was a brilliant politician, able to maintain a peaceful and mutually beneficial relationship with Rome, and he was a visionary architect, but he was also a depraved and cruel ruler. Some of Herod's brutality was calculated. For example, he wanted complete autonomy regarding secular matters, and he tolerated no interference from the religious leadership. When the *Sanhedrin* tried to apply Mosaic Law to secular issues, he executed forty-six of its members to demonstrate who was in charge.

Fear of losing power made Herod wary of the surviving Hasmoneans, and he embarked upon a mission to kill as many of them as he could. Unfortunately, this meant doing away with some of his immediate family. Herod had married ten times and one of his wives, Mariamne, was a Hasmonean—she was a granddaughter of Hyrcanus II. Deeming her a threat, Herod issued the order to kill both his wife and their two sons, Aristobulus and Alexander. He also ordered the execution of Antipater, his son from his first wife, when he discovered that Antipater had been complicit in certain intrigues regarding evidence against Aristobulus and Alexander. The bloodshed went to such an extreme that it has been suggested that Herod may have suffered from paranoia or a psychosis.

©Israel Ministry of Tourism. Courtesy of the Israel Ministry of Tourism.

▲ During the Roman control of Judea, the Romans constructed the Caesarea Aqueduct, which brought water from Mount Carmel to the city of Caesarea.

The Kingdom Is Divided

When Herod died in 4 B.C.E., the Jewish kingdom he controlled was divided among three of his sons. His son Archelaus ruled much of Palestine until 6 C.E., when Rome deposed him after receiving so many complaints from his subjects. From that point on, this area (referred to by the Romans as Judea) would be ruled directly by the Romans.

Another son, Herod Antipas, was the tetrarch of Galilee and Peraea and achieved notoriety in executing John the Baptist. He fell out of favor with his subjects after repudiating his wife to marry his niece, and he was banished by the Emperor Caligula in 39 C.E.

FACT

According to Flavius Josephus, a Jewish historian who wrote the history of the Jewish people (see pages 154-155), John the Baptist was a Jew who preached "virtue, righteousness toward one another and piety toward God." His influence over the Jewish people became threatening to Herod Antipas, who ordered John the Baptist's death.

The eldest son, Herod Agrippa I, actually ruled with some competence in the northern part of his father's kingdom until his death in 44 C.E. The last son, Herod Agrippa II, was also a poor monarch who briefly reigned over Judea between 41 and 44 C.E., the year Jerusalem fell at the hands of the Romans.

Pharisees, Sadducees, and Essenes

By the time of Herod the Great's reign, the schism that had formed during the Hellenist period between the Hellenists and the traditionalists became even deeper, and three major groups emerged—Pharisees, Sadducees, and Essenes. All three drew many followers, but only one of the groups, the Pharisees, would survive and continue in existence after the end of the Second Temple Period.

The Sadducees

The term "Sadducee" derives from the Hebrew name of Zadok, who was the high priest at the time of David and Solomon. The Sadducees called themselves the sons of Zadok—they were a sect of priests and other upper-class Jews who did not believe in the oral Torah and insisted that all law must be written and remain unchanged. Moreover, their interpretation of the Mosaic code was narrow and conservative. The center of the Sadducee worship was the Temple. Consequently, when the Romans destroyed the Temple in 70 C.E., the Sadducees disappeared.

The Pharisees

The Pharisees were a more numerous group than the Sadducees. It has been estimated that by the time of Herod the Great's reign, near the end of the first century before the Common Era, about 6,000 Pharisees lived in Judea.

The term "Pharisee" is derived from the Hebrew *parush,* or "separated." Some have suggested that this word is applied to the sect because the Pharisees separated themselves from the masses by virtue of their holiness. Another possibility is that the Sadducees used this term to accuse their opponents of separating from the Torah.

The Pharisees believed that both the written and oral Torah came directly from God and were therefore valid and binding. In accordance with the Torah, the Pharisees began to codify *Halakhah* (the Law), insisting upon its strict observance. However, they encouraged debate among scholars regarding the finer points of the Law.

In contrast to the royal religious establishment with its high-priest Sadducee aristocracy, the Pharisees democratized Judaism. By liberalizing the laws and making their observance less onerous and by extending to all Jews some of the *mitzvot* that had been reserved for the priests to obey, the individual's relation to God was enhanced.

The Essenes

The Essenes were actually a radical branch of the Pharisees. This group was comprised of a wholly devout and pious people, mostly men, who formed an ascetic and mystical order and took an oath of celibacy (although one group of Essenes did marry). Celibacy was just one of the ways of maintaining ceremonial purity, as it was understood by the Essenes—other laws such as *Kashrut* (dietary laws) were practiced with utmost care.

Members pledged piety toward God, justice to men, and adherence to the order and its doctrines. As a sect, the Essenes disappeared sometime in the second century C.E., due to the practice of celibacy and lack of new converts.

ALERT!

The Essenes accepted the authenticity of several men who claimed to be messiahs. This ardent belief in the true messiah's imminent arrival might have played a role in the emergence of Christianity.

Jesus of Nazareth

The Essenes were very much a presence during the first century of the Common Era, during the lifetime of Jesus of Nazareth, believed by the Christians to be the son of God and the Messiah. (While the Jewish tradition does accept the actual existence of Jesus, it rejects the opinion that he was the Messiah.)

It is possible that Jesus had some contact with the Essenes. As with so much history up to this point, what we know for certain about the life of Jesus is limited. Jesus grew up in the village of Nazareth and spent much of his life in the Galilee, where he was regarded as a healer and preacher who called for repentance. He attracted disciples from the common people. His charisma may have earned him animosity from certain Jewish circles. Around 35 C.E., Jesus was crucified in Jerusalem on false charges of being a rebel against the Roman Empire. Subsequently, his followers believed he had risen unto heaven.

The early adherents of Jesus were Jews and, in fact, they remained a sect within Judaism, observing most of the Jewish religious practices, laws, and customs. They even participated in the rituals at the Temple. Only when Paul, a Jew from Tarsus, joined the movement and convinced the followers of Jesus to accept non-Jews into their ranks, did the birth and rapid growth of Christianity take place.

The Teachings of Hillel and Shammai

Learned men emerged among the Pharisees as well. Hillel and Shammai were both scholars whose pharisaic tendency toward spirited discussion gave rise to two distinguished systems of thought in the early years of the first century C.E.—the school of Shammai and the school of Hillel.

The School of Shammai the Elder

Shammai the Elder lived between 50 B.C.E. and 30 C.E. A man of learning, he was known for his great wisdom—and a quick temper. In his approach to students and others, he tended to be very pedantic.

Shammai believed that the essence of Torah could be discovered in the details of the text. Together with his followers, Shammai adopted a strict view of *Halakhah,* particularly on matters having to do with cleanliness. Ultimately, this perspective took the school of Shammai out of rabbinic Judaism and, like the Sadducees, this group eventually disappeared.

The School of Hillel the Babylonian

Shammai's great adversary in matters of interpretation of the Torah and the Law was a man by the name of Hillel (30 B.C.E.–10 C.E.), sometimes referred to as Hillel the Babylonian. According to Jewish legends, Hillel was a Diaspora Jew who appeared in Jerusalem one day and began to teach Jewish Law, and in a way markedly different from Shammai.

In fact, the two men disagreed on almost all scholarly and religious matters. Furthermore, their personalities could not have been more different. Hillel was an unassuming man who displayed patience even with the slowest of learners. He sincerely believed in the worth of each individual, and this was reflected in his approach to Judaism. Hillel embraced a universal and humane interpretation of the Torah. Unlike Shammai, he was of the opinion that the essence of Torah could be found in its spirit.

FACT

Hillel had an enduring influence on Judaism, and he is regarded as the forebear of the later sages who led the Jews of Judea until 400 C.E. One of his important contributions was to create a new (and easier) way for people to convert to Judaism.

Many of Hillel's aphorisms have lasted down to the present day. One of the most renowned is his response to a pagan who said he would become a Jew if he could be taught the Torah while standing on one foot. Hillel's famous reply was: "What is hateful to you, do not unto your neighbor: this is the entire Torah. All the rest is commentary—go and study it."

Revolts Against Rome

During the years 6–41 C.E. Judea was controlled by a series of seven Roman prefects (Pontius Pilate of New Testament fame was one of the prefects). Then, after a three-year rule by Herod Agrippa II, the power reverted to Rome, and Judea would be ruled by seven consecutive Roman procurators until 66 C.E.

The Roman rulers had no real interest in governing the Jews, and political, social, and economic conditions quickly deteriorated under their insensitive rule. That first year, under the rule of the Roman prefect Coponius, the Jewish populace rose up against what they perceived as unjust taxation. The rebellion was led by two men known as Judas the Galilean and Zadok the Pharisee, who urged the people not to pay taxes. The revolt was repressed, and the Romans inflicted severe penalties upon the population. This pattern of insurrection, defeat, and repression would continue throughout the period of Roman rule.

Judas the Galilean's rebel group became known as the Zealots. This faction took their name from the biblical description of Pinhas—a man who had saved Israel from a plague—as "zealous for his God" (the Book of Numbers).

Most revolts were small in both size and duration; the largest revolt occurred in 44 C.E., when a mob of thousands of Jews let by Theudas conducted a particularly violent uprising—it, too, was crushed. Yet, despite the passion, resolve, and cost of human lives with which these acts of resistance were conducted, they could not rival the insurrection that is often called the Roman Jewish War of 66–70 C.E.

The Roman Jewish War

The direct cause of the conflict had to do with the respective rights of the Jews and the pagans living in Caesarea, which served as headquarters for the Roman administration. Gessius Florus, who had been serving as the procurator for two years, sided with the pagans and subsequently ordered his troops to Jerusalem, where they crucified a number of eminent Jews. This was more than the Jewish population would tolerate.

The Roman garrison in Jerusalem was massacred, and when the new Roman force arrived to put down the rebellion, they met the same fate. For a short while, it seemed that the power was with the Jews, just as it had been during the times of the Maccabees. But this situation would not last. Eventually, Rome reacted to the defeat by dispatching to Judea one of its greatest generals, Titus Flavius Vespasian, along with four legions of well-trained Roman soldiers.

Vespasian was an astute and patient military strategist. He chose to avoid taking the direct route to Jerusalem and the treacherous mountains that favored guerrilla warfare. Instead, he concentrated on clearing the coast and then the surrounding regions near Jerusalem of all rebel forces. In 69 C.E., before he could complete his task, he was recalled to Rome to become emperor. His son, Titus, was left in charge to capture Jerusalem.

FACT

The Jewish revolt was no small matter to Rome since it has been estimated that 8 million Jews (including 2.5 million in Palestine) lived within the Empire—that's 10 percent of its population. And yet, the odds were insurmountable; the rebellion was doomed from the start.

Destruction of the Second Temple

In April of the year 70 C.E., Titus approached Jerusalem with 60,000 soldiers and blockade equipment. The city was held under siege until September, when the battle began in earnest. Twenty-five thousand Jewish defenders fought a violent and bloody struggle, making the Romans pay dearly for every street and alleyway. Unfortunately, tens of thousands of civilians were caught in the crossfire, and the population suffered horrible losses. Finally, on the ninth day of *Av* according to the Hebrew calendar—the same date as the destruction of the First Temple, mourned during Tisha B'Av—the Second Temple was burned.

It took another month for the Roman troops to capture west Jerusalem. In the end, a vindictive Titus ordered the razing of the entire city with the exception of the towers of Herod's palace. The Temple was gone. Jerusalem was leveled to the ground.

The Final Stand at Masada

Following the fall of Jerusalem, three areas of resistance remained. Herodium was taken relatively quickly by the Romans, and Machaerus fell in 72 C.E. One stronghold of Jewish autonomy stood alone—Masada. Masada was hardly an important city. It was a fortress constructed by Herod the Great, an imposing structure atop a 1,300-foot rock in the Judean desert, near the Dead Sea. Later, Masada became the center of the Zealots, who established a community there under the leadership of Menahem, son of Judas the Galilean (founder of the Zealot movement).

©Itamar Grinberg. Courtesy of the Israel Ministry of Tourism.

▲ The fortress at Masada, where Zealots took their last stand in the year 74 C.E.

After Menahem was killed in the battle for Jerusalem, his nephew Eleazar ben Jair became the leader of the contingent at Masada. This small group was not much of a threat to Rome, and none of these people had participated in the rebellion against Rome. Nevertheless, their independence would not be tolerated. Troops under the command of the Roman general Flavius Silva placed the stronghold under siege in 74 C.E. Subsequently, Masada fell to the Romans, but when the soldiers entered the compound, what they discovered must have been horrendous.

The Zealots' Final Act of Resistance

Rather than surrender, the 960 insurgents and refugees—men, women, and children—had all committed mass suicide. (Two women and their five children survived by hiding in a cave.) These Jews chose to pay the ultimate price for freedom.

Events that took place at Masada have been permanently etched into the collective memory of the Jewish people. Masada has served as a source of inspiration to the modern state of Israel. Today, soldiers serving in the Israeli Defense Forces swear their oath of allegiance at Masada before beginning their tour of duty.

Although the Jewish tradition does not glorify mass suicide, it should be remembered that Romans were barbarous in their treatment of captured Jews. Many were killed on the spot, while others were sold into slavery. Many of the slaves ended up in the Coliseum, where they were forced to fight as gladiators or were simply thrown to the lions. The Jews of Masada chose death rather than submission to the Romans and a life of slavery, unable to even practice their religion.

The Legacy of Josephus

Most of what we know about the Jewish rebellion against the Roman Empire comes to us from the Jewish historian Josephus (37–100 C.E.). Born Joseph bar Matthew into a priestly family, possibly of Hasmonean descent, Josephus was a precocious youth who ultimately associated himself with the Pharisees. At the age of thirty, after the fall of Jerusalem where he participated in the insurrection, he was taken to Rome as a hostage.

Josephus's account of the Jewish rebellion appears in his book, *The Jewish Wars,* the only surviving contemporary account of what happened in Judea. He also wrote a multivolume account of Jewish history, known as *The Antiquities.*

However, Josephus was soon declared a free man and granted Roman citizenship. He became well respected in Roman circles and was a protégé of three different emperors. Although he gave his children gentile names, Josephus remained proud of his Jewish heritage. He spent the rest of his life writing major works that tried to explain the rebellious Jews to the Romans while maintaining strict adherence to the facts as he knew them.

The Jewish Diaspora

The destruction of the Second Temple and the fall of Jerusalem to the Romans in 70 C.E. marks the beginning of what has been called the Diaspora, which would last for almost 2000 years, until the establishment of the modern state of Israel in 1948. However, it is important to note that many Jews remained in Judea, and economic reconstruction began almost immediately. Indeed, Jews still represented the largest segment of the community in the region.

It is also incorrect to consider this the only Jewish diaspora. The first diaspora (exile) had taken place when the Jews were sent to Assyria; another diaspora had landed many Jews in Babylon. And even before the dispersal in the year 70, many of the Jews were already in the diaspora, residing throughout all parts of the Roman Empire, from Egypt and Spain to Greece and Asia Minor.

Loss of Jerusalem as the Spiritual Center

However, the Diaspora that began in 70 C.E. was unique because up until that point, the communities in exile—though self-governing and independent of Judean Jews—looked to Jerusalem as the hub of the Jewish people. The Temple had been their spiritual center, and many made pilgrimages that reaffirmed their faith and sense of community. This sense of centeredness was taken from every Jew when Jerusalem was razed, and for 2,000 years the Jewish people were to keep alive their hope to one day return to Jerusalem.

Chapter 14

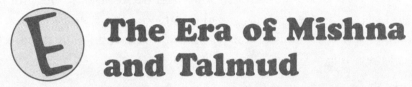

The Era of Mishna and Talmud

The first few hundred years after the destruction of the Second Temple and the dispersal of the Jews were a time of trials and tribulations for the Jewish people. Yet despite all of the upheavals and obstacles in their way, they persevered. One of the greatest achievements of this period was the compilation of the Talmud, a collection of Jewish law and commentaries to which Jewish scholars would continue to add material until as late as the fifteenth century.

Dispersed Throughout the Roman Empire

Rome had been ruthless in suppressing the rebellion of 66–70 C.E. and barbaric in its treatment of the survivors. So it should have come as no surprise to the Romans that the Jews were bitter and did not make for loyal subjects.

Repression of Jews became common practice. By the beginning of the second century, Jews were attacked throughout the Roman Empire for acts of subversion and introducing ideas considered hostile to the Roman way of thinking.

FACT

Maltreatment of Jews living in diaspora communities and in Judea reached a peak in the year 115, when mobs rampaged through the Jewish quarter of Alexandria, an Egyptian city home to a quarter of a million Jews, and burned its great synagogue, which had been the largest in the world. The Jewish community in Alexandria never fully recovered from that attack.

In response to the violent acts, Jewish uprisings took place throughout the Roman Empire, particularly in Egypt and Cyprus, and as a result many Jewish communities were decimated. The fighting in Rome was particularly bloody as well.

Under the Leadership of Emperor Hadrian

When Hadrian became emperor of Rome in 117 C.E., conditions did improve for a brief period. An atmosphere of tolerance prevailed and there was even consideration given to allowing the Jews to rebuild the Temple.

However, for reasons unknown, Hadrian soon changed his approach and became antagonistic to the Jews. He adopted a plan to transform Jerusalem into a pagan city-state based on the Greek *polis* model, with a shrine to Jupiter on the site where the Temple had stood. He also issued a ban on male castration, which included prohibition against male circumcision.

▲ Ruins at Qumran, an archaeological site where the Dead Sea Scrolls were found.

The Bar Kokhba Revolt

Hadrian's anti-Jewish policies aroused the anger of the Jews, and in the year 132 a Jewish uprising led by a man widely known as Bar Kokhba broke the uneasy peace in Judea.

The Man Behind the Revolt

Until recently, not much was known or written about Bar Kokhba. However, in 1947, archeologists working in the Dead Sea region in Israel uncovered evidence of this man's existence, including some of his letters and documents related to the rebellion.

Many Jews believed that Simon was the messiah, and they called him Bar Kokhba, "son of the Star," a reference to a verse in the Book of Numbers (24:17), "There shall come a star out of Jacob," an allusion to the arrival of a messiah.

Bar Kokhba's birth name was Simon Bar Kosiba, and he was an imposing man both in physical size and stature as well as in his abilities as a leader. In his writing, he referred to himself as Simon Nasi, "prince of Israel." He was a secular ruler and governed an area of Israel before the revolt took place.

Spiritual Guidance

The spiritual guide of the insurrection against Rome was Rabbi Akiva (50–135), Bar Kokhba's religious adviser and one of the wisest men of the age. There is an interesting story about how Akiva became a scholar. Because he came from a humble family, he spent his youth working as a shepherd and disliked scholarly pursuits. However, he fell in love with a woman who only agreed to marry him if he would study. As a result, Akiva became an eminent rabbi. Although he is famous for his legal systematizing and formulation of a new method of biblical interpretation, Akiva is better known for his compassion and concern for the poor, which had led him to support Bar Kokhba's rebellion.

A Temporary Victory

Rabbi Akiva was convinced that God would come to the rebels' aid and help them regain control of Judea, and so Bar Kokhba led an armed force of as many as 100,000 men to fight the Roman troops. For a time, it seemed like victory was on the side of the Jews—Judea was free of Romans, and Jerusalem was reoccupied, though practically defenseless without its walls. Bar Kokhba was so confident of having succeeded that he declared independence from Rome and even had new coins minted.

But Hadrian was not to be intimidated by Jewish insurgents. Under the command of Rome's best general, Julius Severus, twelve legions—half of the entire Roman army and three times as many soldiers as those who had destroyed Jerusalem in the year 70—marched on Judea to put down the rebellion. Despite the advantage in numbers, Severus wisely decided to avoid major battles with Bar Kokhba's troops. Instead, he eliminated the enemy one by one, isolating and destroying bands of guerrillas, burning down villages and towns, and taking over fortresses and strongholds. Gradually, he starved and exhausted the insurgents into submission.

Defeat of the Jewish Rebels

Jerusalem fell. The major fortresses, including Herodium, were captured as well. The end came in 135, in a village southwest of Jerusalem called Betar, where Bar Kokhba and the last of the rebels made their stand. Bar Kokhba was killed in the battle, and Rabbi Akiva was captured and imprisoned. Akiva's death is an example of the ferocity with which Rome treated Jewish prisoners. Rabbi Akiva's execution was by flaying—his flesh was torn from his body by iron combs until he died an agonizing death.

FACT

The losses in terms of human life, on both sides, were staggering. It has been estimated that 585,000 Jews were killed, and casualties on the Roman side were equally high. In total, fifty Jewish outposts and almost 1,000 towns and villages were razed. By the time the revolt ended, nearly all of Judea lay in waste.

For all intents and purposes, this marked the end of the Jewish state. More than eighteen centuries would pass before a modern Jewish nation would arise in its place. What held the Jewish people together in the Diaspora was the Torah.

The Oral Law

By that time, the Jewish people had the written Torah, which had been recorded during the Babylonian exile. In addition, there was the Oral Law, or Oral Torah, sometimes called the *Torah Sheb'al Peh,* which served a very important purpose—it provided detailed explanations of the Law as it is presented in the Torah. Traditionally, it was believed that these explanations had been provided to Moses by God to be passed down orally from teacher to student, because the Oral Torah was intended to be flexible so its principles could be debated among the religious scholars and adapted to new situations.

All this worked very well while the Jews had a land of their own (even if under foreign rule), where institutions like the judicial council of the *Sanhedrin* remained intact and could conduct their activities at a specific site.

However, after the destruction of many Jewish centers of learning in the year 70, the chances of the survival of the Oral Law seemed slim. Luckily, a man known as Johanan ben Zaccai managed to convince Vespasian to allow a Jewish center for study to be established in the city of Yavneh. There, Johanan reassembled the Pharisaic sages and scribes, as well as the council of the *Sanhedrin*.

Less than a century later, after the staggering defeat of the Bar Kokhba rebellion, many Jewish sages were forced into hiding, and during the first half of the second century, they gathered at different locations in their efforts to study and apply the Law. It was time to codify and write down the arguments of the Oral Law so that it could be preserved intact for future generations.

Codification of the *Mishna*

The remarkable man who emerged to lead the project of reducing the Oral Law to written form was Rabbi Yehuda Ha-Nasi (Yehuda the Prince), the son of Rabbi Shimon Ben Gamliel II. Ha-Nasi was born into a wealthy family, and he became the leader of the Jewish community in the Galilee and southern Judea in the second half of the second century.

FACT

Rabbi Yehuda Ha-Nasi was addressed as rabbi (wise man) because he taught the Torah and was designated Ha-Nasi ("the Prince") because he was elevated and made the prince, an honorific term in Israel. Many Jews also called him "our Master the Saint," because it was said that his body was as pure as his soul.

Ha-Nasi was both a great scholar and a strong, effective leader. He used his wealth to get things done on behalf of his constituents. Not only was he able to obtain a consensus from the diverse segments of the Jewish community, but he worked well with the Roman authorities, maintaining friendly relations with the three Roman emperors who followed Hadrian—one of them, Marcus Aurelius, went so far as to consider Ha-Nasi his confidant.

It is said that Ha-Nasi was dedicated to the study of the Torah and that he spent a substantial portion of his personal wealth to support scholars, whom he exempted from paying taxes. During times of food scarcity, he saw to it that the scholars were fed although he did not show a similar compassion for the uneducated. It is therefore not surprising that it was Ha-Nasi who undertook the mammoth project of codifying the Oral Law into what is known as the *Mishna* (from the Hebrew for "repetition").

Completion of the *Mishna*

Redacting the Oral Law was a monumental undertaking. The first step involved obtaining all written interpretations, rulings, and illustrations. Even more challenging was the task of interviewing as many rabbis as possible and asking them to recall what they knew about the legal traditions. Then, Ha-Nasi combined these recollections with the written documents he had gathered, edited everything, and by 200 C.E. he and his school produced the *Mishna*.

No sooner had the *Mishna* been completed than the rabbis realized more had to be done. Over the next several centuries, questions regarding the Torah as well as the Oral Law continued to be raised and explanations and clarifications provided. The two main centers for these activities were Judea and Babylon. As a result, in addition to the *Mishna,* we also have the commentaries of the *Gemara,* also known as the Jerusalem and Babylonian Talmuds.

The Jerusalem Talmud

After the Bar Kokhba revolt, the *Sanhedrin* and therefore the center of rabbinic study moved to Tiberias, a city in the Galilee region north of Judea. It was here, about 200 years following the *Mishna*, that the Jerusalem Talmud, *Talmud Yerushalmi,* was completed.

Because of the unsettled conditions in Judea following the Bar Kokhba insurrection, the rabbis in the various academies in the Galilee did not have the luxury to spend as much as time they would have liked deliberating on each point. As a result, the Jerusalem Talmud is considerably shorter than the Babylonian Talmud—even though the multivolume Jerusalem Talmud is 750,000 words long!

The Babylonian Talmud

By contrast, the Jewish community in Babylon was much more prosperous and stable. They could afford to take their time in adding commentary to the *Mishna*. Hence, the Babylonian Talmud, or *Talmud Bavli*, was not completed until the beginning of the sixth century and consisted of two and a half million words. This work was more polished and extensive than its Jerusalem counterpart, and it is in wider use today.

One of the reasons for the stability of the Jewish community in Babylon was that country had been governed by the Persian Sassanian dynasty since the third century. During this period, the official head of the Jewish community, the *exilarch,* established rabbinic academies in central Babylon.

As many as 1,200 scholars gathered at the academy in Sura that was founded by Rabbi Abba Ben Ibo (known as the Rav). By and large, these rabbis considered themselves as the repository of the strictest Jewish tradition. Consequently, the Babylonian Talmud is much more detailed than the Jerusalem Talmud.

However, this is not to say the undertaking did not face obstacles. During the years 455–475, before the sages could finish the project, most synagogues and academies were closed by the authorities. The repression was prompted by the Persian priests who were growing anxious over the encroaching Christian missionaries, and the reaction also extended to the Jewish community. However, the Jewish institutions were re-established by 500, and shortly thereafter, the Babylonian Talmud was completed.

A Foundation for Judaism

The commentaries contained in the Babylonian and Jerusalem Talmuds are known as the *Gemara*. In Hebrew, *Gemara* means "completion"; in Aramaic, it means "tradition." While the Jerusalem Talmud was written in Hebrew, the Babylonian Talmud was written in Aramaic, the idiom commonly spoken by the Jews during that time. Together, the commentaries of the *Gemara* and the codified laws of the *Mishna* comprise what we commonly refer to as the Talmud. The term "Talmud" means "study" or "learning," and it is in fact the main source of instruction for Jews who wish to learn the finer points of Jewish Law.

FACT

If you examine a page in the Talmud, you will see the Hebrew text of the *Mishna.* Surrounding and interspersed among the *Mishna* are explanations written in Aramaic—the commentaries of the *Talmud Bavli.* Additionally, the Talmud contains commentaries of rabbis who lived between the sixth and fifteenth centuries. These rabbis are known as *Rishonim* or "the first ones."

A Guide for All Areas of Life

The Talmud is a record of the way rabbis, scholars, and jurists have applied the laws of the Bible to all aspects of their life. Consequently, it encompasses everything that went on in those people's daily existence. Themes include the social and the private, urban and rural, civil and criminal, public and domestic, everyday and ritual. Virtually nothing was overlooked.

All of this information is divided into six sections, known as the *sedarim* (orders):

1. *Zera'im* (seeds): Deals primarily with agricultural laws but also laws of prayer and blessings.
2. *Mo'ed* (season): Addresses celebration of the Sabbath and festivals.
3. *Nashim* (women): Deals with the laws of marriage and divorce.
4. *Nezikin* (damages): Discusses civil law and ethics.

5. *Kodashim* (holy things): Considers sacrifices and the Temple.
6. *Toharot* (purities): Deals with laws of ritual purity and impurity.

Each of the *sedarim* contains several books called *masekhtot* (tractates), for a total of sixty-three. Although the respective *sedarim* seem to address rather specific and narrow topics, in fact, each *seder* contains diverse and assorted subjects.

A Work of Literary Complexity

Despite the fact the Talmud addresses legalisms and specific issues, it is not a code or catechism that lays down the law in summary categorical form. In fact, the Talmud is filled with legend, folklore, parables, reminiscences, prayers, theology, and theosophy. Moreover, the Talmud contains numerous stories called *agadata* (allegorical stories), which are intended to illustrate important points of Jewish law.

In the pages of the Talmud, not only is the law made clear but the tensions, conflicts, and arguments of its collaborators come alive before the reader's eyes. The explications of the rabbis are the most important parts of the Talmud.

Engaging the Talmud can be a fascinating experience, for it is like coming face to face with the living and breathing people who left a little of themselves dispersed throughout the pages.

Chapter 15

E The Medieval Period in Western Europe

By the time the Diaspora had begun, many Jews were already living throughout the Roman Empire. However, what had once been a mighty power was undergoing a decline. Ravaged by war and internal conflicts, by the fourth century the Roman Empire was no more—replaced by the Byzantine Empire and other Christian states of Western Europe. Suddenly, the Jewish people living in Europe found themselves a persecuted minority living under Christian rule.

The Rise of Christianity in Europe

As discussed in Chapter 13, Christianity originated in Judea, but it gained momentum and spread throughout the Roman Empire after St. Paul began to accept non-Jews into the fold. Soon, Christians dropped many Jewish practices; from that point on, the majority of the new converts to Christianity would be former pagans, not Jews. And although the Gospels may have been written in Aramaic, the idiom of the Jews, they were soon translated into Greek for the benefit of the gentiles.

Unfortunately, the Gospels do not give a clear account of the events surrounding the life of Jesus of Nazareth. They downplay the fact that Jesus and his followers were Jewish, while making the term "Pharisee" synonymous with "evil" and laying the blame for Jesus' death on the shoulders of the Jews.

The rapid spread of Christianity became a threat to the empire, and persecution of Christians was routinely practiced by various emperors in the second and third century. However, in 313 C.E. Emperor Constantine issued the Edict of Milan, which formally granted Christians the right to practice their faith in peace. Only a few years later, in 325, the Council of Nice formally declared Christianity to be the one and only official religion of the empire. The following year, Constantine moved to Byzantium (which would be renamed Constantinople in his honor), and the Roman Empire was no more.

By the tenth century, the Jewish population in lands that had once been the Roman Empire decreased to no more than 1,500,000 Jews. The dramatic drop in population was the result of persecution, conversion (often forcibly), assimilation, and murder.

The tables had turned. The Christians, now a powerful majority, wanted to eradicate paganism, and they did not take well to Judaism. It's likely that they resented the Jews' rejection of the Christian belief that

Jesus was the Messiah and the son of God. Although the Jewish people were permitted to remain and were not forcibly converted, they were no longer equal citizens. For centuries to come, they would suffer violence and oppression at the hands of their Christian neighbors.

The Ashkenazic Communities

Gradually, the Jews spread from the areas formerly belonging to the Roman Empire through the rest of Europe. The first group of Ashkenazim were Jewish traders who had followed the Roman Legions into Gaul (France), where they settled along the Rhine Valley and later in northern France.

QUESTION?

Who are the Ashkenazim?
The Ashkenazim or Ashkenazic Jews are those who settled in Germany, France, and later in Eastern Europe. The Ashkenazim share a common language, Yiddish, as well as Yiddish culture. The term *Ashkenaz* is the Hebrew word for "Germany."

When Charlemagne the Great established the Carolingian Empire in 800 that ruled for the next 200 years over Western and Central Europe, Jews were encouraged to settle as traders. Following Charlemagne's death, his son, Louis the Pious, placed the economic activities and the properties of Jewish merchants under the protection of the monarchy. By the turn of the millennium, numerous Jewish communities were established along European trade routes. In 1066, following the Norman Conquest, some French Jews had also arrived in England.

The Jewish communities were generally small and homogeneous villages where many Jews were artisans and craftsmen. The Jewish communities were governed by an elected board known as the *Kahal* or *Kehillah*. Biblical and Talmudic studies were undertaken with intensity, and a number of eminent scholars and literary figures emerged at this time. Probably the most famous of his age was Solomon ben Isaac of Troyer (1040–1105), also known as Rashi.

A New Language Emerges

It wasn't long before the Ashkenazic Jews began to converse in their own language. Originally, they spoke in a combination of Hebrew and Old French; later, German dialects were incorporated as well. When the Jews migrated to Austria, Bohemia, and northern Italy in the twelfth century, they took this new language, Yiddish, with them. When they were later invited to enter Poland to engage in commerce, Yiddish also absorbed the influence of Polish, Czech, and Russian.

FACT

In its more recent form, Yiddish is composed mostly of Middle/High German, with a measure of Hebrew and touches of Slavic tongues and Loez (a combination of Old French and Old Italian). In its written form, Yiddish uses the Hebrew alphabet.

Yiddish became the language of Ashkenazic Jewry. It served them well because it was an adaptable and assimilative language that was flexible enough to incorporate some traits of the tongues spoken in the places Jews lived.

Surviving the Crusades

Up until the eleventh century, things were relatively calm. Although some Christian clerics were hostile to the Jews, for the most part conditions remained tolerable because the secular rulers wanted to preserve the economic advantages they received from their Jewish subjects. However, circumstances changed beginning with the Crusades.

The First Crusade

It all began at Clermont-Ferrandin in 1095, when Pope Urban II called on Christian nobles and knights to beat back the "infidels"—the Muslims—who were winning one victory after another in the Middle East and were successfully spreading the influence of Islam. The fate of the Holy Land and Christian sacred sites were at stake.

An armed contingent of 5,000 knights and 10,000 infantry answered the Pope's call and set out on their holy mission. Along their journey through Europe, they were joined by thousands of peasants.

The Crusades were intended to be a holy endeavor. Those who joined the Crusades became known as "Crusaders" because each one completed the ceremony of "taking the cross" and because they wore a red cross on their outer garments.

One particular goal was to save the Church of the Holy Sepulchre, which had been constructed on the site where the Empress Helena (Emperor Constantine's mother) had determined Jesus had been buried following the crucifixion. The Christians could not bear the thought that one of their holiest sites would be destroyed by the Muslims, or even that it would fall into disuse and disrepair.

Christians were in fact successful in reclaiming and rebuilding the Church of the Holy Sepulchre. Today, thousands of Christian pilgrims visit the site every year. At least in this respect, the Crusades proved to be successful.

But there were less noble incentives as well. The Church wanted to acquire new lands in order to keep its power, and it needed money to finance its projects. Monarchs, noblemen, and knights also had their sights set on securing land and wealth.

A Time of Religious Hate

The Crusades stirred religious fervor among the populace and religious indignation against the unbelievers soon turned to violence. The primary targets of the Crusaders were the Muslims, but the Jews—accused of being Christ-killers—were marked as well.

The Jewish people were subject to unspeakable acts of violence during the years that encompassed the Crusades. In the Holy Land, they were seen as collaborators of the Muslims and many were massacred. The Jews in Europe suffered as well. Each time fervent preaching sent a new wave of soldiers on a Crusade to save the Holy Land from the hands of the infidels, the Crusaders would also make stops on the way to attack the infidels in their midst—the Jews. Usually, the local populace would enthusiastically participate in the carnage. The anti-Jewish sentiment that already existed before the end of the eleventh century was reignited with each new Crusade. It has been estimated that 10,000 Jews, more than a third of the Jewish population in Western Europe, were killed during the Crusades.

©Israel Ministry of Tourism. Courtesy of the Israel Ministry of Tourism.

◀ Remains of a fortress in Caesarea, originally constructed by the Christian Crusaders.

One account of the violence directed against the Jewish people describes the massacre of Mainz, a city in Western Germany located on the banks of the Rhine that had been home to one of the oldest Jewish communities in Western Europe.

Trying to avoid the fate of their brethren in other towns, the Jews of Mainz bribed the local bishop to have his guards protect them in the great hall of his mansion. Unfortunately, this did not spare them from an attack by a crazed mob of thousands. On May 27, 1096, 700 Jewish men, women, and children were slaughtered despite their resistance.

FACT

In England, the Third Crusade, led by Richard the Lionheart, was particularly devastating to the Jewish community of 4,000 people. In the year 1190, the Jews of York found themselves under attack and took refuge in a castle. When they saw that their situation was hopeless, they committed mass suicide.

Two Centuries of Violence and Bloodshed

In total, as many as ten Crusades spanned the twelfth and thirteenth centuries. Historians disagree over the exact count because it isn't always clear when each particular Crusade began and ended. It is generally believed that there were five major Crusades:

- The First Crusade (1095–1099) culminated with the conquest of Jerusalem and the slaughter of its Muslim and Jewish inhabitants.
- The Second Crusade (1147–1149) unsuccessfully attempted to recover lands from the Turks.
- The Third Crusade (1189–1192) was undertaken after Saladin recaptured Jerusalem. This Crusade, led by King Richard the Lionheart, failed in its quest.
- The Fourth Crusade (1202–1204) succeeded in capturing Constantinople.
- The Children's Crusade (1217–1221), led by a young boy named Stephen of Cloyes, was a misguided effort to lead the young of

France and Germany to the Holy Land. Most of the children never returned; those who did not perish from hunger or disease were supposedly sold into slavery.

In addition, there were five minor Crusades that took place in 1217–1221; 1228–1229; 1248–1254; 1270; and 1271–1272. The Crusades came to an official end in 1291, when the last Crusader stronghold at Acre (a fortress on the coast of the Mediterranean in Palestine) fell to the Muslims. But the problems the Jewish people would have to contend with did not end there.

Jewish Involvement in Money Lending

Two main factors pressed the Jews into the business of lending money. With the rise of exclusively Christian trade guilds, the Jews were forced out of commerce and no longer able to earn a livelihood at the occupations they had filled in the past. And because they were prohibited from owning land, they could not be farmers.

The second catalyst that drove the Jews into money lending occurred in 1179, when the Church forbade Christians to lend money to other Christians and charge interest. Interestingly enough, Jews were likewise prohibited by *Halakhah* to collect interest from fellow Jews. However, there was no prohibition against charging gentiles. Moreover, given their experience as merchants and traders, Jews had grown adept at drafting business letters, calculating exchange rates, and conducting commercial dealings, all of which made them well suited to extend credit. By the end of the twelfth century, a good many money-lenders were Jews.

Christian Resentment

Needless to say, this enterprise caused more than a good deal of resentment among the Christian population. Money lending was an important institution when kings and nobles needed money for military undertakings, public projects, or personal aims. However, when the debtors were unable to pay back the loans, they often saw it as more convenient to have the debts wiped out and the lenders exiled—or eliminated. Unfortunately, there was a useful set of accusations that could easily be leveled against any Jewish community.

False Accusations

One outrageous charge that was leveled at the Jews became known as the Blood Libel. The first recorded accusation took place in Norwich, England, in 1144. It was claimed that the Jews purchased an innocent Christian child by the name of William, tortured him in some satanic Passover ritual, and then killed him for the purpose of draining his blood to be used at the Passover *seder*. Another Blood Libel occurred in England in 1217; thereafter, similar charges became rampant throughout Western Europe. With each new accusation of blood libel, the vigilante mobs rose up to attack Jewish communities.

Some Christian leaders tried to counteract the allegations. In 1247, Pope Innocent IV specifically denied the validity of the Blood Libel, but to no avail. The irony of accusing Jews of drinking human blood is that Jews are forbidden to consume blood in their food, and meat must be drained of blood before it is considered kosher.

FACT

Another form of accusation had to do with the wafer of the Host (representing the body of Christ) used during Communion— supposedly, the Jews would kidnap the wafers for the purpose of torturing Christ. The first of these allegations took place in the early thirteenth century in Germany and Switzerland.

The Bubonic Plague

The Jews were blamed for the bubonic plague—known as the Black Death—that swept through Europe in the fourteenth century, killing as many as 25 million people (half the entire populace). Today, we know the plague was brought about by bacteria carried on fleas and spread by rats, but at the time the cause was unknown, and some superstitious people decided that the fault lay with the Jews.

Tens of thousands of Jews were viciously murdered because it was believed they were responsible for the Black Death—despite the fact that they were equally vulnerable to the epidemic. In Mainz alone, 6,000 Jews were killed. Of 350 localities in Germany, 150 of the smaller villages were eradicated. In all, more than 300 Jewish communities were wiped out.

A Vicious Cycle

In the period after the fall of Rome and until the Renaissance, Jewish people were victims of all kinds of accusations—ritual murder, drinking Christian blood, poisoning wells, destroying the Host, causing the bubonic plague, and many other imaginary crimes. Usually, the only recourse from the mobs of angered citizens was to flee to another area until the following wave of accusations and repression. With a history like this spanning over centuries, it is astounding that the Ashkenazic Jewish community survived at all—and with their faith intact.

State-Sanctioned Discrimination

By and large, violence against the Jews erupted when mass hysteria overtook the street mobs, who needed an easy target for their problems. However, there were also times when discrimination was perpetrated by governments. The most drastic measure taken against the Jewish communities by the monarchs of Europe was exile. Other measures included heavy taxation and discriminatory laws.

The So-Called Jew Taxes

To many monarchies, the Jews were a source of wealth. In spite of all they suffered, the Jews still managed to be productive citizens. They generated substantial income for their sovereigns and local rulers through the payment of special taxes, sometimes referred to as "Jew taxes."

In Germany, thirty-eight special taxes were imposed upon the Jews, covering such occasions as birth, death, marriage, and circumcision. In England, in order to finance the enormous expenses of the Third

Crusade, Jews were assessed higher taxes than the rest of the citizenry. Although they comprised less than ¼ percent of the population, they paid 8 percent of the taxes.

A Wave of Expulsions

But despite the economic benefits derived from the Jewish communities, expulsion of the Jews became a popular strategy because it generally won sovereigns popularity with the masses, cancellation of all debts owed to Jewish moneylenders, and the acquisition of all properties abandoned by them. Thus, beginning in the late twelfth century and up to the fifteenth century, the Jews were expelled from one country after another.

The first sovereign to exile the Jews was Philip Augustus, King of France. In 1182, all Jews were banished, their property was confiscated, and the debts owed to them were declared to be null and void. In 1198, the crafty monarch saw an opportunity to create a new source of revenue by permitting the Jews to re-enter the country and then charging a royalty tax upon those who took him up on his offer! However, the amnesty was short-lived; in 1306, the Jews were expelled once again, and the French Treasury became the recipient of all debts owed the Jews.

Because there was no centralized authority in Germany, the Jews could only be expelled from individual city-states by local rulers, and there were always some regions where they could find a haven. In fact, Jews remained on German soil throughout the Middle Ages.

In England, the situation was also economically motivated. In 1275, King Edward I began a campaign against usury, with money-lending activities punishable by death. Because all Jewish people were seen as usurers, the monarchy seized their assets and exiled them from England—as many as 16,000 had to find homes elsewhere. Many of these Jews made their way to France, where they settled until being cast out in 1306. For 350 years, no Jew would be permitted to return to England.

England and France weren't the only countries that adopted exile of Jews as a policy at one time or another. The following countries expelled their Jewish populations as well:

- Hungary: 1349, 1360
- German states: 1348, 1498
- Hapsburg city-states (modern-day Austria): 1421
- Lithuania: 1445, 1495
- Spain: 1492
- Portugal: 1497

Whenever one country expelled them, the Jews managed to find another place to live. Moreover, once a country deported its Jews, an economic downturn frequently followed, and it became prudent to readmit them. Of course, once the economy stabilized, the Jews would find themselves being cast out once again.

FACT

In medieval Europe, Jewish sectors were referred to by different designations: *Jewry* in England, *Juiverie* in France, *Judengrasse* in Germany, *Juidecca* in Italy, and *Judería* in Spain.

Confined in the Jewish Ghetto

The marginalization of the Jews in Christian Europe took on a physical component with the establishment of the ghettos, designated districts that were demarcated by a moat, hedge, or some sort of bulwark. During the day, the Jews could leave these areas for work and other activities. But at night, to avoid intermingling, the Jews had to return and stay put. Many ghettos were secured in the evening and guarded by Christian gate-keepers. Although Jewish sectors first appeared in Western Europe as early as the eleventh century, it wasn't until the *Ghetto Nuovo* that the Jews were really forced to the confines of their neighborhood.

The *Ghetto Nuovo* in Venice

In 1509, a group of Jewish immigrants from Germany was granted permission to take up residence in Venice, provided that they live on a small island located among the city's canals and enclosed by a high wall. This quarter was known as the *Ghetto Nuovo,* or "New Foundry," because that was where metal had been smelted for the making of cannons.

Soon, the practice caught on in other cities. In 1555, the Pope decreed that the Jews were compelled to live in a swampy area on the left bank of the Tiber River. The ghetto would be separated from the rest of Rome by an enclosed wall. In the remaining part of the century, other Italian states adopted similar ghettos for their Jews.

Preservation of the Community

Even when they weren't forced to live apart, the Jewish people often clustered together. There was safety in numbers, and those in a Jewish neighborhood had more of a chance to defend themselves when attacked. Furthermore, living within the Jewish community made it easier for the Jews to remain observant and keep Jewish customs such as keeping the Shabbat and maintaining dietary laws of *Kashrut*.

However, the ghetto was a place of confinement, often too small for the number of people living in it. Often, it was placed at the most disadvantageous area of the city. Overcrowding and an unhealthy environment often led to epidemics. Worse, an enclosed Jewish neighborhood was an easy target for the angry masses. Ⓔ

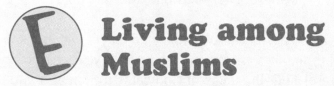

Chapter 16

Living among Muslims

While the Jews living in Europe had to contend with the rise of Christianity and its power over European societies, Jewish communities in the Middle East—in places like Babylon (now Iraq), Egypt, and Moorish Spain—found themselves a minority living among adherents of Islam, another monotheistic religion that emerged from the deserts of Saudi Arabia in the sixth century of the Common Era.

The Rise of Islam

The story of the birth of Islam is narrated in the Qur'an, the holy text central to the Islamic faith, dictated by the prophet Muhammad, who was divinely inspired by God. Muhammad was born in Mecca around 569–570 and grew up an orphan, taken care of by his uncle. In his youth, Muhammad was a shepherd; later, he worked for his uncle as a caravan merchant.

Muhammad eventually became a respected leader within his community and a devout man. When he was forty years old, he experienced a revelation—the angel of God came to him and told him that he would be a prophet of God. These revelations, written down in the Qur'an, would continue until the end of Muhammad's life.

FACT

Islam teaches that Abraham, Moses, and Jesus Christ were some of the many prophets of God, but that Muhammad was the final prophet who revealed God's message to humankind in the most complete and definitive way. This message, contained in the Qur'an, supercedes all previous messages and holy texts.

Slowly, Muhammad began to spread God's message throughout the community. Despite the initial period of persecutions, the message continued to spread, and a Muslim state appeared in Medina in 622 C.E. By the time Muhammad died in 632, the Arabian peninsula was under the control of Muslims, and the faith was quickly spreading further.

Growth of the Islamic Empire

By the 640s, much of the Middle East (including Palestine) as well as Egypt came under Muslim domination. In 661, the Umayyad Empire was established, its center in Damascus, Syria. Thirty years later, the Temple Mount in Jerusalem became the base of a Muslim mosque, the Dome of the Rock, which remains there to this day.

Eventually, Muslims conquered North Africa and crossed the Strait of Gibraltar into Spain, establishing a kingdom that would remain under their control for 700 years. In fact, the first few hundred years after Muhammad's lifetime has become known as the Golden Age of Islamic civilization in Spain, Iraq, Syria, and other areas controlled by Muslims.

Jewish and Muslim Relations

Those conquered by Islamic troops quickly became converts to Islam, whether by choice or by force. However, the Jewish communities were generally left alone. Islam's behavior to its Jewish subjects reflected Muhammad's ambivalence toward the Jews. In the Qur'an, Muhammad referred to the Jews as the People of the Book and taught that all Muslims should be respectful of their Jewish neighbors. However, the Jewish refusal to accept Muhammad as God's new prophet angered Muslims.

The Jews living among Muslims endured limitations upon their commercial and civic activities. Furthermore, they were subject to heavy taxation, known as the *jizyah*. The rationale for this tax was that it was paid for the Islamic state's protection of minority communities who did not abide by the state's laws. Despite the taxes and certain limitations, a Jewish middle class consisting mainly of artisans thrived and prospered under Islamic rule.

The Karaite Schism

By the eighth century, Persia (formerly Babylon) was ruled by a Muslim dynasty known as the Abbasids, who had established themselves in Baghdad. As you may remember from Chapter 8, the Jewish communities of Persia had existed and even thrived for many centuries, from the time of the Babylonian exile. These communities continued to coexist with the Muslims, and it was here that the Karaite movement first emerged.

The term "Karaite" is derived from the Hebrew verb *kara* (read) and the noun *mikrah* (scripture). Karaites are known as People of the Scripture because of their devotion to the Torah and the rejection of the Oral Law (the Talmud and other writings).

The catalyst for the formation of Karaism had to do with a dispute over who would become the new leader of the Babylonian Jewish community. But later, profound philosophical differences evolved, and the movement broke with rabbinical Judaism. The Karaites (just like the Sadducees centuries before) disagreed with the validity of the Oral Torah. They claimed that the Written Torah had to be observed literally, without rabbinic interpretation—and if there was any room for clarification, the Karaites maintained, it should be left to the rational thinking process of each individual, and not to the rabbis.

In its formative stages, the Karaites were a small pious and ascetic sect. However, early in the tenth century, the Karaite movement spread beyond Babylon. In fact, Karaites established an academy in Jerusalem. In the tenth and eleventh centuries, the Jerusalem Karaites distinguished themselves as merchants, literary figures, biblical and legal scholars, and philosophers. During this period, a network of Karaite synagogues sprang up all over the Middle East.

FACT

At their peak, it has been estimated that as many as 40 percent of Jews were Karaites. But for the most part, the Karaites represented a small segment of world Jewry. Today, the Karaite population is minuscule, with tiny enclaves in Israel, Crimea, the United States, and Europe. Until recently, a thriving Karaite community existed in Egypt.

The Golden Age in Spain

The Muslim conquest of Spain began in 711 and lasted no more than four years. For the next 700 years, the Muslims would rule a heterogeneous population, and for most of this time, the Muslim and Jewish civilization flourished—so much so that this period has often been referred to as the Golden Age in Spain. Indeed, during this time, the Spanish Jewish population would become the largest Jewish community outside of Persia.

Muslim Spain serves as an example that where the Jews were given a good deal of liberty, not only did they prosper, but so did the country in which they lived. The Jewish contributions to Spain were numerous and widespread. Many Jews served as courtiers to the local monarchs. No longer barred from the practice of medicine, many Jews trained as doctors; one such man, Hasdai ibn Shaprut, served as physician to two caliphs in the tenth century.

Free to become artisans, the Jews became excellent tanners, metalworkers, and jewelers. As in much of Western Europe, Spanish Jews were also active in trade and conducted commerce between the Christian and Muslim countries.

The Sephardic Community

The Jewish community in Spain became so well entrenched that by the fourteenth century, Spanish Jews were distinctively identified as Sephardim and developed their own language, known as Ladino or Judezmo. Ladino is written in either Hebrew or Roman characters and is based upon Hebrew and Spanish. It made its appearance as early as the Middle Ages and is still spoken in Turkey, North Africa, Israel, Brazil, and other parts of South America. In contemporary times, some Sephardic Jews from Arab countries speak a mix of Hebrew and Arabic.

Eminent Sephardic Jews

Over centuries of Muslim rule, many Sephardic Jews distinguished themselves in medicine, religion, and the arts. For example, Samuel ibn Nagrela of Granada (993–1056), also known as Samuel ha-Nagid (Samuel the Prince), excelled in both the religious and secular worlds. He represented the epitome of the Sephardic ideal as a mathematician, philosopher, statesman, and courtier.

Other prominent Jews during this period include the following:

- Abraham ibn Ezra (1092–1167): A physician, philosopher, astronomer, and biblical scholar.
- Bachya ibn Pakuda (1040–1080): A renowned ethicist who wrote *Duties of the Heart,* still read today as a pre-eminent book on Jewish ethics.

- Solomon ibn Gabirol (1020–1057): A philosopher and author of more than 400 poems.
- Moses ibn Ezra (1055–1135): A literary critic, poet, and author of penitential prayers.
- Judah Halevi (1075–1141): physician, poet, and philosopher.

Halevi's most remembered achievement is *The Book of Argument and Proof in Defense of the Despised Faith,* also known as *The Book of the Khazars*—a fictional rendition of a supposedly true incident that occurred in the eighth century. According to the story, the king of Khazars wished to become a servant of God, but he wasn't sure which religion he should accept. To make up his mind, the king gathered together representatives of all the world's notable religions, so that they may each try and convince him which religion is best. After hearing everyone out, the monarch of Khazaria chose Judaism, and he and many of his subjects underwent a conversion. The Khazarian kingdom vanished from history after being conquered by a Byzantine/Russian coalition in the eleventh century.

Rabbi Joseph Caro

Another Sephardic Jew, Rabbi Joseph ben Ephraim Caro (1498–1575), gained fame with the publication of *Shulhan Arukh.* Caro was born in Toledo, Spain. Following the expulsion of the Jews from Spain in 1492, he and his family wandered through Turkey, Bulgaria, and Greece. Ultimately, Caro settled in Safed, Israel. His gravestone is intact to this day, and it is a frequent stop for visitors to Safed.

Caro was a fervent mystic, but he is more famous for his legal writings. When he was in his thirties, Caro began writing his magnum opus, *Beit Yosef* ("House of Joseph"), a detailed commentary on Rabbi Jacob Asher's fourteenth-century code, *Arba'ah Turim* ("Four Rows"), a tractate on Jewish Law. While *Beit Yosef* was a milestone in Jewish legal literature, something concise and more accessible was required to serve as a clear and succinct guide to *Halakha.*

Caro accomplished this task in 1564 with the publication of the *Shulhan Arukh* ("The Set Table"). Initially, some rabbis opposed the *Shulhan Arukh* because it was a summary and did not lend itself to the rabbinical practice of going back to the original sources. However, in time the *Shulhan Arukh* gained acceptance in almost all Jewish communities. Today, it is regarded as a defining criterion of religious orthodoxy and traditionalism.

Moses Maimonides

Arguably the most notable Jew of this period was Moses ben Maimon (1135–1204), also known as Rambam (term formed from the initials of Rabbi Moses ben Maimon) or Maimonides. Maimonides was born in Cordova, Spain, where his ancestors, a distinguished family of rabbis, had lived for many generations. When Maimonides was thirteen, Spain came under the rule of the cruel Berber dynasty of the Alohades, and the Jews were given three options—flee, convert, or be killed. The Maimonides family chose to escape—first to North Africa, then to the Holy Land, finally settling in Cairo, Egypt, where Maimonides spent the remainder of his life and where he gained fame as a physician, scholar, and philosopher.

Maimonides was a cosmopolitan man who believed that a Jew's best weapon was to rely on intellect and reason as opposed to the esoteric. He was an eminent doctor and in 1185, he was appointed court physician to the Muslim ruler of Egypt.

Maimonides was a precocious young man and at the age of twenty-two, he published a commentary on the *Mishna*. Indeed, he later organized a systemization of Jewish Oral Law called the *Mishneh Torah*, which remains the standard compilation of *Halakha* to this very day. Maimonides is also known for outlining the Thirteen Principles of Faith (discussed in his book, *Discourse on the World to Come):*

1. God exists.
2. God is one and unique.
3. God is incorporeal.
4. God is eternal.
5. Prayer is to be directed to God alone and no other.
6. The words of the prophets are true.

7. Moses was the greatest of the prophets; his prophecies are true.
8. Moses received the Written Torah (first five books of the Bible) and the Oral Torah (teachings contained in the Talmud and other writings).
9. There will be no other Torah.
10. God knows the thoughts and deeds of men.
11. God will reward the good and punish the wicked.
12. The Messiah will come.
13. The dead will be resurrected.

©Israel Ministry of Tourism. Courtesy of the Israel Ministry of Tourism.

▲ Excavated entrance of the ancient synagogue in Capernaum, in the Galilee region, which dates back to the fourth century C.E.

Despite Maimonides's fame and high regard, many of his writings became controversial. Indeed, after his death, his works were banned and burned at the orders of the rabbis. Nevertheless, Maimonides's reputation has prevailed. Thousands of people make annual pilgrimages to the Galilee city of Tiberias, where Maimonides was buried.

Kabbalah—Jewish Mysticism

The Sephardic community in Spain also saw the emergence or revival (as you will see, this has yet to be determined) of Jewish mysticism, or Kabbalah, a Jewish mystical tradition that would spread to other Jewish communities. Kabbalah was shrouded in mystery and required years of study for initiation.

QUESTION?

What is Kabbalah?

The term "Kabbalah" comes from the Hebrew verb *lekabbel,* "to receive" or "to accept." Kabbalistic knowledge is said to have been passed down from Abraham through the generations. As with *Halakhah,* Kabbalah evolved by word of mouth, with each kabbalist leaving his own unique imprint.

Mystical Origins

The pre-eminent Kabbalistic writing is the *Zohar* ("The Book of Splendor"). Appropriately enough, its origin is shrouded in mystery. According to tradition, it is believed that following the failed revolt of Bar Kokhba and the execution of Rabbi Akiva in the second century, Rabbi Shimon Bar Yochai, or Rashbi (an abbreviation of his name), escaped with his son and went into seclusion for thirteen years.

Many kabbalists believe that while hiding out in caves, Rashbi had composed the *Zohar,* working it out in his head. Later, he dictated it to Rabbi Aba, who transcribed the material in the form of parables. However, not long after the time of the Rashbi, the *Zohar* mysteriously vanished.

Kabbalists claim that the *Zohar* remained hidden until it was found again in Spain. Others, however, believe that *Zohar's* origins are a fable, and that it was written sometime in the 1280s by Moses ben Shem Tov, a leading Spanish kabbalist. Regardless of its origins, however, the *Zohar* is the foremost tome on Kabbalah.

A Secretive Tradition

Kabbalah interprets the Torah in a way so as to focus on its concealed significance, which is usually discerned through the hidden meaning of the words and letters. Kabbalah addresses questions relating to human existence, the purpose of life, and similar profound concerns. It teaches how one's life can become empowered in order to reach the spiritual world. By studying Kabbalah, it is believed that a person's soul will widen to the point of allowing the surrounding holy light that exists in the world to enter it.

FACT

The basic ideas of Kabbalah with which we are familiar today first appeared in Provence in southern France near the end of the twelfth century, with the appearance of an anonymous book called *Bahir* ("Brightness"). In this book, the Ten Sefirot of the Godhead (ten emanations of God's essence) are clearly delineated.

The method of Kabbalah may be compared to mathematics of emotions. It takes the total of all feelings and desires, divides them, and then provides an exact mathematical formula for each and every circumstance. This is why the Hebrew letters are so important—because each one represents a numerical value. Kabbalah combines emotions and the intellect and infuses an element of spirituality to study.

Distinguished Students of Kabbalah

There have been many distinguished kabbalists throughout Jewish history. One such person was Rabbi Moshe Cordevero of Safed (1522–1570), known as the Ramak. In his work, *Pardes Rimonim* ("The Pomegranate Orchard"), Cordevero rationally systematized Kabbalistic thought and organized the material into a coherent system.

Another kabbalist, Rabbi Yitzhak Luria (popularly called the Ari), was born in Jerusalem in 1534 and was raised in Egypt, where he moved with his mother as a young child after his father's death. In 1570, Rabbi Luria returned to Palestine, settling in Safed, where he taught Kabbalah. His brilliance was immediately recognized. Although he died only two years later, at the age of thirty-eight, his system of study is still practiced today.

The Inquisition and Expulsion from Spain

The Golden Age in Spain would not last forever, and the end was drawing near. From the time when the Muslim Moors acquired their first foothold in Spain in the early eighth century, the Christians were determined to regain their lost territory and drive out the infidels. The final victory finally came in 1492, when Granada fell to the Christians and the last Muslim ruler was defeated.

The Christians viewed both Muslims and Jews as infidels, and both groups became targets during their quest to regain Spain. With each territory captured by the Christian forces, Muslim and Jewish citizens were slaughtered. In Barcelona, the entire Jewish community was murdered by the Christian armies.

In the new Christian Spain, the Jews had few options—conversion, death, or exile—and many Jews did convert, continuing to practice Judaism in secret. The *conversos*, as they were known, were despised by the populace, and discrimination was not uncommon. An even more contemptuous term, *marrano* (the Spanish word for "swine"), was used as well. Estimates vary, with the most conservative in the tens of thousands—perhaps as many as 600,000 Jews converted during this period in Spain.

The Spanish Inquisition

In 1478, at the instigation of Queen Isabella, the pope in Rome issued the papal bull *Exigit Sincere Devotionis*. The bull called for an inquisition into the sincerity with which all Christians—and Jewish converts in particular—held their Christian beliefs. In 1480, Ferdinand and Isabella established the Spanish Inquisition by formal decree to investigate the charges against lapsed Christians as well as heretics. A Dominican named

Tomás de Torquemada, who was Isabella's personal confessor and a rabid hater of Jews—some believe he had Jewish ancestors who had converted—was appointed as the chief inquisitor. This marked the beginning of a brutal and pervasive persecution of the Spanish Jewish community.

The Inquisition was carried on unrelentingly for more than 150 years, though investigations continued to be conducted until early in the nineteenth century, when it was officially abolished. Everyone was vulnerable to accusations of anti-Christian activities or beliefs, and the Jewish *conversos* were an easy target. During investigations, the accused were tortured. Those who did not "confess" were burned at the stake or hanged as unrepentant heretics.

FACT

In the first twelve years, more than 13,000 *conversos* were condemned. It has been estimated that there were 341,000 victims of the Inquisition. In all, more than 32,000 people were burned at the stake, with the rest given lesser punishments.

Sephardim Leave Spain

The monarchy allowed the converted Jews to remain in Spain, but they had other plans for those Jews who refused to give up their faith. On March 31, 1492, the Edict of Expulsion provided a "final solution" to the Jewish question.

At the time the royal seal was set to the edict, 200,000 unconverted Jews lived in Spain. About half that number went to Portugal, although they would be expelled from there five years later. About 50,000 Jews traveled to Turkey or North Africa. The remainder found homes in Palestine and elsewhere. In less than four months after the Edict of Expulsion became effective, all of Spain's Jews were gone.

Jews in the Holy Land

When a few of the Sephardim left Spain, they made their way to Palestine, where they found a small Jewish presence. The region was ruled by

Muslim caliphates until 1516 (with the exception of the period during the twelfth century, when the Crusaders briefly controlled the Holy Land).

ALERT!

Until the late nineteenth century, when secular Jewish settlers began to arrive with the hope of eventually establishing a Jewish homeland, most of the Jews chose to live in the Holy Land for scholarly and religious reasons. Many eminent rabbis and kabbalists emerged from the small Jewish community in Palestine.

From 1516 until the end of World War I in 1917, Palestine was ruled by the Ottoman Empire, a Muslim empire centered in Istanbul, Turkey. During this period of time, the Jews were looked upon favorably because of their wide experience in commerce and trade and the wealth they generated for their Ottoman rulers. Within a century after the Ottomans took control, the tiny Jewish community in Safed grew tenfold to 10,000 people and became a major intellectual center. The Jewish population in Jerusalem increased dramatically as well.

Chapter 17

Jewish Life in Eastern Europe

From the thirteenth century and onward, the Jewish community also appeared in Eastern Europe. Jewish towns and villages, known in Yiddish as *shtetls*, prospered. Despite the persecution and violence that the Jewish people periodically had to face, these communities survived for centuries and have left behind a rich heritage of Yiddish culture.

The Jews Arrive in Poland

In the year 1264, a very unique event took place. King Boleslav, the monarch of Poland, invited the Jews into his kingdom and granted them a charter unprecedented in its scope in terms of the rights it conferred. In this document, among other privileges, Jews were granted equal status with Christians in all forms of commerce. Christians who attacked Jews and their cemeteries would be punished, and Christians were obligated to protect their Jewish neighbors from any acts of violence—failing to do so constituted a crime. In exchange for royal protection and the granting of autonomy in running their lives, the Jews paid a tax rate of 30 percent.

FACT

In 1567, the Polish King Sigismund II Augustus issued another invitation to the Jews. In 1569, when Poland absorbed Lithuania, additional management and vocational opportunities arose for the Jews in these newly acquired lands.

It may be that this benign attitude toward the Jews had to do, at least in part, with the fact that Poland did not become a Christian nation until late in the eleventh century and that the Jews' reputation as Christ-killers had not yet become ingrained in the people. It is also likely that the primary motive behind the issuance of the charter and the invitation to the Jews was the belief that they would prove a boon in developing the commerce of Poland, just as they had in other regions where they had lived. Finding themselves no longer limited to money lending, Jews in Poland became fiscal agents, tax collectors, managers of the nobles' estates, craftsmen, and farmers.

A Center for Ashkenazim

At first, Jews trickled into Poland from Crimea, the Russian steppes, the Middle East, and Spain, but most of the arrivals were Ashkenazim, who migrated from the west as a result of expulsion. As a result, the Jewish population in Poland increased dramatically, from 20,000 in the year 1500 to 150,000 in 1575, representing 5 percent of the entire Polish populace.

Indeed, by 1650, estimates have put the Jewish population in Poland as high as 500,000—the largest Jewish community in the Diaspora at that time.

Many Jews lived in small urban centers or towns *(shtetls),* where they constituted a majority. These independent Jewish communities were governed by their own *kehillah,* just as they had been centuries earlier, in the small towns in France and elsewhere in Western Europe. The *kehillot* collected the taxes to remit to the Polish nobles and monarchs and governed the Jews in all secular matters—the rabbis took care of religious laws. In time, these *kehillot* organized into regional and national federations in order to represent the Jews before the monarchy.

Yiddish Becomes the *Mame Loshen*

It was in Eastern Europe that Yiddish continued its long and colorful history as the *mame loshen* (the mother tongue). It earned this name because it was the language of the home. While men learned Hebrew, *loshen ha-kodesh* (the sacred language) in religious schools, women spoke only Yiddish, and they passed this language on to their children.

QUESTION?

Is "Yiddish" synonymous with "Jewish"?
The word *Yiddish* literally does mean "Jewish," as in "the Jewish language," but Yiddish is not common to all Jewish people. It is only one of several languages (Ladino being another prominent one) that developed in the Diaspora among various Jewish communities.

Yiddish is a very social language, replete with nicknames, terms of endearment, and more than a good share of expletives. There are also plenty of proverbs and proverbial expressions, curses for just about every occasion, and idioms reflecting the fears and superstitions of the times. Although it arose as a spoken language, Yiddish also holds a prominent place in Jewish literature (see Chapter 22).

The Jews used Yiddish in everyday matters. Although a few Jews deemed themselves too sophisticated to speak this language of the common people, it nevertheless gained a prominent place in the hearts and minds of millions of Jews the world over. And in return, this language served the Jewish people well, adapting and changing from community to community, absorbing some traits of the tongues spoken in the places Jews lived. Consequently, even English words and phrases made their way into Yiddish after the waves of immigration into the United States by European Jewry at the end of the nineteenth and early twentieth centuries.

Chmielnicki's Rebellion

Although the Polish crown remained beneficent toward the Jews, there were periodic incidents of violence against them at the hands of their Christian neighbors. Moreover, their position as tax collectors for the local nobles did not endear the Jews to the common folk, nor were they appreciated for their business acumen and skills as artisans, which made them formidable competitors in commerce.

Until the middle of the seventeenth century, by and large, conditions for the burgeoning Jewish community in Poland were mostly agreeable. But as had happened repeatedly throughout Jewish history, good times were often followed by bad.

When Lithuania had joined Poland in 1569, what we know today as the Ukraine and portions of Belarus also became a part of Poland. The Ukrainians did not like this change, and there was a popular revolt in 1635. Although the revolt didn't succeed, a second rebellion followed in 1648–1649. This time, the Ukrainian populace was led by a petty Ukrainian aristocrat by the name of Bogdan Chmielnicki.

With his army of Ukrainian peasants and aided by Cossacks and Tartars from the Crimea, Chmielnicki waged a bloody campaign against the Polish nobility, the Catholic Church (Ukrainians themselves were Eastern Orthodox), and the Jews.

FACT

The number of Jews murdered in this two-year period was astounding. Estimates vary, but it is possible that as many as 100,000 Jews met hideous deaths at the hands of Chmielnicki, who justifiably earned a reputation in Jewish history equaled only by Hitler.

Slaughtered by the Rebels

Thousands of *shtetls* were pillaged or abandoned in the path of Chmielnicki's marauders. The Jews fled to fortified towns that turned into death traps. Frequently, they were denied admittance and left to stand helpless outside the ramparts to be slaughtered. On other occasions, if they were permitted entry, they were handed over to Chmielnicki's forces to be killed once the city came under siege. In those instances where the Jews were granted complete asylum, once the town was seized by Chmielnicki, they met agonizing deaths.

Chmielnicki's rebellion was staggering in its barbarity toward the Jews. Written accounts exist to this day describing how Jews had their flesh flayed or their limbs severed and their torsos thrown into the road to be trampled by carts. Children were murdered in front of their parents; pregnant women had their bellies slit open and the unborn babies tossed into their faces; many victims were buried alive.

Following the bloodshed, many Jews remained in Poland, and the Jewish population increased during the eighteenth century. However, the Jews never regained their prior standard of living, and many lived in poverty.

The Hasidic Movement

Chmielnicki's carnage left in its wake a Jewish population decimated both physically and psychologically. Most of those who did survive found themselves living in dire poverty. To add to their woes, acts of violence and discrimination against them became everyday incidents for Eastern European Jews.

During such times, it is common for people to seek salvation and solace wherever they can find it. Many Jews came to prefer the spiritual nature of Kabbalah, Jewish mysticism first developed in the Sephardic community (see Chapter 16), to the legalistic approach of rabbinic Judaism.

Many of the common people deeply resented the authoritarian and sometimes oppressive manner in which the rabbis controlled Jewish society.

In reaction to this, rabbinic studies became even more focused on *Halakhah* and conventional Talmudic rumination. The religious establishment grew fearful that the masses would flock once again to a false messiah—as they had in the seventeenth century, when many Jews became followers of Shabbetai Zvi. And indeed, a messianic pretender did appear in Poland during the eighteenth century. Jacob Frank had garnered a large following among the Jews, until he converted to Christianity.

QUESTION?

Who was Shabbetai Zvi?
Zvi was a Jew from Smyrna, a town in Turkey. A charismatic, fervently religious man, he was proclaimed to be the messiah. And yet, when forced to choose between conversion and death, Shabbetai Zvi chose conversion, renouncing Judaism in favor of Islam.

As a pious fervor spread among the masses in Poland, who were often ignorant of formal religious learning, a deep schism developed between them and the rabbinical authorities. Out of this chasm emerged Rabbi Israel ben Eliezer (1700–1760), who became known as the Ba'al Shem Tov ("Master of the Good Name") or Besht.

The Ba'al Shem Tov

The Besht was born in Okup, a small town in Western Ukraine. He was an orphan who at various times supported himself by helping in the ritual slaughterhouse, digging for lime in the Carpathian mountains, serving as a watchman in the synagogue, and as an innkeeper.

The Besht had very little formal education and ultimately chose to roam the countryside, believing that it was the best way to commune with God. While many holy men at that time also performed practical Kabbalah that included dispensing folk medicine, amulets, and incantations, the Besht soon rose above their ranks, in part because of his genuine charisma and also because he never hesitated to criticize the pedantic reiterations of scholars and the rabbinical emphasis on formal learning.

The Hasidic Movement

When the Besht died, he left behind no written work of his own, except for a few letters. However, after his death, his oral teachings began to appear in stories that were circulated about him. These teachings or principles, which had been established by the Besht, remain the core of Hasidism today.

FACT

The Hebrew word *hasid* means "pious" or "pious one." In classical Jewish sources, it referred to any person whose spiritual devotion extended beyond the technicalities of *Halakhah*. With the rise of the Hasidic movement over the last 200 years, the term "Hasid" is now used to describe a member of the movement.

The Ba'al Shem Tov conceived a revolutionary form of popular prayer conducive to ordinary and humble Jews, with the aim of breaking down the barriers inhibiting one from entering the divine world. How one prays, the Besht emphasized, is more important than where it is done. Sincerity is required not only in prayer but in all of life's actions. This is accomplished through the following:

- *Kavana* (pure intention)
- *Devekut* (clinging—devotion to God's presence)
- *Hitlavut* (enthusiasm—joy in performing all deeds)
- Sincere prayer

Simply put, the goal is to hallow life and thus awaken the holy reality in all things.

The Besht also revived the ancient concept of the *tzaddik* (the righteous one). Since the average Hasid could not be expected to achieve full religious perfection, he would devote himself to a particular *tzaddik* and obtain vicarious fulfillment through him. The different Hasidic sects can trace their roots to a specific *tzaddik*, often from a particular village or town in Eastern Europe.

©Israel Ministry of Tourism. Courtesy of the Israel Ministry of Tourism.

◀ A Hasidic Jew praying at the Western Wall.

Hasidim and Mitnagdim

The Hasidic movement met with intense opposition from many rabbis. Hasidism's foremost adversary was Rabbi Elijah ben Shlomo Zalman (1720–1797), who was known as the Vilna Gaon (the Genius of Vilna). Zalman and those in support of traditional rabbinic Judaism—the *mitnagdim* (opponents)—feared the deintellectualization of Torah and the possibility of the Besht becoming a false messiah (though he never made such a claim). Many Hasidim were excommunicated for their practices, but ultimately, the *mitnagdim* disappeared, and Hasidism became a part of Orthodox Judaism.

Jewish Presence in Russia

Some of the Polish Jews came under Russian rule as a result of the partitions of Poland, between 1772 and 1795, and the awarding of the Napoleonic Duchy of Warsaw by the Congress of Vienna to Czar Alexander I. Up until this point, Russia had essentially kept Jews out; now, it found itself ruling over a Jewish population.

At first, Catherine the Great, whose rule extended from 1762 to 1796, did not view her new Jewish subjects unkindly. For the most part, they continued to live just as they had before—in Jewish *shtetls,* where they constituted a majority. However, at the instigation of Christian merchants in Moscow, who were concerned about competition from Jewish traders, limitations were established regarding the extent to which the Jews could participate in the economy.

At the turn of the nineteenth century, the Russian monarchy prohibited the lease of land by Jewish people. Commencing in 1804, Jews were expelled periodically from various villages, regions, and cities, including Moscow and St. Petersburg, and were consigned to reside in specific areas, known as the Pale of Settlement.

The Pale of Settlement

By 1812, the borders of the Pale of Settlement were finalized. From that point on, the Jews were limited to the twenty-five western provinces from the Baltic Sea in the north to the Black Sea in the south, in areas known today as Ukraine, Lithuania, Belarus, Crimea, and a portion of Poland.

Although it was possible to obtain special permission to live outside the Pale, only a few select Jews actually managed to do so—fully 95 percent of all Jews in Russia were confined to the Pale of Settlement.

Things were getting more and more difficult for the Jewish community, which was socially marginalized and economically restricted, but Russian Jews learned to make the best of their situation. Cut off from the mainstream of the Russian economy, it was difficult to earn a living, and many Jews became destitute.

However, it is a *mitzvah* and a cornerstone of Jewish tradition that the poor and unfortunate be cared for by those in a position to provide assistance. Charitable societies made sure that there was adequate food, clothing, shelter, and even a basic education for those who were in need. The only people who didn't give to charities were those who benefited from their generosity. The Jewish community also saw a religious revival, with a resurgence in Torah study and adherence to Jewish religious practices.

Persecution and Pogroms

Unfortunately, the Pale of Settlement was one of the first injustices in a series of many that marred Jewish life in the nineteenth century. Czar Nicholas I, who reigned from 1825 to 1855, was exceptionally harsh. Because he feared that the changes and new ideas that had begun to appear in western and central Europe might spread to Russia, his regime was both repressive and reactionary. The Jews made the Czar especially apprehensive.

In 1844, Nicholas decreed the elimination of *kehillot,* or Jewish councils, and he placed the Jews under the direct supervision of the police and local municipal authorities where they lived.

The Cantonist Decrees

In 1827, Nicholas issued the Cantonist Decrees ("canton" means "military camp"). These edicts conscripted many Jewish males between the ages of twelve and twenty-five into military schools and military service for twenty-five years. Because the conditions were harsh, many of the Jews died before they could return home.

The purpose behind the Cantonist Decrees was to convert the Jewish conscripts, and this was often accomplished by forced baptism. While in the military, the Jews were unable to fulfill the commandments of *Halakhah*: Jewish soldiers were forced to eat pork, and they could not observe the Shabbat or other holidays. Those who were lucky enough to survive the service lost their Jewish identity.

Conditions improved somewhat during the reign of Alexander II (1855–1881). When he emancipated the serfs, he also ended the forced conscription of Jews. He also allowed specific groups of Jews—wealthy merchants, university graduates, and certified artisans—to live outside the Pale of Settlement.

New Restrictions

In addition to forced conscription, a great deal of legislation was enacted to restrict the lives of Russian Jewry. Jews were banned from the civil service and could not teach non-Jews. Owning property outside the Pale was illegal. Strict quotas governed the number of Jewish children allowed to study at public schools. The wearing of yarmulkes was banned in public places. Jewish activities of all sorts was severely restricted or prohibited altogether.

Jews were classified as either "useful Jews" or "useless Jews," with certain opportunities available to those in the former category. Sometimes, Jews could obtain a higher education or engage in a commercial enterprise by bribing officials—bribery was a way of life in corrupt czarist Russia.

FACT

Despite all the difficulties, the Jewish population in Russia continued to increase. In 1825, the 1.6 million Russian Jews represented about 3 percent of the total population. By 1850, this figure grew to 2.35 million; by 1880, 4 million Jews resided in Russia.

A Wave of Pogroms

The first modern Russian pogrom took place in 1871 in Odessa and was incited by Greek and Slav ethnics who hated the Jews. The state-sanctioned pogroms commenced in 1881, when Alexander III ascended the throne following the assassination of Alexander II.

Pogroms were a result of the Russian peasants' growing dissatisfaction with their standard of living and injustices. Hoping to provide an outlet for their frustration and anger, the Czarist government offered a scapegoat—the Jews.

The police instigated hundreds of violent pogroms; many others were the result of the clergy preaching against the Jews, particularly around Christian holidays. The Jewish community suffered great losses—property was destroyed, and thousands were maimed and killed. There was no relief and no safe place in Russia for Jews to feel secure. As a result, Jews began leaving Russia at the rate of 50,000 annually. Many of them made it all the way to the United States.

Jewish Revolutionaries

Meanwhile, the dissatisfaction within the Russian populace continued to rise. New ideas and modes of thinking made their way into Russia. The time was growing ripe to cast off the yoke of Czarist oppression. Revolutionary movements appeared throughout Russia; many of the revolutionaries were Jewish. Moreover, many of these Jews later aligned themselves with the Bolsheviks, the radical faction led by Vladimir Lenin that was successful in overthrowing the monarchy in 1917.

We don't know why so many Jews joined the movement, though many reasons have been suggested. However, it's important to realize that the Jewish Communists were nonobservant; many of them rejected Judaism, and some even grew to disdain their Jewish heritage. These people fought for social equality, even at the expense of their Jewish culture, and they accepted Karl Marx's view that religion is the opium of the people, a way to keep them enslaved and obedient.

One such Jewish Communist was Leon Trotsky. Born Leon Davidovich Bronstein, Trotsky gave up his Jewish identity in favor of the Communist cause. At the time of the Revolution, Trotsky was at the helm, working closely with Lenin and the other leaders.

ALERT!

Trotsky took no interest whatsoever in anything Jewish or with the suffering of the Jews. His solution to end Jewish misery was assimilation. Eventually, the Communist regime adopted this policy, forbidding the practice of Judaism and labeling Zionism "Jewish Imperialism."

Meanwhile, the Russian Revolution was followed by the Civil War. The Red Army fought against the White Russians and other factions that opposed the Communist regime, and the Jewish population was caught in the middle. For instance, the anarchist group led by Nestor Makhno in Ukraine was virulently anti-Semitic and supported Jewish pogroms, spreading rumors that all Jews were secretly Bolsheviks.

Some Jews did in fact join the Red Army. They accepted the Communist promise that in a communist society all people would be equal and that all the restrictions of the tsarist era would be lifted from them. One such revolutionary, Isaac Babel, worked as a journalist for the Red cavalry. His experiences led him to write several novels known, collectively, as *Red Cavalry*. However, Babel did not give up his Jewish identity. Some of his best stories recall the Odessa ghetto of his early childhood. Although Babel's works were met with critical acclaim in the early 1930s, he became one of the victims of Stalinist repressions. Convicted of Trotskyite conspiracy, Isaac Babel died in a prison camp in 1941. Collections of his short stories have been translated into English, and he has received international acclaim posthumously.

Life Under Communism

During the first decade of Communist rule, Jewish life did improve. Jewish people were permitted to live in cities anywhere in Russia—even in Moscow; they could study at any institution and work in any position they merited. After the end of the Civil War, the pogroms became a thing of the past, partially due to the government's strict control of the peasants, which were suffering collectivization (giving up all personal property to the collective farms).

The Jews were also allowed to maintain their distinct identity as a secular ethnic group. In Jewish public schools, children were taught in Yiddish; Yiddish Communist newspapers were widely available; the National Yiddish Theater toured all over the Soviet Union, giving performances in Yiddish. However, subsequent to the campaign against religion, which was anathema to communist doctrine, Jews were no longer allowed to practice Judaism. In 1919, all Jewish religious communities were dissolved. The study of Hebrew was banned, and Zionism was denounced.

Creation of the Jewish Autonomous Region

Because the Jews were regarded as an ethnic group, the government decided to create a Jewish region. In 1930, they mapped out a small section in the southeastern part of Russia and gave it the name of Birobidzhan, the Jewish Autonomous Region, a secular Zion where the Jewish settlers were encouraged to go.

Unfortunately, this was a misguided idea at best and a cruel one at worst. The Jewish settlers, mostly idealistic communists, found themselves in an undeveloped region, previously occupied by native tribes and exiled Russians, with harsh winters and a poor soil that they were expected to cultivate. Many families faced starvation, and those who could leave eventually did. Today, the official language of the Jewish Autonomous Region remains Yiddish, but you would be hard pressed to find a Jew there.

There is evidence that shortly before his death, Stalin began working on plans to exile all of the Soviet Jews to Birobidzhan. The infamous Doctors' Trial, in which Stalin's Jewish doctors were accused of conspiracy against him, was meant to bring out the people's outrage against the Jews, which would facilitate the mass exile.

The Years of Repression

After Lenin's death in 1924, there was a power struggle between Trotsky and Stalin. Stalin emerged victorious, and his quest to consolidate power intensified over the years. Perhaps because many Jews were in positions of leadership within the Communist Party, they suffered more than other groups. In the years of the Great Terror of 1934–1939, all Jewish institutions were destroyed and activities banned. During Stalin's infamous purge of the Communist Party, Jews were specifically targeted; by 1945, very few Jews remained in the Party.

Stalin's anti-Semitism was becoming increasingly obvious. In 1948, Yiddish schools were closed, and beginning in the late 1940s—only a few years after the Holocaust—Jewish writers, artists, poets, musicians, and intellectuals were attacked as "cosmopolitan snobs." Their work was discredited, and thousands were imprisoned or executed.

After Stalin's death in 1953, conditions for the Jews did not improve. Under Khrushchev, most of the surviving synagogues were closed; by some estimates only sixty synagogues remained open in the entire country. Education quotas were established in colleges and universities, which made it very difficult for Jewish students to enter the school of their choice. And although officially there were no laws that prohibited Jews from certain areas of employment, it became increasingly difficult for Jews to find work without relying on bribery or family connections.

FACT

There was a brief respite in 1964 with the ousting of Khrushchev, but after Israel's dramatic victory in the Six-Day War in 1967, anti-Semitism resumed in the USSR. This time, however, Soviet anti-Semitism appeared under the guise of anti-Zionism.

Jewish Emigration

In spite of oppression, the Jews nonetheless managed to prove themselves beneficial and useful to the USSR, constituting a significant percentage of its best and brightest citizens—scientists, doctors, educators, and other professionals. So, when the Russian Jewish community saw the rise of the Zionist movement in the sixties, the government did not allow emigration.

In 1971, Brezhnev opened the gates for a time, and as many as 250,000 Jews were able to make their escape. As a result, more restrictive policies were reimposed in 1980, and those Jews who expressed a desire to leave the country were generally denied immigration. These people, known as the "refuseniks," suffered discrimination—many could not find work and were socially ostracized.

However, through the efforts of the Jewish communities around the world, particularly the American Jewry, the Russian government was pressured to concede. In the mid-1980s, Mikhail Gorbachev finally agreed to allow Jewish emigration in return for economic assistance. As a result, the Jews left the USSR in large numbers, with most choosing the United States and Israel as their destination. Today, Russian Jews constitute as much as 20 percent of the population in Israel.

Chapter 18

Enlightenment and Emancipation

Now it's time to go back in history and return to Western Europe, where important changes were taking place during the eighteenth and nineteenth centuries. As Enlightenment brought modernization of European societies, the Jewish communities in France, Germany, and other Western European countries were affected as well. Finally, the Jewish people had the opportunity to be integrated with the rest of their countrymen and fully participate in the economic, social, and even political life of their country.

Spinoza, World Thinker

As the Enlightenment dawned on the horizon of the eighteenth century, one of its principal forerunners was Benedict Spinoza, born Baruch Spinoza in 1632 into a former Marrano family active in Amsterdam's Jewish community. Young Baruch received a traditional Jewish education, gaining proficiency in Hebrew and the Bible as well as Talmudic literature. He also studied Latin and philosophy, including the works of Descartes, Hobbes, and other writers of his time.

Spinoza began to develop some rather unconventional views, and when they assumed an appearance of atheism, he came to the attention of Amsterdam's Jewish leadership. At the age of twenty-three, Spinoza was questioned by the rabbinical court and offered a stipend of 1,000 florins to keep quiet, which he refused.

FACT

On July 27, 1656, Spinoza was excommunicated by a Rabbinical Pronouncement of Excommunication that included, among other charges, his denial of angels, the immortality of the soul, and the divine inspiration of Torah.

When his father died, Spinoza gave his share of the inheritance to his sister and went off to live in various cities in Holland, ultimately settling in the Hague. Spinoza led a simple life, eking out a living as a lens grinder. He declined a professorship at the University of Heidelberg and refused all awards and honors. Nonetheless, he had a wide range of correspondence, and other philosophers often visited him. In 1677, Spinoza died of tuberculosis, which was probably aggravated by his occupation.

A Distinct Philosophy

The only work Spinoza published during his lifetime was *A Treatise on Religious and Political Philosophy*. This work, which examined the relationship between religion and the state, earned Spinoza the reputation of an atheist in the Christian community. However, his major treatise was *Ethics,* probably written in 1665 but published posthumously.

In *Ethics,* Spinoza rejected the conventional concept of God, insisting instead that God was in everything, just as everything was in God. According to Spinoza, the highest good one could hope to achieve was knowledge of God. More than any of the philosophers of his era, Spinoza cherished freedom from passions and fear and the freedom to think. It is precisely the independence Spinoza exhibited both in his work and in the way he lived his life that makes him one of those distinguished individuals responsible for ushering in the age of Enlightenment.

The Enlightenment

Spinoza was one of many Europeans who began to question the old ideas and who relied on reason above all else. The new ideas of the time, now known as the Age of Enlightenment or the Age of Reason, affected the way people in the West came to view religion, and the Jewish community was affected as much as its Christian neighbors.

The Enlightenment, which came into full swing in the eighteenth century, allowed the emergence of liberal democracy, helped start the scientific revolution, and began the movement toward secularization (less emphasis on religion). The proponents of these ideas sought to establish universal principles governing humanity, nature, and society. With less importance assigned to religion, which became a personal concern rather than the official dogma of the state, the Jews were no longer seen as enemies. Consequently, the Jews emerged out of the ghettos, becoming full citizens in the countries in which they lived. Unfortunately, many were becoming too secularized and were giving up the strict beliefs of orthodox Judaism in return for full assimilation.

ALERT!

The Jewish communities in western and central Europe were not immune to the ideas of the Enlightenment. Try as they might, the rabbis and councils could not keep new thoughts at bay. An encounter between Judaism and secularism was inevitable.

Mendelssohn and the *Haskalah*

The architect who envisioned and built the bridge spanning Jewish life and the Enlightenment was Moses Mendelssohn (1729–1786). Mendelssohn was born in the central German state of Dessau, the son of a poor Torah scribe. He received a conventional Jewish education, but also excelled at secular subjects such as Greek, Latin, mathematics, and philosophy. When still a young man, Mendelssohn became friends with Immanuel Kant, who would gain recognition in philosophy; another friend, dramatist and literary critic Gotthold Lessing, remained Mendelssohn's lifelong confidant.

In 1750, Frederick the Great (the monarch of Prussia) bestowed upon Mendelssohn the status of "Jew under extraordinary protection," which gave him the right to live in Berlin. Mendelssohn earned a living first as a teacher and later as a successful merchant, all the while writing about art, literature, and religion. Lessing helped Mendelssohn publish his philosophical writings and immortalized his friend in a play *Nathan the Wise,* in which Mendelssohn served as the model for the protagonist, a Jew promoting universalism and humanism.

A New Approach to Judaism

To his credit, Mendelssohn did not see an "either-or" choice having to be made between secularism and Judaism. Throughout his life, he was at home among gentile philosophers and scholars as well as his compatriots in the Jewish community. To many modern Jews, Mendelssohn served as an example of a Jew who successfully made the transition from ghetto to modernity without leaving his people—in contrast to those who converted in order to further their secular careers.

In 1769, Mendelssohn received a challenge from a Zurich pastor, John Lavater, to defend Judaism as compared to Christianity; much of Mendelssohn's subsequent work involved explaining and extolling Judaism to the gentile world. Mendelssohn did not take Lavater's bait by arguing that Judaism was superior to other faiths. Instead, Mendelssohn wisely called for good relationships between Jews and Christians and urged for mutual tolerance.

The Birth of the *Haskalah* Movement

Moses Mendelssohn is often regarded as the father of the *Haskalah* movement. In its most restrictive sense, *Haskalah* refers to a phase of Hebrew literature in which Jewish writers diverged from the traditional paradigms. In its broadest sense, however, *Haskalah* is the Jewish Enlightenment—a nineteenth-century doctrine whose adherents were referred to as *maskilim* (enlighteners). Inspired by Mendelssohn, the *maskilim* believed that Jews needed to modernize their style of life and become more receptive to new ideas.

The goal of the *maskilim* was not to abandon Judaism or their Jewish identity, but to integrate their religion and laws with that of the general European culture. Indeed, for these Jews, Judaism was compatible with the Enlightenment's emphasis on tolerance, reasonableness of thought, and universal humanism.

To promote their objective, the *maskilim* established Jewish schools and wrote new textbooks in Hebrew. The disciples of Mendelssohn opened a center in Prussia, and in the 1820s the movement spread to Austria and later to Russia. Although it may not seem like a radical change, this was a very important step in the Jews' integration into the society where they lived.

The Consequences of the French Revolution

There were changes in the French Jewish community as well. Following the success of the French Revolution in 1789, the French people, including the 34,000 Jews living in France (mostly Ashkenazim residing in the northeastern provinces), had great expectations for a better life. Although the Reign of Terror followed, there were nevertheless positive changes as well.

In 1789, the National Assembly issued the Declaration of the Rights of Man, which proclaimed that "all men are born, and remain, free and equal in rights." A second decree, which did not pass without a great deal of resistance some two years later, completed the emancipation of the Jews.

The Spread of Revolutionary Ideals

The spirit of the French Revolution spread through Europe both by the exchange of ideas and by the sword—the French Army's conquests in pursuance of Napoleon's expansionist plans. Wherever Napoleon and his troops marched, Jews were treated with fairness and liberated from their ghettos. However, within France, Napoleon did nothing to promote equal opportunities for the Jews; in fact, some historians believe that he reversed the progress.

FACT

In 1799, Napoleon Bonaparte (1769–1821) became the First Consul of France; five years later, he proclaimed himself Emperor. Napoleon conquered the Austrian-Hungarian Empire, Italy, and almost defeated Russia, which would have made him master of Europe.

Napoleon and the Sanhedrin

Like many other monarchs, rulers, and statesmen who sincerely desired parity for the Jews, Napoleon believed this could best be accomplished if these stubborn people would just give up their unique identity and become like everyone else. To look into the feasibility of such a plan, in 1807, Napoleon convened a gathering of prominent Jewish rabbis and laymen that has been called a Grand *Sanhedrin*.

The Jewish delegates at this congress found themselves in a quandary. On the one hand, they did not want to antagonize this powerful European ruler; on the other hand, they did not wish to acquiesce to anything that would result in restricting the practice of Judaism. As a result, very little of any consequence actually transpired. In diplomatic jargon, the delegates pledged loyalty to Napoleon and made a vague renunciation of any Jewish tradition that would conflict with French citizenship.

Following the Grand *Sanhedrin*, Napoleon issued two edicts. In one decree, he established a system of councils of rabbis and Jewish laymen to supervise Jewish affairs. In the second edict, he suspended or reduced debts owed to Jews and limited their rights in specific areas.

ALERT!

It's hard to predict what more Napoleon would have done to affect Jewish lives and which direction his inconsistent policy was heading. However, this became moot when he was defeated at Waterloo in 1815 and exiled to the island of Saint Helena, where he died.

Emancipation and New Opportunities

The spirit of the French Revolution opened doors for Jews throughout Europe. Within four years, all French and German ghettos were abolished. Jews were granted complete citizenship in Holland (1796) and in Prussia (1812). But the liberalization of laws and lifting restrictions on the Jews did not proceed rapidly or smoothly—there were reversals as well. There were centuries of hatred and hostility to surmount. Prejudice and anti-Semitism couldn't simply vanish from the European continent.

In Germany, where 300 German principalities had joined to make up thirty-nine states at the Congress of Vienna held in 1815, a reactionary mood prevailed. Renewed German patriotism and nostalgia for the German folk spirit sparked hostility toward the non-Germans. The Jews— perceived to be "Asiatic aliens"—were particularly vulnerable. Only after 1830 did liberalism begin to take hold; by the mid-nineteenth century, all German states had extended equal rights to the Jews.

In 1848, following the Austrian revolution, religious equality was established and it was not rescinded even after the Hapsburg monarchy was restored. In 1867, Austria declared the permanent emancipation of the Jews.

In Italy, following the fall of Napoleon, there was an increase in antagonism toward the Jews. It was not until 1848 that the Jews in Tuscany and Sardinia were granted permanent emancipation. Other Italian cities followed suit until Rome bestowed full citizenship upon its Jewish residents in 1870. The Jews in Switzerland did not receive citizenship until 1874, and the Jews in Spain had to wait until 1918.

Once open, the doors could not be completely shut again. With the right to participate fully in their society, the Jewish people of Europe saw many opportunities open to them. They were free to obtain higher education (though, in some countries, quota systems persisted) and pursue all aspects of commerce and other professions.

Jewish Progeny of the Enlightenment

The Age of Reason and the new freedoms it offered spawned generations of thinkers, artists, politicians, and cosmopolitan citizens who assiduously clung to the tenets of the Enlightenment. With Emancipation, Jews found themselves faced with new opportunities in the professions, commerce, the arts, and society in general.

Although Jews were fully emancipated throughout all of western and central Europe (except for Spain) by the end of the nineteenth century, prejudices still remained and for all intents and purposes, they were barred from entry into certain levels of society. Consequently, some Jews made the decision to convert in order to attain secular success (others were children of converts). On the other hand, many Jews retained their Jewish identity and achieved levels of prominence nonetheless. Indeed, more than a few reached the apex of their chosen fields.

Sir Moses Montefiore (1784–1885)

Moses Montefiore established a stock exchange business in London and served as the sheriff of London, at which time he was granted knighthood. Eventually, Montefiore chose to retire in order to devote himself to oppressed Jews everywhere. During his visit to Israel, he founded a hospital and a girls' school in Jerusalem. By the time he returned from the Holy Land, Moses Montefiore had become a devout observant Jew. His 100th birthday was celebrated by Jewish communities all over the world.

Benjamin Disraeli (1804–1881)

Though born a Jew and proud of his Jewish heritage, Disraeli's father had the thirteen-year-old Benjamin baptized, and he became a practicing Anglican. Although Benjamin Disraeli had a keen interest in literature—in fact, he wrote a number of novels that were well received—he made his mark as a statesman and politician.

In 1868, Disraeli founded the modern Conservative party and served as prime minister of Britain, though only for one year. However, in 1874, he became the prime minister once again; this time he served a six-year term.

Gustav Mahler (1860–1911)

An outstanding musician, Mahler distinguished himself as composer and conductor of the Budapest Imperial Opera (1888–1890), the Hamburg Municipal Theater (1891–1897), the Vienna State Opera (1897–1907), and the New York Philharmonic (1909–1911). Today, Mahler is considered to be one of the last great romantic composers in the tradition of Beethoven and Brahms.

Sigmund Freud (1856–1939)

Freud was born in Moravia (now part of the Czech Republic) to a devoutly religious family and spent much of his life as a psychiatrist and professor in Vienna. While critical of Judaism and all religions, Freud was proud of his Jewish heritage, which he credited with providing the traits he needed to develop psychoanalysis, the science and movement he founded, and with enabling him to withstand the ostracism he faced from the scientific establishment. Freud's theories of the unconscious and repression remain cornerstones in the field of psychology and the treatment of mental illness.

Albert Einstein (1879–1955)

Born in Germany to Jewish parents, Einstein was not an observant Jew, but he considered himself a religious man and was a proponent for the Jewish people, helping Jews escape the Holocaust and supporting the modern state of Israel, which offered him the presidency (he reluctantly declined).

Albert Einstein is considered one of the greatest physicists of our time, and his achievements were recognized with a Nobel Prize in physics. One of Einstein's most famous achievements is the formulation of the special and general theory of relativity.

FACT

The Enlightenment and Emancipation affected many Jews in their secular lives—the way they thought, the occupations they pursued, their style of dress, and the degree to which they mixed with gentile society. It was not long before these attitudes had an effect on their religious beliefs and practices as well.

Changes in the Jewish Faith

For the first time in Christian Europe, Jews found themselves on equal footing—at least legally, if not always in practice—with their Christian neighbors. Moreover, they were allowed to observe their religion without interference. Interestingly, change was about to come to Judaism—but from within.

Judaism was never a static, inflexible religion. Over the centuries it has changed and evolved, and sometimes there were divisions along the way: between the Essenes, Pharisees, and Sadducees; Karaites and Rabbinical Jews; Hasidim and *Mitnagdim*. However, up until the end of the eighteenth century, all observant Jews—the remaining Karaite communities notwithstanding—adhered to the essential principle that both the Written Law (Scriptures) and the Oral Law (rabbinic interpretation and commentaries) is derived from God and must be obeyed. Those Jews who embraced this basic premise became known as Orthodox to distinguish them from the new movements that arose in Judaism during the nineteenth century.

The Introduction of Reforms

Enlightened German Jews grew chagrined at their religious services with its clamor, informality, spontaneity, and unseemly manner of prayer. They desired to bring Judaism into closer harmony with contemporary European standards of decorum. They sought to show the world that the

Jews were not strange and alien but very much the same as their Christian neighbors, except for the religion they practiced: "German in the streets; Jewish in the home." They no longer wanted to be embarrassed by their religious practices at home or in the synagogue.

Those Jews who embarked on putting these changes into effect were called "Reformers," and the movement which they spawned became known as Reform Judaism. The first Reform Temple was built in 1810 by Israel Jacobson (1768–1828), one of the most active reformers in Westphalia, central Germany. In 1818, another Reform Temple opened in Hamburg; others soon followed.

Initially, the reformers didn't act together. The Reform movement emerged as a unified branch of Judaism under the direction of Samuel Holdheim (1806–1860), who became head of a Reform congregation in Berlin.

In the mid-nineteenth century, as some of these reformers emigrated to the United States, Reform Judaism became the dominant belief held by American Jews. It would remain the most commonly practiced form of Judaism until the turn of the twentieth century, when a wave of Orthodox immigrants arrived from Eastern Europe.

The Nature of Reforms

In keeping with the decorum desired by the reformers, services were conducted in a more seemly manner. The new movement replaced most of the Hebrew liturgy with services conducted in the German vernacular. Mixed-gender seating replaced the practice in which women sat in a separate section of the synagogue. The Reform movement also adopted some of the features of Christian churches, such as organ music, choral singing, and sermons. Indeed, some of the rabbis became so adept at sermonizing that it was not unusual to find Protestant pastors attending Jewish services to listen to the sermons.

All of these changes were made possible because Reform Judaism rejected the underlying premise to which the Orthodox adhered so resolutely. Reform Jews believed that while the Torah was divinely inspired, it was written by a number of individuals and then revised and edited. In keeping with the spirit of the Enlightenment, Reform Jews held that while most of the values and ethics of the Torah should be revered and retained, each individual was free to follow those practices that were most likely to advance a meaningful and ethical life and enhance his or her relationship to God.

A Second Movement Emerges

It did not take many years for a breach to occur within Reform Judaism. Despite its many supporters, some Jews felt that Reform Judaism had admirable intentions, which it simply took too far. A more reasoned and less extreme break from Orthodox Judaism was appropriate. Out of this middle-ground approach came Conservative Judaism.

In 1845, Rabbi Zacharias Frankel (1801–1875) withdrew from the emerging European Reform movement when he insisted that the liturgy should be conducted in Hebrew. A decade later, Rabbi Frankel became the first head of the Jewish Theological Seminary of Breslau that served as the pre-eminent center for the training of Conservative rabbis in Europe.

The Tenets of Conservative Judaism

Like Reform Jews, Conservatives believe that the Torah was divinely inspired but authored by humans. However, they believe that the *Halakhah* is binding, although adaptations may be made based as long as they remain true to the spirit and values of the Jewish faith.

FACT

Conservative Judaism made its way over the Atlantic to America with the founding of the Jewish Theological Seminary of America in 1886. However, it was not until the early twentieth century that Conservative Judaism truly became organized under the aegis of the United Synagogue of Conservative Judaism.

In the area of the service, Conservative Judaism provides a distinct middle ground. The liturgy is conducted in Hebrew, but the native language of the worshippers is used as well. Men and women sit together; and many congregations have choirs and organs. Ⓔ

Chapter 19

Jewish Life in America

The story of Jews in America is one of the most successful chapters of Jewish history. The United States, the land of opportunity and freedom, became a safe haven for hundreds of thousands of Jews, who finally found a home where they can freely practice their religion while fully participating in the life of their country.

Arriving with Columbus

The Jewish people were among the first Europeans to arrive in the New World after Columbus's voyage. In fact, there has been speculation that Columbus was of Jewish heritage or possibly even a *marrano,* though nothing has ever been conclusively proven. The last name Colombo (Columbus's name in Italian) was common among Jews in Italy. And although he was a legal citizen of Genoa, he was fluent in Spanish and apparently didn't know how to write in Italian, perhaps because he was a son or grandson of Spanish Jews.

Columbus relied upon two Jews in planning his voyage—Abraham Zacuto, who drew the tables, and Joseph Vecinho, who had perfected the instruments which Columbus used to navigate. What is more, the first member of Columbus's expedition to set foot in the New World was his interpreter, Luis de Torres, a Jew who had been hastily baptized before the voyage.

FACT

Just four days before Christopher Columbus set sail to discover a new world that would become a haven for millions of Jews, the last group of Jews left Spain in compliance with the Order of Expulsion.

The Jews of South America

Jews who had been expelled from Spain and Portugal were not permitted to live in the Spanish and Portuguese colonies in the New World. But this did not prevent *marranos* from undertaking the voyage, several of whom were among the first Spaniards to reach Mexico with conquistador Hernando Cortez in 1519. Suspicious of the Jewish *conversos,* an Inquisition soon sent out its own representatives, and many *converso* settlers were burned at the stake as the Church spread its control throughout the Spanish colonies in the New World. However, in 1577, Spain rescinded its laws forbidding Jews to emigrate to its colonies.

Many Jews also emigrated to the Portuguese colony of Brazil. Indeed, its first governor, Thomas de Souza, was of Jewish origin. Jews established sugar plantations and engaged in the trading of precious and semiprecious stones. Sephardic merchants settled in Brazil in 1630 and conducted trade. However, in 1654, repeating the practices established in Europe, Brazil expelled its Jews. As we shall see, some Jews would go to North America while others went to Barbados and Jamaica.

During the eighteenth century, Jews also began settling in the English, Dutch, and French colonies of the Caribbean: Barbados, Martinique, Curacao, Jamaica, and Surinam. Early in the nineteenth century, the Spanish colonies in South America and the Portuguese colony of Brazil rebelled and gained their independence. The Inquisition in those countries was subsequently abolished, and numerous Jewish communities were founded.

Substantial immigration by Jews to South America did not take place until the last decades of the nineteenth century, when Ashkenazim from eastern Europe settled in Argentina. Near the end of the twentieth century, more than 600,000 Jews lived in South America, half of them in Argentina.

Throughout most of the Diaspora, Jews concentrated in cities, and South America was no exception in this regard. The South American city with the largest Jewish population is Buenos Aires in Argentina (250,000), followed by the Brazilian cities of San Paulo (75,000) and Rio de Janeiro (55,000), Montevideo in Uruguay (48,000), Mexico City (32,000), and Santiago, Chile (25,000).

Early Jewish Communities in North America

The first account of a Jewish presence in North America dates back to 1654, when twenty-three Sephardic refugees arrived in the Dutch colonial town of New Amsterdam after they had been expelled from Brazil. The city's governor, Peter Stuyvesant, strenuously objected to the presence of these Jews whom he regarded as "enemies and blasphemers of Christ." However, mindful of its commercial ties to Jewish merchants and financiers, the Dutch West India Company overruled Stuyvesant and the small Jewish contingent was admitted, though they were afforded no rights as citizens. In 1664, New Amsterdam fell in battle to the English, who renamed the town New York. Jews were granted religious freedom and all the advantages of full English citizenship.

Another Jewish community was formed in 1677, when a group of Jews from Barbados arrived in Newport, Rhode Island. In the middle of the eighteenth century, the Jews of Newport organized a congregation with its own cantor—Isaac Touro—who had been summoned from Amsterdam. On December 2, 1763, the congregation of twenty families dedicated its synagogue. A decade later, the congregation had grown to 200 families.

The Touro Synagogue

During George Washington's visit to Newport in 1781, a town meeting was held in the synagogue, and a letter Washington wrote to the congregation in 1790 remains posted on its wall today. In the years following the Revolutionary War, the Jewish population in Newport dwindled, and by 1822, no Jews remained in the city. However, the Touro Synagogue was preserved from funds bequeathed by Isaac Touro's son.

The Touro Synagogue is considered the oldest synagogue building in the United States and was designed by Peter Harrison, a leading eighteenth-century American architect. In 1946, the synagogue was designated a national historic site.

Jewish Communities Throughout the Colonies

As the Jewish communities continued to spread to other colonial cities like Savannah, Charleston, and Philadelphia, the Jewish people established themselves as full citizens with all rights and privileges of other colonists. Because there was no state religion and religions did not determine secular law, Jews had no need to maintain their separate legal system or councils to govern themselves, as they had done in Europe. Consequently, Jews became integrated into mainstream society and did not live as a people apart from the general populace.

Jewish Canadians

It was not until 1759, after the British conquered New France (French Canada) during the French and Indian War, that Jews began to emigrate to Canada. The Jewish population grew very slowly; in 1881, the Canadian Jewish community was made up of approximately 2,000 Jews. However, with the waves of Jewish immigration from Eastern Europe that commenced in 1881 and continued for several decades, 300,000 Jews came to make Canada their home.

Citizens of the United States

When the Revolutionary War began in 1776, it is estimated that 2,000 Jews (most of them Sephardim) lived in the thirteen colonies. The majority of these Jews supported the rebel cause and some fought as officers, soldiers, and militiamen. Indeed, the first fatal casualty on the side of the insurgents in Georgia was a Jew, a man by the name of Francis Salvador.

ALERT!

Jews played a major role in financing the war for independence. Possibly the leading individual financier of the war was Haym Solomon, whose entire personal fortune went to the war efforts, leaving him to die a pauper.

The Arrival of German Jews

After the victory over the British and the creation of the United States, the new nation was the land of opportunity for European Jews, although several states had not yet extended rights of citizenship to the Jews. From the 1820s to 1881, most of the Jewish arrivals came from German-speaking lands. These immigrants generally began life in the new land as peddlers, but they soon established themselves as proprietors of small businesses and shopkeepers.

Some of these Jews went far beyond mere success in commercial enterprises and became quite well known both in their own times and to subsequent generations. Here are several of these prominent individuals:

- *Levi Strauss*: Founder of Levi's Jeans credited with the invention of blue jeans.
- *Charles Bloomingdale*: Founder of the department store that bears his name.
- *Marcus Goldman*: Founder of Goldman Sachs, an investment banking firm.
- *Jacob Schiff*: Led the investment house of Kuhn, Loeb & Co.
- *Julius Rosenwald*: Developed the mail order business and catalog of Sears, Roebuck & Co.
- *Joseph Seligman*: Banker and financier for the North during the Civil War. After the war, President Grant offered Seligman the position of Secretary of the Treasury, which he chose to decline.

The German Jews frequently settled in new communities like Albany, Syracuse, Buffalo, Rochelle, Chicago, Detroit, Cleveland, Milwaukee, and Cincinnati. In fact, at one time Cincinnati was second to New York City in having the largest Jewish population.

FACT

In 1820, 4,000–6,000 Jews lived in the United States. Twenty years later, the Jewish population increased to 15,000; before the outbreak of the Civil War, 150,000 Jews were United States citizens. By 1860, 40,000 Jews resided just in New York City.

Most of these Jews epitomized the spirit of the Enlightenment. By and large, they were liberal, rational, unassuming, and respectable in their demeanor and conduct. The Reform movement had made its way from Germany to the United States, so by 1860 almost all observant Jews considered themselves Reform. Indeed, of the 200 synagogues in the United States in 1880, 90 percent were Reform, and Temple Emanuel in New York was the largest Reform synagogue in the world.

A New Wave of Jewish Immigrants

In the sixty-year period before World War I, 30 million immigrants entered the United States. They were anything but a homogeneous group consisting of Irish, Swedes, Germans, Italians, Poles, Slavs, and others. Among these emigrants were 2.5 million Jews.

> Give me your tired, your poor
> Your huddled masses yearning to breathe free. . . .

These are the first lines of the poem inscribed on the Statue of Liberty, which greeted millions of immigrants who disembarked at Ellis Island in New York Harbor. Appropriately enough, these words were written by Emma Lazarus (1849–1887), the American Jewish poet who was so moved by news of Russian pogroms in 1881, she devoted the remaining years of her life to writing poems and essays on behalf of Jews and Judaism.

After the wave of pogroms of 1881, Jews left Eastern Europe at the rate of 50,000 every year, until 1914. Most of these Jews chose the United States as their destination. During the first two years, 38,000 arrived in the United States; in the next ten years, the average was 37,000 annually; and from 1903–1914, on average, 76,000 Jews entered the United States each year.

Despite the pogroms, not all Jews chose to leave Europe. To the most religious and pious people, America was like a golden calf—tempting with its promises of economic advancement but hollow in its spirituality and posing a threat of assimilation. The rabbis warned that it would be far too difficult to maintain and practice Judaism in America, and to some extent they were correct. Most Jews did ultimately stray from Orthodox Judaism to practice Conservative or Reform and later Reconstructionist Judaism; others left Judaism entirely.

Some Jewish immigrants decided to return home when they realized that life in America wasn't conducive to the observance of Judaism and the Jewish way of life as they knew it.

The relatively prosperous and genteel Jews of German origin who had become respectable American citizens did not know what to make of the destitute Eastern European newcomers they referred to as *Ostjuden*. The new arrivals spoke only Yiddish, were superstitious, and observed Orthodox Judaism. Frequently, the German Jews were ashamed of the recent Jewish arrivals, and they often kept their distance from the immigrant neighborhoods where the Eastern European Jews took up residence.

A Different Kind of Life

After disembarking from the German or British ships that had carried them across the Atlantic—generally in steerage—most of these immigrants settled in the Lower East Side of New York. The rest settled in other major cities of the Northeast.

By 1910, 540,000 Jewish immigrants were crowded into the tenements of the Lower East Side, with entire families sometimes cramped into one room. Over half of these Jews worked in the clothing industry as tailors, seamstresses, contractors, and entrepreneurs. For most, the pay was low and the hours long—usually seven days a week and ten hours a day. The conditions were horrendous, and it was not without justification that these plants became known as sweatshops.

FACT

A preponderance of Jews constituted not only the rank and file but also the leadership of the labor movement that was dedicated to improve terrible working conditions—most notably in the International Ladies Garment Workers Union and the Amalgamated Clothing Workers of America.

But in their shared poverty, the Jews continued the tradition of helping each other. Immigrants from various locales in Europe formed *landsmanshaften* (a Yiddish term for "hometown associations") together with their former townsmen. These associations maintained synagogues and provided sickness and burial insurance.

Nor was the quality of life barren. Yiddish newspapers and theaters flourished. On Sabbath and Jewish holidays, entire neighborhoods would close to observe and celebrate. The Jews created a world to themselves in the Lower East Side and other Jewish neighborhoods throughout America.

New York became the largest Jewish city in the world. By 1920, 1.64 million Jews made up 29 percent of New York's total population. The Jews dominated the newspaper and publishing industries. Arthur Hays Sulzberger and Arthur Ochs headed the *New York Times*. Viking Press, Simon & Schuster, Alfred Knopf, and Random House were founded by Jews. In addition to Bloomingdale's, Jews opened other major department stores: Altman Brothers, Macy's, Gimbels, Sterns, and Abraham & Straus.

By hard work and sheer determination, the first generation of Jews struggled to climb the rungs on the ladder of opportunity in America. They moved to better neighborhoods—in the case of New York, from the Lower East Side to Harlem. They made sure their children received a good education, becoming teachers, doctors, and lawyers. Many also entered the political arena, because by this time religion was not an obstacle to attaining elected office—at least not officially.

Benign public policy and laws notwithstanding, anti-Semitism reared its monstrous head and extended its tentacles to block the way of Jewish upward mobility or mixing in with mainstream America. It was an obstacle that had to be overcome if the Jews were to truly succeed in their new home.

Surmounting Anti-Semitism

But despite the official acceptance of the Jews as full members of American society, anti-Semitic sentiments were pervasive and worked to block the Jews' upward mobility and integration into the American mainstream. The old European prejudices and hatred was transplanted to the New World, reinforced with each new wave of immigrants. The basic principles of religious freedom and equality guaranteed in the Bill of Rights prevented anti-Semitism from becoming official government policy, but they could not eradicate it from American society.

Through the end of the seventeenth century, Jews in America enjoyed religious and economic equality, though they were denied political office. After the American Revolution, anti-Semitism was not tolerated by the new federal government. However, substantial authority remained with the states, so that each state could make its own decisions regarding the extension of civil rights to the Jews. It was not until after 1820 that all the states extended full citizenship to the Jews.

Anti-Semitism on the Rise

However, anti-Semitism became more evident in the United States after the Civil War. Some have suggested that following the war, many Americans thought that the Jews profited from the war. But probably more controlling was the fact that with Jews on either side of the conflict—Northerners hating Southern Jews and Southerners hating Northern Jews—the centuries' old notion of the Jew as inherently evil, demonic, and not to be trusted became prevalent among large portions of the population.

Which side did the Jews support during the Civil War?
The Jews generally supported the states in which they lived. Seven thousand Jews fought for the North, and 3,000 Jews fought for the South.

QUESTION?

Other factors contributed to the rise in anti-Semitism around this time. There was a growing belief among the American people that the United States was a Christian nation, and consequently the Jews were viewed as outsiders. We have seen that in the time between the Civil War and World War I, 30 million immigrants entered the United States. Many millions of these newcomers were Polish and German Catholics who carried with them the image of Jews as Christ killers. Compounding matters was the poverty that permeated American society during the Depression: One common accusation was that the Jews controlled the financial markets and were the culprits of the stock market crash.

In the Twentieth Century

In the first half of the twentieth century, anti-Semitism could be discerned in many ways including the following.

- Quotas on immigration.
- Denial of admission to many prestigious universities and professional schools, social clubs, hotels, and even neighborhoods.
- Overt acts of anti-Semitism in the military.
- Numerous physical assaults.
- Refusal by businesses, banks, hospitals, and law firms to hire Jews.

But with the exception of immigration quotas, all these actions were in the private sphere. As a matter of public and government policy, there was never discrimination sanctioned against the Jews, and no major political party ever adopted an anti-Semitic agenda.

FACT

To ensure that American Jews had access to education, in 1948 Abram Sachar founded Brandeis University, a secular university that guaranteed a first-rate education to Jewish students. The university was named in honor of Justice Louis Brandeis, the first Jewish Supreme Court Justice.

Not until after World War II did matters improve. No doubt, reaction to the Holocaust tempered anti-Semitism. The American troops had a hand in the liberation of concentration camps, and when they returned they shared what they saw with the rest of the country. While anti-Semitism still existed, it became more subtle.

Jews in Contemporary American Society

In 1970, 5.8 million Jews lived in the United States, and this number has remained stagnant since that time. In fact, the 1990 National Jewish Population Survey had reported a decrease to 5.5 million Jews; in 2001–2002, they reported that the number had again decreased, to 5.2 million.

Ironically, the decrease in population has nothing to do with the usual reasons that existed throughout Jewish history, when Jewish populations were decimated by forced conversions, expulsions, and murder. Today, the chief explanation for the decline is that American society is so open to the Jews, assimilation and intermarriage has resulted in new generations losing their Jewish identity.

Consistent with Jewish population patterns throughout American history, most Jews still reside in major cities. In metropolitan New York alone there are almost 2 million Jews; there are 455,000 in Los Angeles, 295,000 in Philadelphia, 250,000 in Chicago, and 225,000 in Miami. With the exception of California, most Jews populate states along the eastern coast: New York, Pennsylvania, Maryland, New Jersey, and Florida.

Today, Jews have never been more at home, secure, and prosperous in the United States. Hardly an avenue exists in American society that is not open to the Jews. The only issue today is the rising anti-Israel sentiments that are more common in Europe but have also appeared in the United States.

Active in Politics

In the realm of holding public office, Jews have come a long way from 1826, when Solomon Etting finally succeeded in removing the barrier preventing Jews from holding public office in Maryland and was elected to the Baltimore City Council. Jews have served in the cabinets of presidents and have distinguished themselves as justices on the U.S. Supreme Court.

Jews have held elected positions on the local, state, and federal levels, often reflecting a higher percentage than their numbers in the general population would seem to indicate. For the first time in history, in the 2000 presidential election, a Jew, Senator Joseph Lieberman, ran on the national ticket of a major political party (Democrat) as the vice-presidential candidate. Indeed, the idea that a Jew could ever be elected president of the United States is no longer a pipe dream—as will be seen during the 2004 election. Ⓔ

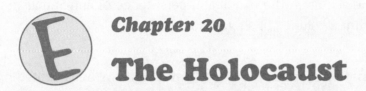

Chapter 20

The Holocaust

The word "holocaust" is derived from the Greek and means "sacrifice by fire." After 1945, the term Holocaust came to refer to the systematic extermination of 6 million Jews by the German Nazi regime and its collaborators. The *Shoah* (Hebrew for "calamity") is another term that refers to this tragedy.

The Hatred of the Jews

Many have wondered how Germany, one of the most cultured and civilized countries in the world, could have transformed itself into the purveyor of the most incomprehensible, colossal, and senseless act of brutality perpetrated upon millions of defenseless men, women, and children. And yet, given the extent and persistence of anti-Semitism in Europe over the centuries, it should not come as a total surprise.

FACT

Appropriately enough, the word "anti-Semitism" was coined by a German journalist, Wilhelm Marr, in 1879 to denote abhorrence of Jews. The term carried a racial connotation, in reference to the Jews as Semites, a group that also includes Arabs and North Africans and that shares a family of languages.

Hatred of Jews had existed for various reasons and in manifold ways throughout the millennia, well before the term "anti-Semitism" ever came into use. A principal feature of anti-Semitism that paved the way for the Holocaust had to do with the portrayal of the Jews as demonic—that they were literally agents of the devil. There have been more than a few well-circulated caricatures of Jews with horns and cloven feet.

Thus, the horrific acts committed against the Jews had a justification—the rest of the human race had to be cleansed of them. Needless to say, this image of the Jews as a people who are inherently evil and in collusion with Satan, the archenemy of God, was further supported by the common belief that the Jews were the killers of Christ.

The Jewish Conspiracy Myth

Around the turn of the twentieth century, a new dimension was added to anti-Semitism—the idea that the Jews controlled the world by way of a grand conspiracy. This was supposedly proven with the revelation of a document known as the *Protocols of the Elders of Zion*, which purported to represent the minutes of a clandestine meeting of Jewish leaders that takes place every 100 years to devise how they will control the world for the next century.

Though proven a forgery, the *Protocols* were used by anti-Semites to support their contention that all Jews were enemies of the nations in which they lived and that they could not be trusted. Many otherwise intelligent and respected people, blinded by anti-Semitism, believed in the authenticity of the *Protocols;* one of these people was Henry Ford, an American automotive pioneer.

The Politics of Discrimination

With the rise of nationalism throughout Europe in the last decades of the nineteenth century, a number of political parties denounced the Jews as disloyal citizens and urged that restrictions be placed upon them or that they be expatriated. The growing hatred of Jews continued into the early decades of the twentieth century and spread through Europe as well as the United States.

This resurgence of anti-Semitism helps explain why the world sat idly by as millions of Jews were murdered. Indeed, non-Germans actively participated in carrying out the slaughter of Europe's Jews—particularly in Austria and the Eastern European nations.

Anti-Semitism in Hitler's Germany

Before World War I, there was not a nation in the world where the Jews were as established and successful as in Germany. But after the war, Germany was particularly vulnerable to anti-Semitism. The Germans suffered a humiliating loss both on the battlefield and at the peace table and were struggling to survive the economic chaos of the postwar depression. They needed an outlet to vent their frustrations and anger. The "powerful" and "alien" Jews were the perfect scapegoat.

Hitler's Vicious Beliefs

The man who managed to capitalize on the hatred of Jews was Adolf Hitler (1889–1945). Hitler was Austrian and grew up in Vienna, a city permeated with anti-Semitism. As a child, he was no doubt also influenced by his anti-Semitic father. Many have and will continue to speculate as to why he hated the Jews with such fervor. Whatever the reason, Hitler's hatred had become a lifelong obsession.

Hitler's anti-Semitic stance was made clear in 1924 with the publication of *Mein Kampf* ("My Struggle"), which he wrote in prison as a result of participating in the Munich Putsch. Hitler's anti-Semitism provided a *weltanschauung* (world outlook) that made hating the Jews the core of the Nazi agenda. He fused German and Austrian anti-Semitism by taking the German fear of Jewish/Bolshevist Russia and the *Protocols of the Elders of Zion,* and mixing it with the Viennese apprehension of the *Ostjuden*—a dark and inferior race corrupting Germanic blood and responsible for everything decadent from the white slave trade to syphilis.

ALERT!

What made Hitler's brand of anti-Semitism especially insidious was that it was carried out in a "rational" demeanor reflecting his belief that the elimination of the Jews should be conducted by degrees and careful planning.

Hitler added a new dimension to the demonic portrayal of Jews and vilified them as lethal vermin. To bolster his contentions, he enlisted and received the support of scientists, philosophers, physicians, and teachers, so that his depiction of the Jews would be accepted by Germany's intelligent citizenry. Indeed, university students were the first to organize boycotts and force the Jews out of government.

Hitler's Plan for Elimination of the Jews

There were three distinct phases to Hitler's nonlethal persecution of the Jews:

Phase I: Non-Aryans were eliminated from the civil service, legal and medical professions, educational institutions, and the public sphere.

Phase II: Jews were reduced to second-class citizens in September 1935 with the enactment of the Nuremberg Laws, which effectively nullified the progress the Jews had made during the Emancipation.

Phase III: Commencing in 1938, all Jewish communal bodies were placed under the auspices of the Gestapo. Jews had to register their property, which made it difficult to produce the assets and capital required to emigrate, despite the fact it was the Nazi government's policy until 1939 to encourage Jews to leave the country.

QUESTION?

What was the Nazi definition of a Jew?
A Jew was any person with at least one Jewish grandparent. Consequently, intermingling of Aryans and Jews was prohibited. This included both marriage and sexual relations.

In the event these "legal" restrictions placed upon German Jewry did not prove daunting enough to motivate them to leave, Hitler had more violent means at his disposal. By 1932, the *Sturmabteilung* (Storm Troopers, or SA, also known as the Brownshirts) was half-a-million strong and all were willing henchmen at Hitler's disposal to beat up and even murder Jewish civilians.

On a more official level, Hitler had also established the *Schutzstaffel* (SS), the Nazi Party's police and security service under the command of twenty-nine-year-old Heinrich Himmler, the son of a Bavarian schoolmaster. The SS, which had all the powers of a police force, would enforce the restrictive laws, and later would carry out and supervise the genocide of the Jews.

Kristallnacht

Despite the sporadic violence and increasingly restrictive conditions in which the Jews found themselves, it was not until November 9, 1938 that everything became clear to the German Jews and to those in the rest of the world who paid any attention. On that night, which became known as *Kristallnacht* (the night of the broken glass), a well-orchestrated pogrom was unleashed by the SA and assorted thugs and hooligans across Germany. Hundreds of synagogues were burned, tens of thousands of homes invaded, many Jews were killed, women were raped, and 30,000 Jews were arrested.

Nowhere to Go

There is a Yiddish song called *"Wie a heen zul Ich gayn?"* ("Where shall I go?"). The Nazi regime encouraged emigration from 1933–1939 as a way of ridding itself of its Jews. Many Jews remaining in Germany wanted desperately to get out, but there were few places for them to go.

FACT

When Hitler came to power, 525,000 Jews lived in Germany. By 1939, 300,000 Jews managed to emigrate from Germany and Austria. The biggest obstacle to emigration for those remaining, however, was finding a country to take them in.

At the Evian Conference in 1938, no nation except the Dominican Republic increased their immigration quotas. Indeed, countries frequently did not fill those slots that were available for entry. For example, while the United States did admit 85,000 Jewish refugees during 1938–1939, during the war period only 21,000 Jews entered the United States—merely 10 percent of the permitted quota. Switzerland took in 30,000 Jews, but turned away countless thousands at its borders. Great Britain limited the number of Jews that could emigrate, but made a one-time special exception when accepting 10,000 Jewish children in what has come to be known as the *Kindertransport*.

Simply put, just when the German Third Reich was about to begin a more lethal approach to dealing with its Jews, doors all over the world slammed shut and the Jews had nowhere to go. Alone and helpless, they faced a systematic genocide.

ESSENTIAL

A logical choice and popular destination among European Jews was Palestine. But in accordance with the White Paper of 1939, immigration restrictions severely limited the number of Jews who could obtain entry into British Palestine—the British did everything in their power to enforce the quota.

Confinement to Ghettos

Ghettos, whose walls were broken down in the nineteenth century, once again made their appearance in Nazi Germany and the countries it occupied during World War II. More than 400 ghettos restricted the area in which Jews could live. But these were no ordinary ghettos, like those in the past where the Jews were confined at night but were permitted to leave for work during the day. The new ghettos presented the first step in a well-conceived plan for the annihilation of the Jewish people.

Most ghettos were located in Eastern Europe and were bound by walls, barbed-wire fences, or gates. The ghettos were purposely designed to be too small, to ensure overcrowding, which created unsanitary conditions, malnutrition, disease, and epidemics that led to high rates of mortality.

FACT

Even though only Jews lived in the ghetto, they were made to wear identifying armbands emblazoned with the Star of David. Life within the ghetto was governed by a council of Jewish leaders, known as the *Judenrate*. There was also a Jewish police force to enforce order.

The largest of these ghettos was the Warsaw Ghetto, which actually consisted of two ghettos referred to as the "large ghetto" and the "small ghetto." Four hundred and fifty thousand Jews were packed into 1.3 square miles within the city limits of Warsaw. Other major ghettos were located in Lodz, Krakow, Bialystok, Vilna, Lvov, Czestochowa, and Lublin. In 1944, ghettos were established in Hungary to facilitate the collection and subsequent liquidation of the Hungarian Jews.

Life in the Ghetto

Within the ghetto, life went on as best it could. When possible, the Jews conducted cultural activities, continued to provide education for their children, and of course, continued to observe Jewish religious practices. Illegal activities were common, particularly the smuggling of food and weapons, to be used in armed resistance. But with passing weeks and months, conditions invariably would deteriorate until the ghettos were finally empty and all its Jewish inhabitants were dead, either from starvation and disease or from being transported to the death camps.

Concentration Camps

The first concentration camps like Dachau, Buchenwald, and Sachsenhausen were established on German soil. Initially, these camps were used as detention facilities for those considered enemies of the Third Reich. In addition to the Jews, the concentration camps also held communists and other political prisoners, gypsies, Jehovah's Witnesses, and homosexuals.

Following the annexation of Austria and *Kristallnacht* in 1938, thousands of Jewish males were periodically rounded up and incarcerated in these camps, generally for months at a time. These camps were supervised by the SS, who exercised absolute authority and exhibited unimaginable cruelty, often assaulting or even killing the prisoners at whim. Physicians used the prisoners as guinea pigs for medical experiments that usually ended in disfigurement or death.

Labor Camps

In 1939, the Third Reich began to employ the inmates of these camps, as well as Jews in ghettos and in the areas under Nazi occupation, for forced labor to meet labor shortages. Commencing in 1942, thousands of Jews were conscripted as forced labor in German industry and sent to work for private companies such as I. G. Farben. Hundreds of plants began production in the camps to produce goods for the German war effort.

ALERT!

Many of the labor camps served another function as well. Tens of thousands of inmates were literally worked to death, dying from exhaustion and starvation, often laboring for no productive purpose whatsoever other than fulfilling the German policy of "annihilation through work."

Transit Camps

A number of camps were utilized as transit camps, where Jews would be held until the time was ready to send them off to the extermination camps. The best known of these transit camps was Theresienstadt (Terezin), located in Czechoslovakia. At first, only privileged German Jews (World War I veterans and those who had connections or wealth) were consigned there; later, Jews from other countries were also sent to Theresienstadt.

Because Theresienstadt was the "showcase" camp that Hitler allowed the Red Cross to inspect to prove nothing harmful was being done to the Jews, conditions were a cut above the other camps. Nonetheless, even in this "model" camp, of the 141,184 Jews who passed through its gates, only 16,832 were found alive when it was liberated on May 9, 1945. Of those survivors, more than a quarter died of dysentery and disease.

Einsatzgruppen—Mobile Killing Units

Between 1941 and 1943, Hitler deployed *Einsatzgruppen* (action groups) in Poland and the Soviet Union under the command of Reinhard Heydrich, chief of the Nazi Security Service or SD. Heydrich took his orders directly from Himmler, who in turn received his orders from Hitler. The Einsatzgruppen were mobile killing units organized into four battalions (A, B, C, and D), consisting of approximately 3,000 men, generally high-ranking officers of the SS, Gestapo, and police.

Many of these murderers were intellectuals and professionals—lawyers, architects, economists, and other well-educated men. Otto Ohlendorf, who commanded Battalion D, held three degrees, including one in jurisprudence. One of the commanders of Battalion C was Ernst Biberstein, a Protestant pastor and church official.

Nightmarish Destruction

In May of 1941, the battalions began their training. Two months later, they received their orders to follow the advancing German army into the Soviet Union and kill all the Communist officials and Jews they could find.

After the German army secured a city, town, or village, the *Einsatzgruppen* would round up all the Jews and tell them they were being transported for resettlement. Quickly and efficiently, they marched the Jews out or took them out in trucks to a site where they ordered the men to dig trenches or pits. The men, women, and children were commanded to strip naked, and then small groups were taken to the pits.

FACT

The number killed varied from several hundred to many thousands. The largest massacre was at Babi Yar near Kiev, Ukraine, where 34,000 Jews were murdered. Generally, each massacre was completed within two or three days. Meticulous records were maintained indicating the number of dead.

It was not long before the Germans found the most efficient way to fill the pits, known as "sardine packing." The first group of Jews would stretch out and lie down at the bottom of the pit, where they would be shot. The second group would lay down on the fresh corpses, with their heads on the feet of those below. The third group would reverse the position. In this fashion, these "killing pits" could contain five or six layers of corpses.

Small children and babies were subject to special treatment. Concerned with ricocheting bullets because cartridges could pass through their tiny bodies, the toddlers were frequently tossed in the air, shot while in freefall, and then allowed to land in the pit. At other times, the killers preferred to save their ammunition, smashing the small heads with a rifle or the butt of a gun.

The Group's Victims

One and a half million Jews—men, women, and children—were murdered by the *Einsatzgruppen*. Despite their proficiency, these 3,000 killers could not have accomplished this feat in such a relatively short period of time without assistance. They frequently received enthusiastic help from the German regular army, Hungarian and Romanian soldiers, and local collaborators, particularly Ukrainians, Lithuanians, and

Moldavians. In other words, many thousands of perpetrators of different nationalities, ranging from peasants to brilliant jurists, eagerly participated in the shooting of 1.5 million Jews, one by one, with an average daily death rate of 2,500.

In 1943, the Nazis abandoned this method of killing Jews. They decided that this system was too inefficient, and there was concern that the task was having negative psychological effects on the soldiers. It was noted that even though many were encouraged to drink schnapps (in fact, they were issued an unlimited supply), they still had difficulty sleeping.

The "Final Solution"

It has been established that the Final Solution to the Jewish question was adopted on January 20, 1942, when representatives of the SS, the Gestapo, and the government ministries met in suburban Berlin. This meeting has gone down in history as the Wansee Conference, named after the street where the meeting was held. Under the leadership of Reinhard Heydrich, those assembled agreed that all Jews should be killed and that this be accomplished at specific sites.

However, this measure had been foreshadowed many years earlier with the publication of *Mein Kampf* and Hitler's rise to power. In a sense, the decision made at the Wansee Conference was nothing more than the reaching of a consensus. The *Einsatzgruppen* had already begun its bloody work during the previous year.

The System of Slaughter

We know that in June 1941, Hitler instructed Himmler to establish extermination camps in fixed centers and that Himmler had told Rudolf Hoss, the commandant at Auschwitz, to enlarge his labor camp so that it could also be deployed for killing. On July 31, 1941, Reinhard Heydrich, the head of the SD, told Adolf Eichmann, the man responsible for the administration of the extermination of the Jews, that he had just met with Himmler and was informed that Hitler had ordered the physical annihilation of the Jews.

In the fall of 1941, Himmler assigned SS General Odilo Globocnik to the task of implementing *Aktion Reinhard* (named after Reinhard Heydrich), which called for the systematic murder of all the Polish and Soviet Jews. To accomplish this directive, construction of the death camps commenced in earnest.

The Death Camps

Nazi concentration camps served several distinct purposes. Some were transition points that held people en route to other camps. Others were labor camps designed to rely on free labor to produce goods for the war effort. While tens of thousands of Jews died in these transit and labor camps, six camps had the sole function of extermination: Belzec, Sobibor, Majdanek, Treblinka, Auschwitz-Birkenau, and Chelmno.

All six death camps were in Poland. The first one to open was Chelmno, near Lodz. It began its gruesome work in December 1941. Between 150,000 and 340,000 Jews were gassed in mobile vans until the camp closed in the spring of 1943 (estimates vary).

The second camp placed in operation was Belzec, where 600,000 Jews were killed by carbon monoxide poisoning between March 1942 and the spring of 1943. A quarter million Jews died in Sobibor between May 1942 and October 1943. During the year Majdanek was functioning (1942–1943), 170,000 Jews were gassed. At Treblinka, 800,000 Jews were killed by gas between July 1942 and October 1943.

Auschwitz-Birkenau

The largest and most infamous of the death camps was Auschwitz-Birkenau, a concentration camp that expanded its operations in January 1942 and continued its grisly work until November 1944. While most of the victims at other death camps were Eastern European Jews, Auschwitz became the graveyard of hundreds of thousands of Jews from Western Europe as well. At the height of Auschwitz-Birkenau's operation, four gas chambers gassed 8,000 Jews a day with a gas known as Zyklon B (hydrogen cyanide). The total number of Jewish victims of Auschwitz is estimated to be one million.

FACT

Disposing of three million corpses was no easy task. Special units of prisoners, called *Sonderkommandos,* removed the bodies from the gas chambers and cremated them. In many of the death camps, the only prisoners to survive did so because they belonged to a *Sonderkommando.*

The German Involvement

After the war was over and the world learned about the death camps, the German citizenry expressed shock and insisted that they knew nothing about the systematic murder of the Jews, but it is hard to accept their assertions. About 900,000 Germans served in the SS and were directly involved in the execution of the Final Solution, and many of them were proud of their service to their country. In fact, some even bragged of their exploits to friends and family, sending photographs of the murders taking place at the killing pits. And soldiers in the German army also knew what was going on—many of the troops were in close proximity to the *Einsatzgruppen* as it was conducting mass executions of 1.5 million Jews.

Well over 1 million Germans were employed in the rail system that transported the Jews to their deaths. Without the efficient operation of the transport trains, death camps such as Auschwitz would never have admitted so many victims. German citizens also received the belongings of the Jews—jewelry, watches, and other valuables—as they entered the camps.

Jewish Resistance

Over and over again, the question has been raised why the Jews did not resist. Why did they allow themselves to be led to the slaughter? How could several thousand Jews permit themselves to be shot, one by one, with no more than thirty or forty rifles aimed at them?

There are several explanations that may provide at least a partial answer to the questions. First, the Nazis were ingenious in their deployment of elaborate deceptions at every step of the way. Jews were led to believe they were being transported to work sites and received detailed instructions on what to bring with them on the trains. And when they arrived, music would be blaring to "welcome" them inside the camp.

Some also argue that the Jewish religion encourages passivity and abhors violence. Therefore, for most of the Jews, violent rebellion wasn't an option. Many pious Jews were taught to accept God's will, which accounts for Jews praying while at the foot of the killing pits or in the gas chambers.

It wasn't difficult for the Jews to accept these deceptions. After all, there was nothing in the history of the world to prepare them for what awaited. It was possible to believe that they were being taken to labor camps, that the Germans needed them for free labor, but what civilized person was willing to entertain the notion that the Nazis had constructed gas chambers where shower heads spewed deadly gas that would kill innocent men, women, and children, all destined to death for the simple reason of being Jewish? It is human nature to believe what we want to believe, and the Jews were no exception to this rule.

Uprisings in the Ghettos

Nonetheless, Jewish resistance did exist. The largest Jewish rebellion is known as the Warsaw Ghetto uprising, which began in late April of 1943 and lasted until early May. The uprising was led by the Jewish resistance organization known as the *Zydowska Organizacja Bojowa* (Jewish Fighting Organization) or ZOB.

When German forces had entered the ghetto to gather Jews for deportation to Treblinka, the ZOB ambushed the Germans with Molotov cocktails and hand grenades, which they had smuggled into the ghetto. Despite little in the way of weapons, the Jews resisted an overwhelming and massive military response from the embarrassed Germans. They held out for twenty-seven days (longer than the entire Polish nation resisted in 1939) and didn't give in; all of the fighters were eventually captured and executed. In the end, it was impossible for an isolated ghetto to fight the German forces. Other revolts took place in the ghettos of Vilna and Bialystok.

Were there acts of resistance in the death camps?
At Sobibor and Treblinka, prisoners attacked their guards with stolen weapons. Most were killed, but several dozen escaped. At Auschwitz, a number of the inmates blew up one of the crematoriums—all were subdued and shot.

Some Jews managed to escape from the ghettos or avoid the roundups in the towns and cities. Frequently, these Jews joined the resistance organizations of the countries in which they lived or formed their own groups of Jewish resistance fighters—in some areas, Jews were excluded from national resistance groups.

Other Acts of Resistance

Although there were few opportunities for violent resistance, many Jews chose spiritual forms of resistance. In the face of hopelessness, the Jews did not give in to hate and despair. They carried themselves with all the dignity they could muster, trying to ignore the subhuman conditions they were in and looking out for each other. Many Jews did not forsake their religion—on the contrary, they continued to pray and observe Jewish traditions and holidays under the most despairing of circumstances. In fact, many Jews chose to abstain from food and water during Yom Kippur, despite the danger of starvation, to demonstrate their continued commitment to their beliefs. That, too, was a form of resistance, a resistance to become subhuman and to the loss of their culture.

By not giving up hope, these Jews confirmed life and did so under the most horrific and damning conditions ever faced by a people at any time in the history of humankind. This was their ultimate act of resistance.

Those Who Survived

The extermination camps had done their job well. For the most part, when the camps were liberated, few inmates were found alive. Generally, as the Nazis retreated from the advancing Soviet troops, most of the inmates who were able to walk were forced on death marches; those who could not keep pace were shot as they dropped.

Despite the Germans' hasty attempts to conceal their crimes, the American and Soviet troops who liberated the death camps found plenty of evidence that mass murders had been conducted at these sites. For example, when the Soviets entered Majdanek, the first of the death camps to be liberated, the crematorium had been destroyed but the gas chambers were left standing. After reaching Belzec, Sobibor, and Treblinka, the Soviets liberated Auschwitz in January 1945, where several thousand emaciated prisoners were barely alive.

The first concentration camp liberated by United States forces was Buchenwald, on April 11, 1945. Encountering 20,000 gaunt figures in the camp, the American troops were overwhelmed.

Well before the camps were liberated by the Allied Forces, there had been sufficient evidence available known to the world leaders and the media that the Nazis were killing Jews at an unprecedented rate.

The first hurdle the survivors had to overcome was not to succumb to illness. For example, after the British entered Bergen-Belsen in April 1945, of the 60,000 prisoners still alive, 10,000 soon died from disease or malnutrition. As for those who managed to stay alive and be restored to some semblance of health, the question was the same as the one that faced the Jews in 1939—where to go?

Looking for a New Home

Most of the survivors rejected the idea of returning to their previous homes. While some gentiles had aided and hid Jews, the majority either did nothing to help, were active in handing the Jews over to the Nazis, or even participated in their murders. The survivors were fearful of returning to this anti-Semitic environment, and they were justified in their concern. After the war, some Jews who returned to their home towns became victims of pogroms. In 1946, the Polish residents of Kielce attacked the Jews who had returned to settle there, killing forty-two Holocaust survivors.

FACT

An estimated 9.2 million Jews lived in Europe before the war. By the end of the war in 1945, 3.1 million Jews survived. More than 6 million Jews were killed by the Nazis and their collaborators. Of these victims, 1 million were children.

Some Jews had no home to return to—many Jewish towns and villages were razed by the Nazis. Others could not bear to return home without their relatives, who did not survive to see liberation. As a result, many survivors were sent to displaced persons (DP) camps; shockingly, some of these camps were organized on the sites of concentration camps, such as Bergen-Belsen. The DP camps were administered by the U.S. army, and Jewish groups such as the American Jewish Joint Distribution Committee provided additional food and clothing.

Few Options

Resettlement wasn't easy. Most countries refused to allow Jewish survivors to enter. The United States still maintained its strict immigration quotas, but it did admit 80,000 Jewish refugees between 1945 and 1952. Britain continued its restriction on the immigration to Palestine, perhaps because it did not wish to offend the Arab residents and neighboring Arab nations, but the Jews living in Palestine organized and undertook the illegal immigration of 250,000 Jews.

Most of the ships carrying these Jewish refugees to Palestine were intercepted by the British. These survivors of the Holocaust found themselves in detention camps located on Cyprus, once again behind barbed wire but this time staring out at a horizon where they could see the coastline of the Promised Land. Ⓔ

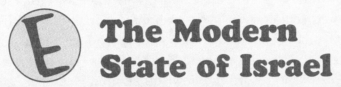

Chapter 21

The Modern State of Israel

During the Diaspora, a few Jews continued to live in the Holy Land in small religious communities. But in the nineteenth century, the Zionist movement inspired thousands of Jews to return to the Promised Land and reclaim their land, which they saw as their birthright. With the creation of the State of Israel, the Diaspora as we know it came to an end as Jews from all over the world were reunited in their ancient homeland.

The First Wave of Immigration

In the early nineteenth century, Palestine belonged to the Ottoman Empire, and the small Jewish community was concentrated in the Jewish Quarter of Jerusalem, a dismal ghetto where scholars and other observant Jews subsisted on charitable contributions sent by their European brethren.

However, toward the end of the century, Palestine saw a different kind of Jews arrive and settle. A wealthy Jewish man, Edmund de Rothschild, had provided financial support to Jewish people who wished to go to Palestine in order to establish agricultural settlements. The purpose of these settlements was to resurrect a Jewish nation in Palestine.

This small group was soon joined by the arrivals who made up the First Aliyah of 1882–1903 (there would be five in total). This first major wave of Jewish immigration was the result of the Russian pogroms of 1881–1882. The Russian and Eastern European Jews did not wish to stay and wait until the next pogrom, and many chose to go to Palestine.

FACT

Aliyah is a Hebrew term that literally means "going up"—that is, going up to Zion. In the synagogue, going up to read the Torah is performing aliyah. Today, Jews talk about immigration to Israel as "making aliyah" and immigrants are called *olim*.

The new settlers struggled against an inclement climate and harsh conditions. Making matters worse was the burdensome taxes levied by the Turkish rulers coupled with mounting hostility of the Arabs, which sometimes turned into violence. Of the 35,000 who made the First Aliyah, almost half returned to Europe within a few years. But new settlers would continue to arrive in waves throughout the first half of the twentieth century, when Israel gained independence and opened its doors to all Jews.

The Dreyfus Affair

Even though immigration to the Holy Land had already begun, it wasn't until the rise of Zionism that the stream of Jews going to Palestine would increase and gain a new legitimacy. As you may remember from Chapter 18, the nineteenth century in Western European was a time of emancipation for the Jews. For a while, it seemed that the danger for the Jewish people was complete assimilation. And yet, the Zionist movement of rebuilding a Jewish homeland in Palestine was born in Western Europe. What had gone wrong?

False Accusations

We may trace the roots of Zionism to the Dreyfus Affair. The allegations grew out of the revelation that a French officer had provided secret information to Germany. Needing someone to charge for the crime, the army authorities decided upon Alfred Dreyfus, a captain in the army and a Jew. He was tried in 1894, convicted, ignominiously stripped of rank, and sent to Devil's Island for life.

FACT

On the most basic level, the affair was a trial of a French Jewish military officer accused of treason. But the event was also a reflection of deep schisms within French society and government involving monarchists and republicans, the Catholic Church, political parties, the army, and vocal anti-Semites.

Subsequently, the chief of intelligence, Lt. Colonel Georges Picquart, though an anti-Semite himself, was not convinced Dreyfus was the right man. He hated the thought of the guilty man going free, so he continued the investigation, concluding that Major Walsin Esterhazy was the culprit. However, despite proof that Dreyfus was innocent, the anti-Semitic faction in the army refused to convict Esterhazy or exonerate Dreyfus. A second trial for Dreyfus was held and he was again found guilty.

What saved Dreyfus is the public outcry in the face of such flimsy and trumped-up evidence, spurred by Émile Zola's publication of an open letter, titled *J'accuse!* Eventually, the authorities relented, and in 1899, Dreyfus was returned to France and pardoned; however, he was not restored to his rank until 1906.

Theodor Herzl, Father of Zionism

The Jews in Western Europe were deeply disturbed by the Dreyfus Affair and its ramifications. Many of them had believed that they were finally full citizens of their countries, but now saw that they were still vulnerable to government-sponsored anti-Semitism. One of these Jews was Theodor Herzl (1860–1904).

Herzl was born in Budapest; at the age of eighteen, his family moved to Vienna, where he had the opportunity to receive a doctorate of law, completed in 1884. Following his studies, Herzl became a writer and journalist. In 1894, he covered the Dreyfus Affair for a liberal Viennese newspaper.

Before the trial, Herzl wrote that the best way to respond to anti-Semitism in Western Europe was to assimilate, but his views changed dramatically in 1894. Hearing the mobs shouting "Death to the Jews," Herzl had cause to rethink his views on dealing with anti-Semitism.

Herzl's Ideas

Two years later, Herzl published a small book, *Judenstaat* ("The Jewish State"), in which he maintained that the Jews are one people and the only solution to their plight is the establishment of their own nation. Herzl suggested that any tract of land big enough to accommodate the Jews would suffice.

Ideas included a tract of land in Argentina, where Baron de Hirsch had funded 6,000 Jewish settlers in an agricultural colony, and Palestine, where Rothschild had provided financing for Jewish settlements. Herzl subsequently wrote a Zionist novel, *Altneuland* ("Old New Land"), which portrayed a new Jewish country he envisioned as a socialist utopia.

ALERT!

Herzl took his cause far and wide—to ordinary Jews, the Jewish elite, foreign rulers, and politicians. Although most of the wealthy Jewish leaders were not receptive to Herzl's proposals, he was popular with the Jewish masses.

Death of a Jewish Hero

Herzl threw himself into his work and it took a toll on his health. At the age of forty-four, Theodor Herzl died of pneumonia and a weak heart. Although he did not live to see the establishment of the Jewish state he envisioned, he was convinced it was only a matter of time before the Jewish people would have a homeland. In 1949, his remains were brought to Israel and reinterred on Mount Herzl in Jerusalem.

Coincidentally, the year of Herzl's death marked the beginning of the Second Aliyah (1904–1914). The majority of the people who arrived during this time were Russians fleeing pogroms. Many of them were socialists, and they founded *kibbutzim* (national farms) based on egalitarian principals.

The Second Aliyah also saw the founding of the first Jewish self-defense group, Ha-Shomer, and settlement of new towns. In a suburb of Jaffa, an Arab town on the Mediterranean coast, the settlers constructed a neighborhood called Ahuzat Bayit, which would one day become Tel Aviv, the first modern all-Jewish city in the world. But despite all the achievements, life in Palestine was difficult. In the face of oppressive conditions, of the 40,000 Jews making up the Second Aliyah, nearly half returned to their previous homes.

©Israel Ministry of Tourism. Courtesy of the Israel Ministry of Tourism.

▲ The skyline of Tel Aviv, a city that represents modernity in Israel.

The Zionist Movement

One of Herzl's legacies was the establishment of the World Zionist Organization. Due in large part to his efforts, on August 29, 1897, the first Zionist Congress convened in Basel, Switzerland. In attendance were approximately 200 delegates from seventeen countries. The congress established itself as the World Zionist Organization and elected Herzl as president.

One of the congress's most significant achievements was the declaration of the goal of Zionism—creation of a home for the Jewish people in *Eretz Yisrael* (the Land of Israel) in accordance with international law. To reach this end, the Congress adopted the Basel Program, which included the following points:

- Eretz Yisrael would be settled by Jewish farmers, artisans, and manufacturers.
- All of Jewry would be united on the local, national, and international levels to accomplish the objective of Zionism.
- Jewish national consciousness would be raised.
- Efforts would be made to obtain the consent and support of governments for the establishment of a Jewish nation.

After centuries of being a "dead" language used only for religious study and prayer, Palestine saw the revival of Hebrew. Ben-Zion Ben-Yehuda (1882–1943), the first son of a Hebrew scholar and linguist Eliezer Ben-Yehuda, is considered to be the first person whose native language was modern Hebrew. Today, Hebrew is the official language of Israel.

Subsequent Zionist Congresses were held every year thereafter until 1901, and then every other year with the exception of a hiatus during World War I. After 1945, meetings have been held approximately every four years. Following the establishment of the State of Israel, the meetings have taken place in Jerusalem.

Points of Controversy

The Zionist movement did experience some deep divisions, particularly in its early years. Some Zionists were secular Jews who supported "cultural Zionism," emphasizing Jewish culture and awareness. Opposing this group were the Orthodox Zionists, who wanted to combine Herzl's political goals with traditional religious identity. In 1902, the religious camp formed the Mizrahi movement.

Another divisive issue occurred at the Sixth Zionist Congress in 1903, when Herzl suggested serious consideration be given to the British recommendation of using Uganda as a place of temporary settlement for the Russian Jewish refugees. For the next four years, Zionists studied and passionately argued for and against the Uganda proposal.

At the Seventh Zionist Congress in 1905, a delegation seceded and formed the Jewish Territorial Organization to seek another location more practical than Palestine. But for most Zionists, Palestine was the only land for a Jewish country, and the Eighth Zionist Congress, held in 1907, rejected the Uganda proposal. Instead, all efforts would be concentrated to create a Jewish homeland in Palestine.

The British Mandate

After World War I, the Ottoman Empire lost control of many of its former territories, including Palestine. In July 1922, the League of Nations appointed Great Britain to oversee the Mandate for Palestine and to facilitate the establishment of "Palestine-Eretz Israel" (Land of Israel) as a national homeland for the Jewish people.

Later that year, all the territory situated east of the Jordan River, representing approximately 75 percent of the land, was removed from the mandate and subsequently became the Hashemite kingdom of Jordan.

The Balfour Declaration

England's intentions concerning Palestine were of considerable consequence in determining whether or not a Jewish state would be established in the region. These intentions had been outlined in a public letter from Lord Arthur James Balfour, the British Foreign Secretary, to Lord Walter Rothschild, head of the English Jewish community, dated November 2, 1917. This document stated unequivocally that the British government supports "the establishment in Palestine of a national home for the Jewish people" and would help achieve this goal without disrupting the rights of existing non-Jewish communities in Palestine.

At the time of the Balfour Declaration, 85,000 Jews and over half a million Arabs lived in Palestine. Most Arabs did not want to share the land with the Jews; nor, for that matter, did neighboring Arab nations desire a Jewish country in their midst.

The Leadership of Chaim Weizmann

Although Balfour was already sympathetic to the Zionist cause, and many British politicians agreed to the idea of a Jewish state in principle, the final language of the letter was the subject of much debate. The person credited with securing the support of Lord Balfour as well as Winston Churchill and Prime Minister Lloyd George was Chaim Weizmann, who was aided by Herbert Samuel, a Jewish member of Parliament.

Chaim Weizmann was born in 1874 in Russia. After high school, he left for Germany in order to study chemistry. Eventually, his job as a professor of chemistry took him to the University of Manchester in England, and Weizmann applied for (and was granted) British citizenship. Weizmann became a Zionist in his youth, and he served as president of the World Zionist Organization for two terms (1920–1931 and 1935–1946). In 1949, Weizmann was honored for his contribution to the creation of the Jewish state with a nomination for the presidency of Israel. He served as the first president of Israel until his death in 1952.

The Jews Continue to Arrive in Palestine

After the end of World War I, even before the establishment of the British Mandate, Palestine saw the arrival of the next group of Jewish immigrants. The Third Aliyah (1919–1923) included about 40,000 Jews, who had come to join the 90,000 Jews already living in Palestine; almost all the new arrivals remained. At this time, the Jews formed the Histadrut (General Federation of Labor) and the clandestine Jewish defense organization, known as the Haganah.

FACT

During the British Mandate (1922–1948), the economy grew and cultural and educational institutions flourished. Both the Jewish and Arab communities were given autonomy regarding their internal affairs. The *yishuv,* as the Jewish community in Palestine was known, established an elected assembly and national council.

The Fourth Aliyah followed in 1924, and new settlers continued to arrive until 1929. This time, most of the arrivals were immigrants from Poland, victims of growing anti-Semitism who were denied entry into the United States. Consequently, many Jewish small-business owners and artisans chose Palestine as their destination, where they established commercial enterprises. During these years, about 82,000 Jews emigrated; about one-quarter returned.

The last wave of immigration before World War II is known as the Fifth Aliyah (1929–1939). The quarter-million Jews who arrived in Palestine with the Fifth Aliyah were fleeing Germany and Austria following the Nazi rise to power and subsequent anti-Semitic policies. Many of the German immigrants were professionals, and their talents and skills greatly improved the quality of life in the Jewish community. The German Jews participated in the establishment of new industries, construction of a port in Haifa, and construction of new towns and settlements. By the end of the Fifth Aliyah, 450,000 Jews were living in Palestine.

Peace Gives Way to Instability

For the first few years of the Mandate, peace and calm prevailed in the *yishuv.* At the helm was a charismatic man by the name of David Ben Gurion (1886–1973). Ben Gurion had come to Palestine from Poland in 1906, but he soon adapted to new surroundings and assumed a position of leadership.

Soon, Ben Gurion had to deal with the erupting violence against the Jews in Palestine. In 1929, the leader of the Arab populace, the Mufti Haj Amin al-Husseini, initiated riots and looting against the Jews in Jerusalem, Hebron, and Safed. Without any protection from the British, several hundred Jews were wounded and over a hundred killed.

©Itamar Grinberg. Courtesy of the Israel Ministry of Tourism.

◀ The Negev Desert covers about half the land of Isreal.

ALERT!

Ben Gurion employed diplomacy when he could but was not afraid to resort to armed resistance when he felt it necessary. His task was daunting. Not only was he faced with a British government growing more conciliatory to the Arab position, but the Arabs were united on two fronts to oppose the creation of a Jewish homeland.

The Jews could not readily defend themselves because Jewish self-defense forces had long been declared illegal by the British. Indeed, in 1920, when Vladimir Jabotinsky reacted to riots in the Galilee by organizing an armed group (a precursor of the Haganah), he and some of his men were arrested by the British and sentenced to imprisonment for fifteen years.

In 1936, al-Husseini organized the Arab leaders within Palestine into a military group, the Arab High Command. Outside the Mandate's territory, the Arab nations met in 1937 at the Pan Arab Conference and declared their unanimous opposition to a Zionist state.

Rioting against the Jews became widespread beginning in 1936. Violence and terrorist attacks by the Arabs were leveled at the *yishuv* and the British. In 1939, the British finally sanctioned the arming of the Haganah and acting together, the violence was quelled in 1939.

Nonetheless, the Arabs made their influence felt. The British issued a new White Paper in 1939 that restricted Jewish immigration to the *yishuv* to 75,000 for the following five-year period. This seemed to satisfy the Arabs, and calm was restored until 1947.

From the Ashes of the *Shoah*

With the murder of 6 million Jews, the world was forced to acknowledge the need for a secure place where Jews could live. On November 29, 1947, the United Nations voted in favor of the partition of Palestine into two states—Jewish and Arab. Almost immediately thereafter, violence erupted in Palestine, with more than 1,000 Jewish, Arab, and British fatalities.

For the next five months, countless assaults were carried out against the Jews. As the British gradually withdrew, they turned over their fortifications and weapons to the Arabs. Although the United Nations held the Arabs responsible for the violence, no action was undertaken to enforce the Partition Plan; while many nations offered verbal support for a Jewish homeland, nothing was done to help the fledgling state. In fact, a number of countries, including the United States, declared an arms embargo to the region, which favored the status quo and the Arabs.

FACT

The Haganah was poorly armed, with 17,600 rifles, 2,700 sten-guns, 1,000 machine guns, and practically no heavy artillery or aircraft. Its forces consisted of between 20,000 to 43,000 men in various stages of training. The Arab Liberation Army was joined by 30,000 well-trained troops from Egypt, Syria, Iraq, Lebanon, and the Arab Legion of Transjordan.

The War of Independence

Despite the chaos and violence, the Jewish leaders pushed for independence. On May 14, 1948, David Ben Gurion read aloud from the Scroll of Independence, declaring "the establishment of a Jewish state in Palestine, which shall be known as the State of Israel." A provisional government was formed, and that night the Jews celebrated the birth of the State of Israel. Unfortunately, that day also marked the beginning of the War of Independence. As the Israelis danced in the streets, Egyptian planes flew overhead, commencing the Arab assault that sought the annihilation of the new Jewish state.

The Haganah, now renamed the Israel Defense Forces (IDF), fought fiercely with the Arab armies, knowing that they were fighting for their very existence. In mid-October of 1948, the IDF launched an offensive in the Negev; and by the end of the year, with a military 100,000 strong, Israel was in control on the ground. It seems miraculous that the Israeli forces not only managed to defend themselves, but also captured the cities of Tiberias, Haifa, Safed, Jaffa, and Acre. Unfortunately, the Old City of Jerusalem was lost after a bitter battle. Jerusalem would remain divided until fighting again began in 1967.

More than 6,000 Jews (1 percent of the Jewish population in Israel) died during the War of Independence. This wore heavily on a nation whose major purpose was to provide a safe homeland for the Jews.

In January 1949, armistice talks were conducted on the island of Rhodes; during the next six months, armistice agreements were signed with Egypt, Lebanon, Transjordan, and Syria. Iraq never signed an accord.

Jewish Immigration to Israel

When David Ben Gurion proclaimed independence, he said, "The State of Israel will be open for Jewish immigration and the ingathering of the exiles [Jews in the Diaspora]." In 1950, the Knesset (Israeli parliament) enacted the Law of Return, which granted every Jew the right to emigrate to Israel and become an Israeli citizen.

In the first three years of Israeli statehood, 687,000 Jews emigrated to Israel, doubling the Jewish population. The majority of these immigrants were survivors of the Holocaust; others came from Libya, Yemen, and Iraq. The following decade, immigrants began arriving from North Africa, Morocco, Tunisia, Egypt, Poland, and Hungary—lands inhospitable to Jews.

Tens of thousands of Jews came from the United States, Canada, South Africa, and Western Europe. They were not looking for safety, but emigrated for idealistic, spiritual, and religious reasons.

Arrival of Soviet Jews

The largest single influx of Jewry, even surpassing the number of Holocaust survivors who had arrived during Israel's formative years, is the modern-day exodus from the Soviet Union. After pressure was brought to bear upon the Soviet Union's policy refusing to allow Jews to emigrate, the Soviet government allowed Jews to leave for the purpose of making aliyah.

By the end of the 1970s, 140,000 Soviet Jews had emigrated to Israel. Emigration was then halted until the late 1980s, when Jews began leaving in unprecedented numbers. After the collapse of the Soviet Union, Jews continued to emigrate. As of the beginning of the new millennium, 1 million former Soviet Jews live in Israel.

ALERT!

More than half a century after its founding as a state, Israel remains a land of ingathering. Three out of every five Jews living in Israel in 2000 were born elsewhere.

Wars and the Quest for Peace

Israel is a tiny country—290 miles long and 85 miles across its widest point, approximately the size of the state of New Jersey. It is barely a speck in a vast region composed of Arab states that for most of the twentieth century were dedicated to the destruction of the Jewish enclave. Even the current record-high Jewish population of 5 million pales in comparison to the 100 million Arabs who are its nearest neighbors.

Compounding this precarious state of existence is the knowledge that should the Arab world decide upon another coordinated attack on the Jewish state, given past experience, Israel can't expect direct help from any other nation, except perhaps the United States. Add to that the frequent terrorist attacks conducted by Palestinians, and you can begin to understand why Israel is a country with a "living under a siege" mentality.

Following the signing of several armistice agreements and the restoration of calm in 1949, the Arabs insisted on two preconditions before they would even discuss peace. First, Israel had to return to the 1947 borders set up in the Partition Resolution that the Arabs had rejected to begin with. Second, the Arabs insisted that Israel repatriate the Palestinian refugees who had left Israel after it declared independence and lived in refugee camps of the West Bank, then belonging to Jordan. With neither condition satisfied, Egypt led the way in maintaining a state of belligerence against Israel.

The Suez War

It was no surprise, then, that fighting broke out in 1956 over the matter of the Suez Canal. The canal had been constructed by the British, and Britain continued to rely on it for a quick passage to the Red Sea and Saudi Arabia. Israel relied on the canal as well, but it was frequently denied passage.

Meanwhile, tensions mounted when the Soviet Union abandoned its support for the Jewish State and aligned itself with the Arab nations. In 1955, Egypt received a shipment of heavy armaments from the Russians. Israel was also suffering from terrorist attacks launched by *fedayeen*, who were trained in Egypt and dispatched from Jordan.

In July 1956, Egyptian President Gamal Abdel-Nasser blockaded the Straits of Tiran and nationalized the Suez Canal. In October, he signed an agreement with Syria and Jordan, placing their forces under his command. It looked like the Arab nations were once again preparing for war.

To pre-empt the attack, on October 29, 1956, Israel attacked Egypt; Britain and France, concerned over blockades of the Suez Canal, joined Israel in the fight. The IDF routed the Egyptians and captured almost the entire Sinai Peninsula. When the United States and the Soviet Union learned of the attack, they pressured Israel, Britain, and France through the United Nations to return the conquered territories. In its place, the United Nations dispatched the U.N. Emergency Force to supervise the vacated territories and guarantee international shipping.

The Six-Day War

In just eleven years, fighting erupted again. In May of 1967, Egypt ordered the U.N. Emergency Force out of the Sinai, and it quickly obliged. Egyptian troops gathered in the Sinai, near the border with Israel, and Syrian troops assembled on the Golan Heights. Approximately 250,000 Arab troops from Egypt, Syria, Jordan, and Lebanon, and 2,000 tanks stood at Israel's borders. Other Arab countries committed troops to the battle, and the Soviet Union was supplying the Arabs with weapons.

What are the Golan Heights?
The Golan Heights, an area that towers 3,000 feet above the Jewish Galilee, was controlled by Syria, who used this strategic parcel of land to shell Israeli settlements and kibbutzim in the valley.

QUESTION?

On May 22, the Straits of Tiran (Israel's only supply route to Asia) was once again closed to Israeli shipping. On June 5, 1967, Israel executed a pre-emptive strike. Israel's victory was swift and overwhelming—stunning the Arab nations and the entire world. The IDF captured the Golan Heights, the Sinai, Gaza, and the West Bank, increasing Israel's territory from 8,000 to 26,000 square miles. The Old City of Jerusalem was seized from Arab control. Hundreds of thousands of Palestinians fled, but three-quarters of a million remained in these territories.

Israel had come within marching distance of the capitals of Egypt, Syria, and Jordan when a cease-fire was invoked on June 10, after six days of fighting. In November 1967, the U.N. Security Council adopted Resolution 242, establishing the principle that Israel would return conquered territories in exchange for peace with its Arabs neighbors. This worked with some countries, though not with others. In 1977, the Egyptian President Anwar Sadat signed a peace treaty with Israel in return for the return of the Sinai Peninsula.

The Yom Kippur War

Although the 1967 war proved to be a failure for Arab nations, they refused to give up. On October 6, 1973, while the Jewish people were observing Yom Kippur, the Day of Atonement and holiest day on the Jewish calendar, the forces of Egypt and Syria attacked Israel. Eighty thousand Egyptian troops stormed the Sinai at a point where 500 Jewish soldiers were positioned. Many Arab and non-Arab nations actively aided the Egyptians and Syrians, with Jordan joining the fighting. Efforts led by the United States to arrange an immediate cease-fire were unsuccessful.

However, once it recovered from the shock, Israel mobilized its reserve forces and recaptured the territory it had lost. Indeed, by the time the U.N. Security Council adopted a resolution calling for a cease-fire, Israel had encircled the entire Egyptian Third Army in the Sinai Peninsula.

Israel Today

The Yom Kippur War was the last war Israel fought in the twentieth century. However, in spite of peace treaties signed with Egypt and Jordan, military campaigns and incursions have continued to occur, particularly with Syria and Lebanon. And during the Gulf War, Israel was bombed by the Iraqis, though it made an agreement with the United States not to retaliate.

FACT

At the turn of the twenty-first century, the population of Israel stood at 6.3 million. Of the total populace, there were more than 1.1 million Arabs (81 percent Muslim, 10 percent Christian, and 9 percent Druze) and almost 5 million Jews, representing more than a third of the total world Jewish population.

Today, the threat to Israel comes from within. So far, the peace process between the Jews and the Palestinians has failed to bring about a long-term solution. The First Intifadah erupted in 1987 in Gaza and the West Bank; the Second Intifadah followed in 2000. In a perpetual circle of violence, as acts of terrorism are perpetrated upon Israeli civilians, the Israeli government takes repressive measures against the Palestinians living in the territories, which in turn leads to further violence. Although Israel has fulfilled the dreams of Herzl and the early Zionists, so far its quest for peace has proved elusive.

Chapter 22

Jewish Culture

We have now completed the 4,000 year saga that is the story of the Jewish people. Jewish history reflects not only the lives of the Jews, scattered to all four corners of the globe, but also the lives of those they have come in contact with and learned from. The Diaspora has certainly influenced Jewish culture, which changed to reflect experiences of particular Jewish communities. Today, we can be proud to have a diverse cultural heritage from the Jews of Europe, Africa, the Middle East, Latin America, and the United States.

A Diverse Mosaic

Culture may be defined as a common set of beliefs and practices that a group of people adopt over time, and there is no question that a Jewish culture does exist. Indeed, for some Jews who are not observant of Judaism, their culture and heritage is what they believe makes them Jewish. However, different communities of Jews living at different times and in different societies have sometimes appeared to have little in common beside Judaism. All of these subcultures make up the mix that we have come to know as Jewish culture.

Given a 4,000-year history and the geographical dispersal that forced the Jews to confront and sometimes assimilate other world cultures, Jewish culture has always been heterogeneous. Yet somehow all the diverse customs and practices have managed to come together, much like Joseph's coat of many colors. And like the variegated hues of Joseph's coat, the result has been a truly wondrous and remarkable synthesis.

The Literary Tradition

Jewish literature, both religious and secular, could easily fill voluminous anthologies, divided by language, subject, or time period when a particular work was authored. In this book, we will have to limit ourselves to a brief survey on this topic, most notably the Yiddish literary tradition and modern works in English and Hebrew.

FACT

Although it was born as a spoken language, Yiddish did eventually make headway in literature. The nineteenth and early twentieth century was the Golden Age of Yiddish literature in Eastern Europe and the United States.

Literary Works in Yiddish

Occupying a singular position in Jewish secular literature are the tales, stories, and novels written in Yiddish that for hundreds of years had a great effect on the Ashkenazic Jews of Europe and the United States.

Unfortunately, while Yiddish literature is rich and immensely attractive, most of it has never been translated—and it is unlikely that it ever will be. Given the nuances and uniqueness of the language, translations from the Yiddish are often found wanting.

Yiddish literature can be divided into three periods: the period of preparation, the classical age, and the postclassical period. The first of these periods was the longest, spanning seven centuries; during that time (between the twelfth and nineteenth century), most Yiddish literature consisted of devotional works whose purpose was to make Judaism more intelligible to ordinary people. Perhaps the most noteworthy of these writings is the *Tz'enah Ur'enah,* a liberal reworking of the stories from the Five Books of Moses, written by Jacob ben Isaac Ashkenazi.

You are probably familiar with the musical *Fiddler on the Roof,* but did you know that it was inspired by the collection of stories titled *Tevye's Daughters,* written by Sholom Aleichem? This talented writer was perhaps unequaled in his ability to depict the authentic human condition of his day with humor and gentleness.

By the fifteenth century, books of poetry, stories, and folktales also began to appear in Yiddish. In 1686, the first Yiddish newspaper was published in Amsterdam.

The classical age of Yiddish literature was brief in duration but brilliant, bold, and beautiful in its bloom. This period in Yiddish literature lasted for a short interval, commencing in the late nineteenth century and ending fifty years later. While there were many distinguished writers of Yiddish literature during this time, three stood at the forefront: Sholom Jacob Abramowitz, best known as Mendele Mokher Sefarim (Mendele the Itinerant Bookseller); Sholom Rabinowitz, known as Sholom Aleichem; and Yitzhak Leib Peretz. These three luminaries of Yiddish fiction wrote about everyday life in the *shtetl* and in the Pale of Settlement in Russia, and each made a unique contribution to the body of Yiddish literature.

In the early part of the twentieth century, many Yiddish writers fled Eastern Europe for the United States. Consequently, New York replaced

Warsaw as the center of the Yiddish literary world. At this time, Sholem Asch and Israel Joshua Singer perfected the Yiddish novel. Israel Singer's younger brother, Isaac Bashevis Singer, emerged as one of the most well known Yiddish writers of short stories and novels. His achievements were recognized with a Nobel Prize for literature. New York also became the hub of Yiddish theater, especially after the Soviet government closed down Yiddish theaters in the Soviet Union.

FACT

In the Soviet Union, Yiddish writers pursued themes of social realism. Among these writers, many of whom were murdered in the purge of Yiddish writers during the Stalin era, were the poet Moshe Kulbak, the novelist David Bergelson, and short-story writer Isaac Babel.

Along with a recent resurgence of the Yiddish language, Yiddish literature has become more accessible, particularly with the publication of anthologies. How long this renaissance will last remains to be seen but it is a renewal of interest among readers—not writers—and little new work written in Yiddish has been forthcoming.

Writing in Modern Hebrew

In the past, Hebrew had been reserved for religious writings. However, one of the objectives of the Zionist movement had been to revive Hebrew as a living language to be used in all spheres of Israeli life. Today, modern Hebrew boasts a sizeable literary tradition, and many of these works have been translated into other languages and are read all over the world.

One of the most distinguished modern Hebrew poets is Hayim Bialik. Talented novelists include Aharon Appelfeld, S. Y. Agnon, A. B. Yehoshua, and Amos Oz. Today, Israel is home to a new generation of gifted Israeli writers such as David Grossman and Etgar Keret.

Jewish Literature in English

Since the middle of the twentieth century, American Jewish literature has flourished as well. While the work of some American Jewish writers has never expressed a Jewish theme or motif, other Jewish writers do include Jewish elements or themes into their writing. These writers include Saul Bellow, Henry Roth, Bernard Malamud, Philip Roth, Joseph Heller, Elie Wiesel, Chaim Potok, Cynthia Ozick, and Leon Uris. With younger writers of fiction such as Michael Chabon, Myla Goldberg, Thane Rosenbaum, Jonathan Safran Foer, and Allegra Goodman, the future of Jewish literature in twenty-first century America is secure.

Jewish Music

Like the Jewish people, Jewish music has its roots in the Middle East, but it cannot be limited to a geographic location. Jewish music has been greatly affected by the Diaspora and as a result, Jewish music is a cross-cultural phenomenon appropriate for a people who have wandered the face of the earth. There are three major classifications of Jewish music: Ashkenazic, Sephardic, and Mizrahi.

Music of the Ashkenazim

A well-known Ashkenazic music genre is klezmer. The term derives from the Hebrew words *klei zemer,* or "instruments of song." Klezmer music was popular among the Ashkenazim in Europe and was played by groups of itinerant musicians who went from village to village entertaining the local populace with folk songs and folk dance as well as traditional music, usually performed in Yiddish.

Following the Holocaust and the devastation of European Jewry, klezmer music almost passed into oblivion. However, in the last decades of the twentieth century, there has been a resurgence of interest in klezmer among Jews, particularly in the United States.

Sephardic and Mizrahi Music

Sephardic music, sung in Ladino, is associated with Sephardic Jews and therefore incorporates some of the melodies and rhythms of

Mediterranean cultures. Mizrahi is the music of those Jews living in North Africa and Arab countries, so the lyrics are frequently in Arabic. Today, both these categories of Jewish music are referred to as Sephardic.

Secular and Religious

Jewish devotional music is present during religious services in the synagogue. In fact, each congregation has a cantor (*chazzan* in Hebrew), who leads the worshippers in chanting prayers. Religious music is not confined to the synagogue. On certain holidays, blessings and prayers are chanted at home. More observant Jews will chant blessings many times a day.

Secular music frequently takes place on special occasions such as weddings, bar mitzvahs, bat mitzvahs, and communal gatherings. At these events, while there is plenty of singing, more reliance is placed on musical instruments. Secular music includes folk music and popular music such as klezmer.

At the Jewish Table

Food is an important part of Jewish culture and religion, serving both secular and devotional functions. First and foremost, there is the matter of *Kashrut*, the Jewish dietary laws observed by Jews to varying degrees (depending on what branch of Judaism they adhere to as well as their personal beliefs). The Torah specifies which foods Jews are permitted to eat and how these foods must be prepared. For example, animals that do not have cloven hooves and do not chew their cud, such as pigs, may not be eaten and only fish that have both fins and scales may be consumed.

But although all traditional Jewish foods complied with the laws of *Kashrut*, they each did so with different ingredients and cooking techniques, depending on what was available locally. That is why Jewish cuisine is really an amalgamation of many cultures—you will find the influence of Middle Eastern, Spanish, German, Mediterranean, and Eastern European styles of cooking in Jewish cuisine.

This also explains why many foods that might be considered "Jewish" are not exclusive to Jewish cuisine. For example, hummus and falafel are common in much of the Middle East; stuffed cabbage is popular in Eastern Europe; and knishes are familiar to Germans as well as to Ashkenazic Jews.

The economic factor also played a role in some Jewish dishes. Where Jews were poor, particularly in the shtetls of Eastern Europe, it was necessary to make a few inexpensive ingredients go a long way and this affected the manner of cooking.

Sephardic and Ashkenazic Cuisine

One way to make sense of Jewish food is to separate it along the cultural break between the Sephardim and Ashkenazim. Sephardic Jewish cuisine, subject to Mediterranean influences, is characterized by the use of spices, olive oil, rice, and lamb. Ashkenazic Jewish cooking reflects the Central, Northern, and Eastern European countries in which they lived.

FACT

The first printed reference to the bagel can be found in the Community Regulations of Krakow, Poland, in 1610. At that time, it was the custom to give bagels as a gift to pregnant women shortly before childbirth, perhaps because the circular bagel represented the circle of life.

The food considered to be "Jewish" by Jews living in the United States corresponds more with the Ashkenazic style of cooking. In some cases, there is an American touch and some Jewish dishes are entirely within the American tradition. Some "typically" Jewish dishes include the following:

- **Bagels:** Donut-shaped rolls that are boiled and then baked. Eating bagels with cream cheese and lox is an American custom.
- **Blintzes:** Crepes or flat pancakes rolled around sweetened cottage cheese, mashed potatoes, fresh fruit, or other filling. The word *blintz* is an Americanized version of the Yiddish word *blintzeh*.
- **Knishes:** Potato and flour dumplings normally stuffed with mashed potato and onion, chopped liver, or cheese.

- **Kreplach:** Another type of dumplings, triangular or square and filled with meat or cheese; kreplach are usually served in soup.
- **Kasha varnishkes:** A mixture of buckwheat and bow-tie macaroni noodles.
- **Kugel:** A casserole (the word "kugel" is German for "pudding"). The two most common types of kugel are the savory kugel with potatoes, eggs, and onions, and a dessert kugel made with noodles, fruits, and nuts in an egg-based pudding.
- **Stuffed cabbage:** Also known as *holishke, praakes,* or *galuptzi,* stuffed cabbage is a popular Jewish food item. It can be prepared in a number of ways, one of which is to fill it with beef and then serve in a sweet-and-sour sauce.

A few of the typical Jewish dishes, like chicken soup, are known for their medicinal value. At the other extreme, however, there is *schmaltz* (chicken fat, fried with onion and garlic), corned beef, pastrami, tongue, and chopped liver—all of which have been part of the American Jewish diet.

Food for Celebration

No Jewish holiday is complete without a *seudah* (feast). Certain Jewish foods, while they may be eaten all year round, are associated with particular holidays. For example, *matzah* (an unleavened bread made of flour and water) is consumed in place of regular bread during the eight days of Passover and is used in cooking instead of flour or even to make stuffing.

ALERT!

There is an increasing awareness of moral issues when it comes to eating animal products. Consequently, there are a number of Jewish vegetarian cookbooks containing recipes of some traditional Jewish offerings without meat, fish, or fowl. Clearly, Jewish food continues to change in accordance with our culture.

At the Shabbat dinner and on other holidays, Jews serve *challah,* a soft, sweet bread glazed with egg white. Since cooking is forbidden on the Sabbath, a popular dish is *cholent,* a slowly cooked stew of beans, barley, potatoes, and beef that can be started before Sabbath begins and left to simmer. Another stew that is traditionally served on Rosh Hashanah (the Jewish New Year) and Passover is *tzimmes,* consisting of carrots, sweet potatoes, and/or prunes.

Jewish Art and Ornaments

Because of the commandment prohibiting the making of graven images, it is sometimes believed that there is no such thing as Jewish art. This is not the case. Indeed, there is a concept known as *hiddur mitzvah*—a commandment that whenever you need to make an object for a specific use, it should be as beautiful as possible, in honor of God's creation, which is beautiful as well.

Jewish art is as old as Judaism itself, dating back to Bezalel, the first Jewish artist, architect, and sculptor, who made the Tabernacle that contained the Ark of the Covenant. Because Judaic art dates back for millennia, most of the early work has been lost to the ages, save for the recoveries made through archeological findings.

It is true that for most of the Diaspora, there was little in the way of distinguished Jewish art, but this changed with the Emancipation of the Jews in eighteenth-century Europe. A number of prominent Jewish artists made their way to Paris to study and hone their skills, with many artists like Chagall, Band, Soutine, and Pisarro achieving international recognition. Throughout the nineteenth century and until World War II, Lithuania was a focal point for Jewish artists. And in the twentieth century, Israeli artists have produced their own unique brand of Jewish art.

Judaica and Art

Returning to the concept of *hiddur mitzvah,* religious objects are often works of art in themselves. Everything in the synagogue—and the building itself—is made to be beautiful. Many religious objects used at home are artistically crafted as well. The Chanukah menorah, the Sabbath candelabra, *Kiddush* cups, and the challah cover are usually beautiful objects that are passed down from generation to generation. The marriage contract, called a *ketubah*, is frequently decoratively inscribed and displayed in the home. Even the mezuzah hanging from the doorpost of the Jewish home is often elaborately made.

©Israel Ministry of Tourism. Courtesy of the Israel Ministry of Tourism.

◀ An ornamental Chanukah menorah.

Some Jews like to adorn themselves with certain symbolic Jewish objects that are beautifully made. The most popular symbol is the *magen david* (the six-pointed Star of David) that is generally worn as a pendant.

Another symbol that appears on necklaces and other jewelry is the *chai,* the two Hebrew letters *chet* and *yud* that make up the word for "life" or "living." Fairly common among Jews, particularly males, is the wearing of a small mezuzah around the neck.

These ornaments aren't meant to be objects of identification. If Jews wear a *magen david* or a *chai* today, it is because it is their way of saying, "I am proud of the history and heritage of the Jewish people."

Jewish Humor

One of the most distinctive traits of Jewish culture is Jewish humor, something that the Jewish people are very proud of. Despite all the hardships of exile and persecution over the centuries, the Jews never lost their particular sense of humor. In fact, laughing at themselves often helped them survive and flourish.

Humor does not become "Jewish" because it is about Jews. Nor, for that matter, are jokes considered "Jewish" because they were told or created by someone who happens to be Jewish. And yet it's not hard to distinguish Jewish humor, perhaps because it always speaks to the existential condition of the Jewish people.

A Coping Mechanism

To a large extent, Jewish humor is the result of the 2,000-year Diaspora. This perpetual exile was a source of both physical and emotional insecurity. While it is true there were shining periods in history when the Jewish people thrived, we have also seen how these epochs were always brought to a painful conclusion.

In the face of misfortune and calamities, Jewish humor evolved to become an affirmation of life. Gaiety and laughter were necessary to offset harsh and despairing conditions. In a way, the laughter generated by their humor was a form of therapy to assuage the pain from persecution, grief, and poverty.

Jewish humor is more than a confirmation of life. It is a defiant answer to the questions of "Why?" and "How to go on?" How else, when confronted by a hostile world for thousands of years, could this small band of people so audaciously cling to their beliefs?

FACT

When God told Abraham that he and Sarah would have a son, Sarah's first reaction was to laugh in disbelief. When the baby was born, his parents named him *Yitzchak* (Isaac), a name that shares its root with *tzechak,* the Hebrew word for laughter.

Laughing at Ourselves and the World

Jews have a way of poking fun at themselves, as if to say to the world, "Hey, you can't malign us, we'll do it to ourselves!" Jewish humor is often incisive and succinct. Henny Youngman's one-liners have their source in hundreds of years of Jewish jokes.

Jewish jokes also deal with the world in which the Jews live and which they love to criticize. Some Jewish humorists are really social critics. Others are more like prophets who carry a certain message or even encourage certain types of moral conduct.

Recognizable Themes

Jewish humor relies on a number of motifs. One recurring theme reminds the Jews of the suffering of those less fortunate and of the *mitzvah* (commandment) to give to the poor. A second motif reflects the iconoclastic disposition imbedded in the Jewish psyche, beginning with Abraham who, when only a child, dared to destroy the idols in his father's house. Consequently, Jewish humor loves to debunk myths and long-held opinions.

Another pattern woven into Jewish jokes reminds the Jews to keep looking on the bright side of things—a disposition so important in surviving the trials and tribulations Jews often faced. And more than a fair share of Jewish jokes emphasize the importance of diligence and hard work to achieve success, values learned during centuries of restrictions and discrimination.

Jewish Comedians in America

The story of the American Jewish comic deserves special attention because of the extraordinary role they have played in American humor; it's perhaps no coincidence that so many comic geniuses and innovators of American comedy are Jews. The success of the American Jewish comedian lies in the ability to bring the themes ingrained in Jewish humor to the wider American public.

Given that anti-Semitism is a major motif in Jewish history, it is not surprising that it is also a major motif in Jewish humor. Many Jewish jokes portray the utter absurdity of anti-Semitism while still recognizing its danger.

Whether consciously aware of it or not, many of these comics delivered their jokes in the unique rhythm of the Yiddish language and the style in which Jewish jokes had been bantered about for centuries. In coping with anti-Semitism, which presented a major hurdle to aspiring comics in the first half of the twentieth century (a reason so many changed their names), they adopted the techniques of early Jewish humor by making the Jews themselves the butt of their jokes while at the same time demonstrating the fallaciousness of anti-Semitism. No one did this better than Jack Benny, who played the character of a cheapskate and yet in his personal life was generous to a fault.

By the second half of the twentieth century, feeling more secure in American society, a number of Jewish comics began using humor to challenge the mores and hypocrisy around them. Comics like Mort Sahl and Lenny Bruce were scathing in their criticism of bigotry, politics, and war. Indeed, these comics along with the likes of Alan King, Jackie Mason, and Shelly Berman—just to name a few—took stand-up comedy to a new level.

Despite pushing the boundaries to get Americans to look at themselves and their culture, these Jewish comics were for the most part well received; through them, Jews in general became more accepted by American society. Jews are now so much a part of the mainstream, some of the most popular television shows were made by and about Jews, like Milton Berle's *Texaco Star Theater* (number-one show at one point in the 1950s) and *Seinfeld,* the brainchild of Jerry Seinfeld and Larry David (both Jewish).

FACT

Excluded from gentile country clubs, Jews opened their own country club in Hollywood called the Hillcrest Country Club. Every Friday, comics including Jack Benny, George Burns, George Jessel, Groucho Marx, and Danny Kaye met there regularly for lunch.

The list of outstanding Jewish comics is impressive, but several deserve a special look:

- **Jack Benny** (Benjamin Kubelsky): Despite the aloof and frugal character he portrayed, Benny was beloved by the American public. Few American entertainers have ever made the transition so successfully from vaudeville to radio, and then to film and television.
- **Milton Berle** (Mendel Berlinger): Credited with bringing the fledgling medium of television to the homes of the American public with his zany humor, Berle made his transition from radio to television in 1948; his program, *Texaco Star Theater,* was so popular on Tuesday nights that many restaurants, theaters, and clubs adjusted their schedules so that their customers could watch the show at 8:00 P.M.
- **The Three Stooges:** This comic band of brothers with their slapstick humor has been entertaining generations of Americans. Moe, Curly, and Shemp, who went by the surname of "Howard," were really the Horwitz brothers (Moshe, Yehudah, and Shmuel). The other prominent "stooge" was Larry Feinberg.
- **The Marx brothers:** Groucho, Chico, Harpo, and Zeppo took their unique brand of comedy from the stage to the screen, sometimes poking fun at traditions and society—particularly high-brow culture. In later years, performing on his own and starring in a television series, Groucho Marx used puns and non sequiturs to challenge any smugness people had about themselves. He laid the groundwork for

subsequent Jewish comics, who carried on the tradition of the Jewish iconoclast.

- **Lenny Bruce:** Of all the great comics of twentieth-century America, Bruce might have been the most innovative and daring; as with all trailblazers, he incurred the wrath of the establishment and met a tragic end, dying of a drug overdose. Speaking as a fast-talking hipster and often employing Yiddish expressions, Bruce's material was frequently directed at bigotry and limitations on the freedom of expression. To prove his point, he sometimes used profanity, for which he was arrested and prosecuted.

- **Woody Allen** (Allan Konigsberg): Allen began his career as a comic writer and landed a spot on the writing staff for Sid Caesar (another Jewish entertainer). Caesar's television show was highly popular, and its cadre included many Jewish writers who went on to distinguish themselves—including Mel Brooks and Carl Reiner. Allen made the foray into stand-up comedy, where he tackled the "angst" of life—issues such as marriage, love, sex, and death. These themes would be repeated with humorous and serious deliveries in his subsequent movies.

In the tradition of Jewish humor, Woody Allen has made some memorable one-liners, such as his observation on death: "It's not that I'm afraid to die. I just don't want to be around when it happens."

There are literally hundreds of outstanding American Jewish comics, almost all of whom you would recognize and some of whom, it may surprise you to know, are Jewish. Here is a very incomplete list for you to peruse: Jason Alexander (Greenspan), Richard Belzer, George Burns (Nathan Birnbaum), Rodney Dangerfield, Fran Drescher, Al Franken, Goldie Hawn, Andy Kaufman, Lisa Kudrow, Jerry Lewis (Jerome Levitch), Richard Lewis, Jon Lovitz, Walter Matthau (Matuschanskayasky), Sarah Jessica Parker, Rhea Perlman, Tony Randall (Rosenberg), Carol Reiner, Rob Reiner, Joan Rivers (Molinsky), David Schwimmer, Pauly Shore, Gary Shandling, Jerry Stiller, Ben Stiller, Peter Sellers, Jon Stewart (Leibowitz), Gene Wilder (Jerome Silberman), and Henry Winkler.

Appendices

Appendix A

Timeline of
Jewish History

Appendix B

Glossary

Appendix A

Timeline of Jewish History

The following timeline may serve as a brief overview of Jewish history. Many of the time periods, especially prior to the Common Era, are approximations. The dating system used differs somewhat from the traditional Jewish dating system for ancient history, and there may be discrepancies by as many as 150 years. However, this divergence disappears with the beginning of the Common Era.

2000–1700 B.C.E.	The Age of the Patriarchs—Abraham, Isaac, and Jacob.
1700–1300 B.C.E.	Israelites enter Egypt, are enslaved, and become populous.
1250 B.C.E.	Moses leads the Israelites out of Egypt.
1250–1200 B.C.E.	Israelite conquest of Canaan.
1020 B.C.E.	Saul is anointed the first king of Israel.
1000–961 B.C.E.	David reigns as the second king of Israel, with Jerusalem as his capital.
961–922 B.C.E.	Solomon rules as the third king of Israel and builds the First Temple.
922 B.C.E.	The Ten Northern Tribes secede and form the kingdom of Israel, leaving the kingdom of Judah.
726–722 B.C.E.	The northern kingdom of Israel is conquered by the Assyrians and the Ten Tribes are exiled into oblivion.
587–586 B.C.E.	The southern kingdom of Judah falls to the Babylonians; the First Temple is destroyed; much of the Jewish population is deported to Babylon.
538 B.C.E.	Cyrus's edict permits the Jews to return to Judea.
515 B.C.E	The Second Temple is completed in Jerusalem.
332 B.C.E.	Alexander the Great occupies Israel.
167–164 B.C.E.	Maccabean (Hasmonean) revolt against Antiochus IV. The Temple is seized and rededicated.
37 B.C.E. to 4 C.E.	Herod rules Judea with the support of Rome.
6 C.E.	Rome assumes direct rule over Judea.
66–72 C.E.	Jews revolt against Rome.

70 C.E.	Destruction of the Second Temple marks the beginning of the Diaspora.
73 C.E.	The fall of Masada.
132–135	Jewish revolt led by Bar Kokhba against Rome.
200	Compilation of *Mishna*.
425–450	Jerusalem (Palestinian) Talmud is completed.
500–550	Babylonian Talmud is completed.
762	The Karaites break with the Rabbanites.
1066	Jews settle in England.
1096	Crusaders massacre the Jews in the Rhineland.
1135–1204	The life of Moses Maimonides.
1144	Ritual murder charges at Norwich.
1146	Beginning of persecution of Jews in Muslim Spain.
1171	First Blood Libel charge brought in France.
1182–1198	Expulsion of Jews from France.
1240	Paris Disputation and burning of the Talmud.
1286	Completion of the Zohar by Moses de Leon.
1290	Expulsion of Jews from England.
1348–1349	Accused of causing the Black Death, many Jews are massacred in central Europe and France.
1394	Final expulsion of Jews from France.
1481	Spanish Inquisition begins.
1492	Jews expelled from Spain.
1497	Jews expelled from Portugal.
1516	First ghetto in Venice.
1564	Rabbi Joseph Caro completes the *Shulkhan Arukh*.
1740–1760	Baal Shem Tov founds the Hasidic movement.
1770–1880	*Haskalah* movement.
1791	Emancipation of Jews in France.
1804	Czar Alexander I establishes the Pale of Settlement.
1827	Czar Nicholas I orders Jews to be conscripted into the army.
1830s	German Jews begin to emigrate to the United States.
1840s	Reform movement begins in Germany.
1848	Full rights granted to German Jews.
1866	Emancipation of Swiss Jews.

1867	Final Emancipation of Jews of Austria-Hungary.
1870	Final Emancipation of Italian Jews.
1881–1882	Waves of pogroms begin in Russia.
1881–1924	Mass migration of Eastern European Jews to the United States.
1882–1903	First Aliyah to Israel.
1894–1899	The Dreyfus Affair.
1897	Theodor Herzl convenes the First Zionist Congress in Basel, Switzerland.
1904–1914	Second Aliyah to Israel.
1905	*The Protocols of the Elders of Zion* appears in print.
1917	Emancipation of the Jews in Russia.
1917	Lord Balfour writes the Balfour Declaration; Britain occupies Palestine.
1922	League of Nations establishes British mandate in Palestine.
1929	Arab riots in Jerusalem and throughout Palestine.
1929–1939	Almost 250,000 German and Austrian Jews arrive in Palestine.
1933	Hitler and Nazi party come to power in Germany.
1935–1939	Anti-Jewish legislation enacted throughout many European countries.
1939	New White Paper severely limits Jewish immigration to Palestine.
1939–1945	Holocaust. Six million Jews die at the hands of the Nazis and their collaborators.
1947	United Nations General Assembly votes in favor of the partition of Palestine.
1948	May 14; Declaration of Statehood by the State of Israel.
1948	Israel's War of Independence.
1952	Stalin orders the execution of Yiddish writers and poets in the USSR.
1956	The Sinai campaign.
1967	The Six-Day War.
1973	The Yom Kippur War.
1979	Signing of Israel-Egypt peace agreement.

Appendix B

Glossary

A

Aliyah: *Aliyah* is Hebrew for "going up." It refers to being called to make a blessing over the Torah reading that is held during services. The phrase "to make aliyah" also refers to emigrating to Israel.

Anti-Semitism: Literally, anti-Semitism means being opposed to all Semitic people, but the common usage is being in opposition to Jews.

Ark of the Covenant: The wooden acacia box plated in gold, first carried by the early Hebrews in the Sinai; the Ark served as a sanctuary for God's spirit.

Ashkenazic Jews, Ashkenazim: Jews who lived in France, Germany, and Eastern Europe, as well as their descendants (from the Hebrew *Ashkenaz,* Germany).

Auschwitz-Birkenau: The most notorious of the Nazi concentration camps, located near Krakow, Poland, where one million Jews met their deaths. Originally a labor camp, it was expanded in 1942 to include an extermination camp (Auschwitz II or Birkenau).

B

Babylonian Talmud: Completed in the sixth century by the Jewish scholars and rabbis living in Babylon, it is the most extensive and authoritative Talmud.

Bar Mitzvah: Upon reaching the age of thirteen, a boy becomes a bar mitzvah ("son of the commandment"), a rite of passage traditionally accompanied by a religious ceremony and celebrations.

Bat Mitzvah: Upon reaching the age of twelve, a girl becomes a bat mitzvah ("daughter of the commandment"); the bat mitzvah ceremony and celebrations are often held when the girl is thirteen.

B.C.E.: Before the Common Era, which is the time marked by the beginning of the Christian calendar.

Blood Libel: Claims first made in the twelfth century that Jews killed Christian children to use their blood in the making of *matzah* or to drink as part of the Passover *seder.*

Brit Milah: The covenant of circumcision.

C.E.: Common Era. The date corresponding to the current Christian calendar.

C

Challah: A sweet eggy bread that is usually braided and served on Shabbat and at other holiday meals. The *challah* served on Rosh Hashanah is round, in order to signify the beginning of the cycle of a new year.

Chametz: Leavened grain products that Jews may not eat or even own during Passover.

Chanukah: The eight-day festival that commemorates the rededication of the Temple after the successful Jewish rebellion against the Syrians in 165 B.C.E.

Chazzan: Also known as the cantor, the *chazzan* leads chanted prayers in synagogue services.

Conservative Judaism: While accepting the binding nature of Jewish laws, the Conservative movement believes they are subject to reinterpretation and change because, although divinely inspired, *mitzvot* did not come directly from God.

Conversos: Spanish term for Jews who converted to Christianity and their descendants.

D

Days of Awe: The ten days from Rosh Hashanah to Yom Kippur.

Diaspora: Any place other than Israel where Jews live. Often refers to the time period following the destruction of the Second Temple in 70 C.E. until the establishment of the modern State of Israel in 1948.

E

Eretz Yisrael: Land of Israel, the Promised Land.

Essenes: A mystical and ascetic movement in Judaism that appeared around 200 B.C.E. and vanished after the destruction of the Second Temple.

G

Galut: The Exile; the exiled community. *Galut* expresses the broader concept of Jewish homelessness.

Gemara: Collection of commentaries on the *Mishna* compiled by the rabbis between third and fifth centuries C.E. Taken together, the *Gemara* and *Mishna* comprise the Talmud.

Ghetto: Designated district demarcated by a moat, hedge, or some bulwark restricting where Jews could live.

The Great Assembly *(Knesset Ha-Gadol):* Established by Ezra around the middle of the fifth century B.C.E., this esteemed body of 120 members strengthened Judaism and led the Jewish people.

H

Haganah: The Jewish fighting force in Eretz Yisrael during the British Mandate period, it was renamed the Israel Defense Forces (IDF) with the establishment of the State of Israel in 1948.

Haggadah: The book read during the Passover *seder;* the *Haggadah* includes the Exodus narrative as well as appropriate blessings and prayers.

Halakhah: The religious laws that Jews are obligated to follow.

Hasidism (also Chasidism): A sect of Orthodox Jews with its own distinctive lifestyle. Hasidism was founded in eighteenth-century Eastern Europe by the Ba'al Shem Tov (the Besht).

Haskalah: The Jewish Enlightenment movement

of the eighteenth century; its followers were called *maskilim* (enlighteners).

Ha-Tikvah: The anthem of the Zionist movement and of the State of Israel.

Hebrew: The language of the Torah, in which prayer is recited. Modern Hebrew is the official language of the State of Israel.

High Holidays, High Holy Days: Rosh Hashanah, the Days of Awe, and Yom Kippur.

Holocaust: The systematic extermination of 6 million Jews by the German Nazi regime and its collaborators.

J

Jerusalem Talmud: Completed in the beginning of the fifth century B.C.E. by rabbis and scholars living in Palestine, it is smaller and less sophisticated than the Babylonian Talmud.

K

Kabbalah: Jewish mysticism.

Karaism: A branch of Judaism that rejected the Oral Law and taught following the Torah literally. Today, only tiny Karaite communities remain in Israel, Crimea, the United States, and Europe.

Kashrut: Jewish dietary laws. Food that adheres to all the laws of *Kashrut* is kosher.

Kehillot: Jewish councils that had governed many local Jewish communities in Europe. *Kehillah* is Hebrew for "community."

Kibbutz: A collective settlement in Israel. Most *kibbutzim* are involved in agriculture.

Kiddush: A blessing recited over wine sanctifying the Sabbath and other holidays.

Klezmer: Informal group of Yiddish musicians; the type of music normally played by such a group.

Kohanim: The priestly sect descended from Aaron.

Kol Nidre: The prayer that begins the evening service of Yom Kippur, also known as the *Kol Nidre.*

L

Ladino: The language of Sephardic Jews, it's a mix of Spanish, Arabic, Hebrew, and other languages. Ladino (also known as Judezmo) uses Hebrew script.

Landsman: Yiddish word for someone who comes from the same hometown. In some cases, a Jew may use the term *landsman* to refer to another Jew.

Levite: Descendants from Levi, one of the sons of Jacob (Israel), who had been charged with performing certain duties at the Temple.

M

Magen David **(Star of David):** The six-pointed star emblematic of Judaism, the Jewish People, Zionism, and the modern State of Israel.

Mame loshen: Literally "mother language," this term refers to Yiddish.

Marranos: Spanish and Portuguese Jews who publicly converted to Christianity, but continued to practice Judaism in secret.

Masada: Jewish fortress in ancient Israel that was the last stronghold of the Zealots during the rebellion against Rome in the second century. Rather than surrender to the Romans, the community in Masada committed mass suicide.

Maskil: Member of the Jewish Enlightenment or *Haskalah*.

Matzah: Unleavened bread that replaces regular bread (which is considered *chametz*) during Passover.

Menorah: Seven-branched candelabrum that was used in the Temple. The nine-branched candelabrum used to light the Hanukah candles is the Chanukah menorah.

Messiah: The English word for *moshiach*, which is Hebrew for "anointed" and refers to the messianic king who will usher in the Messianic Age by ending all the world's evil and commencing 2,000 years of justice and peace.

Mezuzah: A scroll of passages of scripture, housed in a case that is affixed to the doorposts of Jewish homes and some of the rooms.

Midrash: The collection of *midrashim* (interpretations) that expand on incidents in the Bible in order to derive principles and moral lessons.

Mishna: Code of Jewish law, edited by Rabbi Judah Ha-Nasi around 200 C.E.; the *Mishna* is based on oral tradition and together with the *Gemara* constitutes the Talmud.

Mitnagdim: Orthodox Jews who opposed the Hasidim.

Mitzvah: Any one of the 613 *mitzvot* (commandments) that Jews are required to obey. It is sometimes used to refer to any Jewish obligation.

Mohel: Person trained in performing ritual circumcision.

O

Oral Torah: Also known as the Oral Law, the Oral Torah includes Jewish teachings and elucidations about the written Torah handed down by word of mouth through the second century C.E.

Orthodox Judaism: The Orthodox branch of Judaism believes that Jewish law comes from God and is not subject to change. The Orthodox branch may be subdivided into the ultra-Orthodox and the modern Orthodox.

P

Pale of Settlement: Twenty-five Russian provinces that demarcated where Jews were permitted to live. The Pale was created in 1812 and lasted until 1917.

Passover, Pesach: A holiday that commemorates the Exodus from Egypt and is one of the three pilgrimage festivals.

Patriarchs: Abraham, Isaac, and Jacob (Israel).

Pharisees: A movement in Judaism that began around the third century B.C.E. The Pharisees saw the Written and Oral Torah as equally important and are considered to be the forerunners of rabbinic (post-Temple) Judaism.

Pogrom: An organized attack on a Jewish community (from the Russian word *pogromit*, "to wreak havoc").

The Protocols of the Elders of Zion: A document that purported to be the minutes of a clandestine meeting of Jewish leaders held every hundred years to devise how they will control the world for the next century. Though counterfeit, it was widely disseminated by anti-Semites, especially in the early twentieth century.

Purim: A holiday celebrating the deliverance of the Jewish population in Persia from annihilation, as recounted in the Book of Esther.

R

Rabbi: A religious teacher who often interprets the application of Jewish law and may be called upon to settle disputes. Today, the rabbi's duties are similar to other clergymen.

Rabbinical Judaism: A term that includes virtually all branches of Judaism that descended from the Pharisees.

Rebbe: A term used for any leader of a Hasidic community.

Reconstructionist Judaism: One of the branches of Judaism, the Reconstructionist movement believes Jewish law was created by people and can be changed to meet new conditions; it emphasizes Judaism's cultural components versus strict adherence to all commandments.

Reform Judaism: A branch of Judaism that emphasizes its ethical teachings. The Reform movement believes Jewish law was inspired by God and is therefore dynamic; each individual has the freedom to determine which laws to practice.

Rosh Hashanah: The Jewish New Year.

S

Sabbath, Shabbat: Sabbath (in English) and Shabbat (in Hebrew) is a day of rest, prayer, and study as well as a time to pursue spiritual and non-worldly matters.

Sadducees: An oppositional movement to the Pharisees that did not embrace the Oral Torah and narrowly interpreted the Written Torah.

Sanhedrin: During the rabbinical period, this judicial body served as the highest Jewish court, dealing with both religious and legislative matters. Traditionally, the *Sanhedrin* had seventy-one members.

Seder: Hebrew for "order," this term refers to the Passover home ritual that includes the reading of the *Haggadah* and the festive meal.

Sephardic Jews, Sephardim: Jews who had lived in Spain, Portugal, North Africa, and the Middle East and their descendants (from the Hebrew *Sepharad*, Spain).

Shavuot: The harvest festival that also commemorates the giving of the Torah at Mount Sinai.

Shekel: A popular silver coin used in biblical times. Today, Israeli currency is based on the new shekel.

Shema: Perhaps the foremost Jewish prayer that embodies the primary statement of Jewish belief.

Shoah: Hebrew for "calamity" or "catastrophe," it is the Jewish term for the Holocaust.

Shofar: A ram's horn that is blown to emit specific sounds; it is used at synagogue services during the High Holidays.

Shtetl: A small Jewish village in Eastern Europe.

Shul: The Yiddish word referring to a house of worship and study, a synagogue.

Shulchan Arukh: A code of Jewish law written in the sixteenth century.

Simchat Torah: The holiday that celebrates the end and beginning of a new cycle in the public reading of the Torah, which takes one year.

Sukkah: The temporary dwelling (booth, hut, or tabernacle) erected and covered with branches that is lived in or visited during the holiday of Sukkot.

Sukkot: The festival of booths that remembers the Israelites' wandering in the desert for forty years after departing Egypt and before entering the Promised Land. Sukkot is one of the three pilgrimage festivals (the other two being Passover and Shavuot).

Synagogue: The common term for a house of worship.

T

Talmud: Collection of the Jewish oral tradition interpreting the Torah; the Talmud consists of the *Mishna* and *Gemara* and was edited around 500 C.E.

Tanakh: An acronym of Torah (Law), Nevi'im (Prophets), and Ketuvim (Writings), the three sections of the Bible.

Temple: Refers to the First and Second Temple, places of worship in ancient Jerusalem. The word "temple" is also generally used in the Reform movement in lieu of the word "synagogue."

Tisha B'Av: The ninth day of *Av,* a day of mourning that commemorates the destruction of both the First and Second Temple, as well as other tragedies in Jewish history.

Torah: The five books of the Bible (Genesis, Exodus, Leviticus, Numbers, and Deuteronomy) also known as the Pentateuch and the Five Books of Moses.

Twelve Tribes of Israel: Reuben, Simeon, Levi, Judah, Issacher, Zebulun, Joseph, Benjamin, Dan, Naphtali, Gad, and Asher.

Tzaddik: A righteous person sometimes believed, particularly by Hasidim, to have mystical powers.

W

Western Wall: The only remaining wall of the Temple in Jerusalem, also known as the Wailing Wall. The site at the Western Wall is the holiest place in Judaism and is in custody of the Orthodox Jews.

Written Torah: The Bible, which the non-Jews call the Old Testament.

Y

Yarmulke: The Yiddish word for the skullcap worn by most Jews during services and more observant Jews at all times. The Hebrew equivalent of yarmulke is *kippah*.

Yiddish: The international vernacular of Ashkenazic Jews, it's a mix of Old German, Hebrew, and Slavic languages and employs the Hebrew script.

Yishuv: The Jewish community in Palestine before the State of Israel was established in 1948.

Yom Ha-Atzmaut: Israeli Independence Day.

Yom Ha-Shoah: Holocaust Remembrance Day.

Yom Ha-Zikkaron: Israeli Memorial Day.

Yom Kippur: The Day of Atonement set aside for fasting, prayer, and introspection.

Z

Zealots: A movement in Judaism that began around 200 B.C.E.; its followers disappeared after the destruction of the Second Temple and the fall of Masada.

Zionism: The political movement that strove for the establishment of a Jewish homeland; Zionism is responsible for the creation of the modern State of Israel.

The Zohar: The primary written work of Kabbalah (Jewish mysticism).

Index

THE **EVERYTHING** JUDAISM BOOK

By Richard Bank

Judaism has survived for 4 millennia—and many of its customs, laws, and traditions have remained exactly the same today as in the days of Abraham, Isaac, and Jacob. From important holidays, such as Passover and Yom Kippur, to symbols and objects, such as the Star of David and the tallis prayer shawl, *The Everything® Judaism Book* with provide Jews and non-Jews alike a new understanding and insight into the rich diversity and seemingly endless complexity of Jewish practices and culture.

Trade paperback
$14.95 ($22.95 CAN)
1-58062-728-5, 304 pages

OTHER *EVERYTHING*® BOOKS BY ADAMS MEDIA CORPORATION

BUSINESS

Everything® **Business Planning Book**
Everything® **Coaching and Mentoring Book**
Everything® **Fundraising Book**
Everything® **Home-Based Business Book**
Everything® **Leadership Book**
Everything® **Managing People Book**
Everything® **Network Marketing Book**
Everything® **Online Business Book**
Everything® **Project Management Book**
Everything® **Selling Book**
Everything® **Start Your Own Business Book**
Everything® **Time Management Book**

COMPUTERS

Everything® **Build Your Own Home Page Book**

Everything® **Computer Book**
Everything® **Internet Book**
Everything® **Microsoft® Word 2000 Book**

COOKBOOKS

Everything® **Barbecue Cookbook**
Everything® **Bartender's Book, $9.95**
Everything® **Chinese Cookbook**
Everything® **Chocolate Cookbook**
Everything® **Cookbook**
Everything® **Dessert Cookbook**
Everything® **Diabetes Cookbook**
Everything® **Low-Carb Cookbook**
Everything® **Low-Fat High-Flavor Cookbook**
Everything® **Mediterranean Cookbook**
Everything® **Mexican Cookbook**
Everything® **One-Pot Cookbook**
Everything® **Pasta Book**

Everything® **Quick Meals Cookbook**
Everything® **Slow Cooker Cookbook**
Everything® **Soup Cookbook**
Everything® **Thai Cookbook**
Everything® **Vegetarian Cookbook**
Everything® **Wine Book**

HEALTH

Everything® **Anti-Aging Book**
Everything® **Diabetes Book**
Everything® **Dieting Book**
Everything® **Herbal Remedies Book**
Everything® **Hypnosis Book**
Everything® **Menopause Book**
Everything® **Nutrition Book**
Everything® **Reflexology Book**
Everything® **Stress Management Book**
Everything®**Vitamins, Minerals, and Nutritional Supplements Book**

HISTORY

Everything® **American History Book**
Everything® **Civil War Book**
Everything® **Irish History & Heritage Book**
Everything® **Mafia Book**
Everything® **World War II Book**

HOBBIES & GAMES

Everything® **Bridge Book**
Everything® **Candlemaking Book**
Everything® **Casino Gambling Book**
Everything® **Chess Basics Book**
Everything® **Collectibles Book**
Everything® **Crossword and Puzzle Book**
Everything® **Digital Photography Book**
Everything® **Family Tree Book**
Everything® **Games Book**
Everything® **Knitting Book**
Everything® **Magic Book**
Everything® **Motorcycle Book**
Everything® **Online Genealogy Book**
Everything® **Photography Book**
Everything® **Pool & Billiards Book**
Everything® **Quilting Book**
Everything® **Scrapbooking Book**
Everything® **Soapmaking Book**

HOME IMPROVEMENT

Everything® **Feng Shui Book**
Everything® **Gardening Book**
Everything® **Home Decorating Book**
Everything® **Landscaping Book**
Everything® **Lawn Care Book**
Everything® **Organize Your Home Book**

KIDS' STORY BOOKS

Everything® **Bedtime Story Book**
Everything® **Bible Stories Book**
Everything® **Fairy Tales Book**
Everything® **Mother Goose Book**

EVERYTHING® *KIDS'* BOOKS

All titles are $6.95

Everything® **Kids' Baseball Book, 2nd Ed.** ($10.95 CAN)
Everything® **Kids' Bugs Book** ($10.95 CAN)
Everything® **Kids' Christmas Puzzle & Activity Book** ($10.95 CAN)
Everything® **Kids' Cookbook** ($10.95 CAN)
Everything® **Kids' Halloween Puzzle & Activity Book** ($10.95 CAN)
Everything® **Kids' Joke Book** ($10.95 CAN)
Everything® **Kids' Math Puzzles Book** ($10.95 CAN)
Everything® **Kids' Mazes Book** ($10.95 CAN)
Everything® **Kids' Money Book** ($11.95 CAN)
Everything® **Kids' Monsters Book** ($10.95 CAN)
Everything® **Kids' Nature Book** ($11.95 CAN)
Everything® **Kids' Puzzle Book** ($10.95 CAN)
Everything® **Kids' Science Experiments Book** ($10.95 CAN)
Everything® **Kids' Soccer Book** ($10.95 CAN)
Everything® **Kids' Travel Activity Book** ($10.95 CAN)

LANGUAGE

Everything® **Learning French Book**
Everything® **Learning German Book**
Everything® **Learning Italian Book**
Everything® **Learning Latin Book**
Everything® **Learning Spanish Book**
Everything® **Sign Language Book**

MUSIC

Everything® **Drums Book (with CD)**, $19.95 ($31.95 CAN)
Everything® **Guitar Book**
Everything® **Playing Piano and Keyboards Book**
Everything® **Rock & Blues Guitar Book (with CD)**, $19.95 ($31.95 CAN)
Everything® **Songwriting Book**

NEW AGE

Everything® **Astrology Book**
Everything® **Divining the Future Book**
Everything® **Dreams Book**
Everything® **Ghost Book**
Everything® **Meditation Book**
Everything® **Numerology Book**
Everything® **Palmistry Book**
Everything® **Psychic Book**
Everything® **Spells & Charms Book**
Everything® **Tarot Book**
Everything® **Wicca and Witchcraft Book**

PARENTING

Everything® **Baby Names Book**
Everything® **Baby Shower Book**
Everything® **Baby's First Food Book**
Everything® **Baby's First Year Book**
Everything® **Breastfeeding Book**
Everything® **Father-to-Be Book**
Everything® **Get Ready for Baby Book**
Everything® **Homeschooling Book**
Everything® **Parent's Guide to Positive Discipline**
Everything® **Potty Training Book**, $9.95 ($15.95 CAN)
Everything® **Pregnancy Book, 2nd Ed.**
Everything® **Pregnancy Fitness Book**
Everything® **Pregnancy Organizer**, $15.00 ($22.95 CAN)
Everything® **Toddler Book**
Everything® **Tween Book**

PERSONAL FINANCE

Everything® **Budgeting Book**
Everything® **Get Out of Debt Book**
Everything® **Get Rich Book**
Everything® **Homebuying Book, 2nd Ed.**
Everything® **Homeselling Book**

All Everything® books are priced at $12.95 or $14.95, unless otherwise stated. Prices subject to change without notice.
Canadian prices range from $11.95–$31.95, and are subject to change without notice.

Everything® **Investing Book**
Everything® **Money Book**
Everything® **Mutual Funds Book**
Everything® **Online Investing Book**
Everything® **Personal Finance Book**
Everything® **Personal Finance in Your 20s & 30s Book**
Everything® **Wills & Estate Planning Book**

PETS

Everything® **Cat Book**
Everything® **Dog Book**
Everything® **Dog Training and Tricks Book**
Everything® **Horse Book**
Everything® **Puppy Book**
Everything® **Tropical Fish Book**

REFERENCE

Everything® **Astronomy Book**
Everything® **Car Care Book**
Everything® **Christmas Book, $15.00 ($21.95 CAN)**
Everything® **Classical Mythology Book**
Everything® **Einstein Book**
Everything® **Etiquette Book**
Everything® **Great Thinkers Book**
Everything® **Philosophy Book**
Everything® **Shakespeare Book**
Everything® **Tall Tales, Legends, & Other Outrageous Lies Book**
Everything® **Toasts Book**
Everything® **Trivia Book**
Everything® **Weather Book**

RELIGION

Everything® **Angels Book**
Everything® **Buddhism Book**
Everything® **Catholicism Book**
Everything® **Jewish History & Heritage Book**
Everything® **Judaism Book**

Everything® **Prayer Book**
Everything® **Saints Book**
Everything® **Understanding Islam Book**
Everything® **World's Religions Book**
Everything® **Zen Book**

SCHOOL & CAREERS

Everything® **After College Book**
Everything® **College Survival Book**
Everything® **Cover Letter Book**
Everything® **Get-a-Job Book**
Everything® **Hot Careers Book**
Everything® **Job Interview Book**
Everything® **Online Job Search Book**
Everything® **Resume Book, 2nd Ed.**
Everything® **Study Book**

SELF-HELP

Everything® **Dating Book**
Everything® **Divorce Book**
Everything® **Great Marriage Book**
Everything® **Great Sex Book**
Everything® **Romance Book**
Everything® **Self-Esteem Book**
Everything® **Success Book**

SPORTS & FITNESS

Everything® **Bicycle Book**
Everything® **Body Shaping Book**
Everything® **Fishing Book**
Everything® **Fly-Fishing Book**
Everything® **Golf Book**
Everything® **Golf Instruction Book**
Everything® **Pilates Book**
Everything® **Running Book**
Everything® **Sailing Book, 2nd Ed.**
Everything® **T'ai Chi and QiGong Book**
Everything® **Total Fitness Book**
Everything® **Weight Training Book**
Everything® **Yoga Book**

TRAVEL

Everything® **Guide to Las Vegas**

Everything® **Guide to New England**
Everything® **Guide to New York City**
Everything® **Guide to Washington D.C.**
Everything® **Travel Guide to The Disneyland Resort®, California Adventure®, Universal Studios®, and the Anaheim Area**
Everything® **Travel Guide to the Walt Disney World Resort®, Universal Studios®, and Greater Orlando, 3rd Ed.**

WEDDINGS

Everything® **Bachelorette Party Book**
Everything® **Bridesmaid Book**
Everything® **Creative Wedding Ideas Book**
Everything® **Jewish Wedding Book**
Everything® **Wedding Book, 2nd Ed.**
Everything® **Wedding Checklist, $7.95 ($11.95 CAN)**
Everything® **Wedding Etiquette Book, $7.95 ($11.95 CAN)**
Everything® **Wedding Organizer, $15.00 ($22.95 CAN)**
Everything® **Wedding Shower Book, $7.95 ($12.95 CAN)**
Everything® **Wedding Vows Book, $7.95 ($11.95 CAN)**
Everything® **Weddings on a Budget Book, $9.95 ($15.95 CAN)**

WRITING

Everything® **Creative Writing Book**
Everything® **Get Published Book**
Everything® **Grammar and Style Book**
Everything® **Grant Writing Book**
Everything® **Guide to Writing Children's Books**
Everything® **Screenwriting Book**
Everything® **Writing Well Book**

Available wherever books are sold!
To order, call 800-872-5627, or visit us at everything.com